THE REALITY OF PERCEPTION

BY JASON WEBB, LCSW, ASUDC

Front cover picture used with permission from Jari Bartschi
(The perception of the front cover looks like a picture from
outer space. Turn the book over and see what reality is.)

Edited by Catherine Langford & Melissa Leatherwood

Special Thanks to Lance Tamashiro

This book is dedicated to those whose heads hang down.

May you find a new perception to

keep your heads up.

Table of Contents

Preface

I begin this book in the middle of the Pacific Ocean on the cruise ship Serenade of the Seas. Listening to the waves lapping against the ship with no land in sight has to be about as peaceful as life can get. I do not recall a time in my life when I have been so much at peace as I am at this moment. Today is Wednesday; and I am not due back home until Saturday. I could not possibly be more thrilled to have a few more days of this.

I have been subpoenaed to appear in court this upcoming Tuesday. My testimony is needed in a case where the State of Utah is planning on revoking the parental rights of a mother addicted to alcohol. The father has already waived his rights. The child is a 3-year-old girl.

As I sit here on the deck of this massive ship, I wonder how can life be so chaotic for one person (i.e., the mother of this child) and so peaceful for others, namely me. How is it that I am at such peace on the ocean when there are people on the same ship who simply cannot wait for the trip to be over? How can life be so unsettled to one person and so peaceful to another?

It is worth noting that many people are consuming alcohol morning, noon, and night on this cruise. I actually heard one person comment that they could not remember what happened the night before. So, some drank themselves into oblivion while others attended Alcoholics Anonymous meetings on the same ship. Why do some people see alcohol as the answer to their problems while others see it as a plague to be avoided at all costs?

Yesterday, we stopped in Ensenada, Mexico. On our excursion, the tour guide mentioned that the population of Ensenada was 400,000. She then indicated that about 60,000 of them were from the United States. She found it ironic that so many Mexicans are putting their lives at risk to immigrate to the United States while simultaneously United States citizens are moving to Mexico. Why is this?

These thoughts occupy my mind while I sit all alone on deck. As I think about each of these questions, the answer comes, and I do know the reason why. It all comes down to perception.

I read a question put forth by Robert Kiyosaki in his book, <u>Retire Young, Retire Rich</u>[1]. The question was, "How can I do what I do for more people with less work and for a better price?" The thought came to me that I could share my knowledge in a book.

Unfortunately, I have seen many people lose their lives to their perceptions. I have seen dreams lost because of perception. I have seen people suffer unneeded pain and sorrow because of their perception. After making the decision to write this book, I started watching people around me even more. I saw their pain and afflictions. I saw some even consider suicide, and I told my wife, "I have to write this book. Too many people are hurting too much because of what is going on in their heads."

In this book, I will be discussing our perception and how it affects every aspect of our lives. In the first section I will show how depression, anger and anxiety are all caused by our perception. I will also give suggestions as to how we might stop them. In the second section I will discuss how our relationships are based upon our perception and again I will offer suggestions as to how we might improve them. The last section deals with personality disorders and how they are created by our perception. Many people believe that we can't change personality disorders but I disagree and share some insight into my thought process. Finally, at the end of the book I've included two papers that I have written that might help change your perception with regards to pride and how we treat women.

Now, I am not claiming that my perception is the best one or that it is reality. It works for me but it may not work for you. In fact, in my work as a Licensed Clinical Social Worker and a Licensed Substance Abuse Counselor, I let my clients know right up front that I am the only normal one in the world, and everyone else is abnormal. At least, that is what I tell myself, and that helps me feel better. In my first meeting with a client, I tell them that in order for us to get along, they must accept that I am a trans-addict (that is an addict stuck in a normie's body). A normie is what addicts call someone who doesn't use drugs. Once my client accepts me for who I am, our relationship flourishes. Usually my client tells me that he is weird too. Rapport is established quickly.

I do not always counsel my clients in the traditional way. Let me explain. I had a client who checked into our rehabilitation program straight from jail. In fact, she is the only person who the police put into our vehicle in handcuffs and leg chains. The police officer did not even bother to remove the handcuffs or take the chains off. He just gave us the keys and left. She was very depressed and so humiliated. When staff members tried to talk to her, she would not even lift her head or answer their questions. I was assigned to be her therapist. I brought her into my office. I asked her to stand on top of my desk (I have a very big desk). I then went to the computer and played the song, "Wake Me up before You Go Go" by Wham[2]. I blasted the music and told her to dance. Understandably, she was very hesitant. When I asked her why she would not dance, she said she was too embarrassed. So I turned my back to her and said, "There, I can't see you now. Just dance." To my surprise, she started dancing and singing and really went crazy on top of my desk. In a later session, she mentioned that she had always wanted to sing and dance on Broadway. She came alive that day and never went back into her shell. I had never used that tactic before in therapy; the idea just came to me. I use it quite often now when people are depressed; and it helps them forget why they are so sad, at least for a couple of minutes. In fact, to make things even more exciting, I have been known to pull out a rock star wig, sunglasses, and a red nose and ask them, "Do you want to wear them, or should I?" Usually they want me to wear them, and so I put them on and dance with them.

I know you do not have to tell me, I am a sick twisted freak. A member of our staff is from Russia, and she told me one day in her broken English, "You're crazy." I whispered to her that this was my secret and I would appreciate it if she did not tell anyone.

Like I stated before, this book is written in three sections. The first section takes a look into reality and perception. Following that is a discussion of ailments that are common (to some degree) to all of us: depression, anger, and anxiety. Section II dives into relationships and how our perceptions affect them. The last section is not meant to be comprehensive but involves a discussion of the personality disorders that some are diagnosed with. The last section should be read with the intent to learn about different criteria rather than the disorder.

My hope in writing this book is to share a perception that works. It is to enlighten the reader to preserve and savor life and enjoy it to the fullest. If this book can help just one person to live a happier more productive life, then it was worth writing. My purpose is to help lift the heads that hang down. I hope you find the peace and happiness life has to offer.

Section I: How Perception Affects Us

What Is Reality?

Truck Accident

Let me start off by telling a story. I was living in Brandon, Florida, during the summer of 1992. That summer my extended family had planned a family reunion to take place in Utah. My parents decided to drive to Utah due to the high cost of flying. One of my sisters decided to pay for her own airline ticket and fly to Utah to avoid the drive. I had never driven that far and clearly did not understand what I was agreeing to. Since then, I have driven across the country three times and have sworn that I will never do it again. My other sister decided to skip the reunion altogether. My brothers were living in Arizona at the time and decided to make the drive up to Utah. So that left my mom, my dad, and I making the drive to Utah from Florida.

My dad purchased his father's pickup truck from his mother after his father passed away. He rented a camper shell to cover the bed of the truck. In preparation for the trip, we put a mattress in the back so whoever had just driven could take a nap. The person who had just taken a nap would rotate into the passenger seat, and the passenger would move into the driver seat. We planned to follow this rotation across the country and make good time by eliminating stops to sleep.

I had just taken my turn driving and was sound asleep on the mattress in the back. My mom was driving through the state of Louisiana, and my father was keeping her entertained from the passenger seat. I was startled awake from my nap and looked out the window to see the trees circling the truck as we hydroplaned on the freeway. I remember smashing my face back into my pillow and clinging to it as if that alone could save my life. Careening out of control, the truck spun a few times and slipped off an embankment. We were just starting to roll when we slammed into a telephone pole, and the truck came to an abrupt stop. The pole hit right next to the passenger door where my father was sitting and just in front of me.

When the truck settled back on all four tires, there was an unusual stillness in the air. I felt a suitcase land with a thud on my back, but other than that, I cannot remember a single sound. After a few seconds my mom yelled, "Jason, are you alright?" I responded that I was. She called to me, "I think your father is hurt." I told her to come around and open the back door of the camper so I could get out, which she did. I stepped out into the rain and ran to the front of the truck and jumped in through the driver's side door.

My father was sitting with his feet on the floor by the passenger door, but his upper body was just behind the stick shift facing the driver's seat. Because the truck was flipping when we hit the telephone pole, it smashed the truck halfway up on the passenger side, and the damage continued up well onto the roof above the passenger door. The impact left a hole in the roof just above my father. His face was bleeding from the shattered window glass. It was raining quite heavily and the water was flowing through the hole in the roof and landing on my father's face giving the appearance that he was bleeding profusely. Being the intelligent one that I am, I observed, "Dad, I think we need to get you out of here." The only comment he made was a whisper, "I just need time to think." I said, "Okay dad. I'll be outside if you need me."

I stepped out of the truck and saw my mom scrambling around frantically like a chicken with its head cut off. Some trucker passing by saw the accident and called 911 for us. My dad managed to remove himself from the mangled truck. Emergency crews arrived shortly thereafter. My dad's chest was hurting badly, and he was concerned with possible broken ribs or a punctured lung. He was able to walk okay and got himself back up the hill to the ambulance. The paramedics allowed my mom and me to hitch a ride with them to the hospital due to a lack of any other form of transportation. While my mom and dad loaded into the ambulance, one of the paramedics helped me retrieve our luggage from the truck. I knew there was a barbed wire fence right near the truck, but unfortunately the paramedic did not and did not duck in time which resulted in an injury to his forehead. We loaded up the ambulance and made our way to the hospital.

The truck we were driving

At the hospital, my father was taken into x-ray while my mom and I showered and changed into dry clothes. Of course my dad could not pass up the opportunity to make a joke and kidded the doctor with, "Will I ever walk again, Doc?" At least he was keeping his wits about him. The x-rays revealed bruised ribs from the seatbelt but no internal damage. The paramedics agreed to drive us and our belongings to a motel, so off we went.

For three days we deliberated at the motel trying to determine how we would get back home. At this point I couldn't help but wonder the obvious, "Why aren't my parents complaining about the accident?" We had prayed about driving out west and thought long and hard about our decision. We all felt good about it, and now look what happened. This was hardly the reunion we were planning on. Everything was ruined, and we were stranded at a motel with no way home. My parents did not complain about the turn of events even one time. At that point, we had decided to skip the trip to Utah altogether. After calling what felt like every car dealership in the area, we finally found a one-way U-Haul truck that would allow us to rent a vehicle to drive home. This truck had one long bench up front with three seat belts. My mother refused to drive because she was still shaken up from the accident. My father could not drive because he could not move without pain. That left only one driver – me.

Every corner I turned, my dad moaned and told me to drive slower and be more careful. He seemed to feel every rock or pebble on the road. Well, after sitting in the truck for a while, we all needed to reposition ourselves. When my mother tried to shift, she bumped my father's shoulder and he cried out in pain which caused my mom to burst into tears. I merely mentioned that I couldn't take them anywhere with me. After driving 18 straight hours the first day, we stopped at a hotel for the night. We arrived home the next day after just a few hours of driving.

Immediately upon entering our home, my dad smelled smoke. After quickly investigating, he discovered a fire in the electrical box. He put the fire out and called his electrician who relayed to us in a most serious way, "If you hadn't come home today, your house would have burned to the ground."

Moral of the Story

At that point, it became unmistakably clear that the accident was not a curse at all but rather a blessing in disguise. Sure we lost the truck, but our home was spared. I learned a valuable lesson that day. I often tell my clients that if we could just learn to postpone judgment about what is happening to us in the present moment and give it some time, we may be able to understand exactly why certain things happen. We might even be able to see it as a blessing rather than the curse we had originally assumed it was.

What needed to be changed to turn this supposed disaster into a turn of good fortune? The situation itself had not changed. We had actually hydroplaned and slid off the road and hit a telephone pole, and our truck was definitely totaled. The difference was our perception.

After we picked up the U-Haul truck and got on our way back home, we drove back by the scene of the accident and saw the telephone pole we crashed into. My dad happened to notice that this particular stretch of freeway did not have telephone poles along it except for about a one-mile span. Within that mile, there were no more than a dozen or so poles. He observed that if we had hydroplaned anywhere else on that freeway, we would have likely flipped and maybe rolled several times which would have popped the top off the back of the truck and sent me flying possibly to my death. Furthermore, had either of my sisters decided to come with us, they most likely would have been sitting in the little chair behind the passenger's seat which is exactly where the pole hit. That impact would have likely killed or at the very least seriously injured them. Of course, saving our home was definitely a blessing, and that was brought about solely as a result of the accident.

So what is real? If we had complained that God was cursing us, would that have made the curse a reality? Or is it true that perception is reality to the beholder? The fact is, the way I see life is real to me, and the way you see life is real to you. So what is reality?

Definition of Reality

According to The Merriam-Webster Dictionary[3], reality means, "1: The quality or state of being real; 2: Something real; 3: The totality of real things and events." Likewise, the word "real" means "1: Of or relating to fixed or immovable things (as land); 2: Not artificial, genuine, not imaginary."

Who Defines Reality?

So who defines what is real? According to the definition above, reality is the quality or state of, or relating to, fixed or immovable things. At one time in history, the world was believed to be flat. Was that reality? It was to them. At that time, it was believed to be an absolute fixed or immovable truth. But we now know how wrong they were. What about the people who used to say man would never land on the moon? Are our ideas ever reality? At one point, it was believed that everything could be broken down to its smallest part (i.e., an atom). Yet today we know we can go much smaller than the atom. How are we to know if today's realities will be uncovered as falsehoods in the future? And if our ideas are found to be false in the future, does that mean they cannot be reality today?

Is reality really in the eye of the beholder? If so, there are billions of realities in the world. If that is the case, whose reality is right especially since they all seem to conflict somewhere? If that is true, then would the definition "of or relating to fixed or immovable things" still apply? Maybe a more correct definition would be, "the quality or state of, or relating to, fixed or immovable things as viewed by an individual." But even with that, we are not quite there. I believe there is a reality out there that is not defined by an individual or by our perceptions. Yet we all live in a make-believe world, a world in which we lie to ourselves that our perceptions are in fact reality.

The Reality of Fairy Tales

Fairy tales are stories that are made-up, fabricated, invented, improbable, and untruthful. The ones we are familiar with may also be romantic and mythical. As you will come to see throughout this book, we live in a world that is made-up, fabricated, invented, improbable, and untruthful according to our perceptions. In other words, we live in a fairy tale. Because of individual perception, the majority of marriages these days do not end "happily ever after." However, because some people's perceptions are different from this staggering majority, their marriages do continue on "happily ever after."

Let us have a look at Pinocchio[4]. Pinocchio was a puppet that wanted to be a boy. He was held up by strings controlled by a puppeteer, Geppetto. Many people today live in codependent relationships and feel that they cannot make their own choices but rather are a puppet with invisible strings controlled by another. I have seen many of these relationships and often ask these people to make their own choices and be accountable. The response I get is often similar to: "Oh, I can't do that. My mom would be so mad." So instead of standing up for themselves, they continue to do whatever "mom" wants. They lack the self-esteem and empowerment that comes from making one's own decisions. They begin to drink or use drugs to deal with their emotions of shame and guilt. Because of their perception, this lifestyle has become a reality to them, and they are in a sense trapped, or at least they feel that way.

So which story is more real: Pinocchio or the co-dependent relationship? You would think that it is the second story because Pinocchio is a made-up story. But the words "I can't do that" are not any more real than a wooden boy who comes to life. Let me illustrate. Let us say the choice this person feels they cannot make is where he is going to eat dinner on Sunday. The reason he cannot make this choice is because his mom expects him to go to her house so the whole family can eat dinner together every Sunday. It simply does not matter that he has been married for ten years. He knows if he misses dinner, his mom will be offended and upset and will likely take him out of her will. The question now arises, "Can he choose to eat somewhere other than mom's house on Sunday?" The answer is yes, but his perception of what will happen if he does not comply is reality to him, and as a result, he is paralyzed in his decision making and is no better than a puppet being controlled by a puppeteer - his mom. He can choose to eat at home if he wants to and if he was willing to accept the consequences. But instead he gives in once again, and it then escalates and spreads into other areas of his life and he gradually gives in to his mother's every wish even at the cost of his marriage. In other words, he drops everything he is doing for his wife and family if mom calls and says, "I really need you to mow my lawn today." His wife will undoubtedly get annoyed (as she should) and will nag him to stand up to his mother (which he has no intention of doing). Before long, he will feel torn between the two women in his life and will likely end up losing his sweetheart for his codependent mother.

He believes his mother needs him. He believes she cannot live without him (as if she had not managed just fine until the time he was born). What would happen if he cut the strings with his mom? She may get very angry at first, but he would become independent and so might she. He would save his marriage and show his companion that she is the most important person in his life. In time, his mom would surely figure out how to get the lawn mowed. She would eventually pay the next-door neighbor boy $10, and he would gladly mow the lawn. She definitely would not die or cease to exist. Rather than the situation escalating and taking over the son's life and ruining his marriage, it would dissipate as the mother takes responsibility for her own wellbeing. In extreme cases, some moms intentionally use their son's attention to make their daughter-in-law jealous. Notice I used the word "make." This too is only a perception because as discussed in a later chapter on anger, the mother cannot *make* her daughter-in-law feel anything.

Now back to the fairy tale. What if the man's perception was that his wife was the most important person in the world to him, and no one could come between them no matter what? With this perception, when his mom calls and asks for help, he would tell her that he needs to discuss it with his wife first and would then get back to her with *their* answer. The love in the marriage relationship would grow, respect for each other would increase, and they would be that much closer to living happily ever after.

Good Days vs. Bad Days

If our relationships can be good or bad, and it is all based on our perceptions, then why would we ever choose to have a bad relationship? My friend Hugh once told me that he loved it when his wife went out for the evening with her girlfriends because she always returned with renewed love and increased appreciation for him. Her perception of him changed as she listened to her friends talk about their husbands in a negative way. Nothing in their relationship changed but her perception had clearly been altered.

If our days can be good or bad – and it is all based on our perception – then why would we ever choose to have a bad day? My company spent a lot of money for me to see Patch Adams[5] in Anaheim, California, a few years ago. The topic he spoke on was how to never have a bad day for the rest of your life. His answer was simple: Wake up in the morning and choose to have a good day. Mr. Adams understands how perception affects our day and our moods.

This morning, if the sun is shining brightly in the east and there is not a cloud in sight, some people would be happy and some would be sad. People with Seasonal Affective Disorder would certainly be happy. Those who are looking forward to going water-skiing or having a picnic outside would be very happy. On the other hand, farmers unable to adequately care for their crops due to a drought would be sad. So here is the question, "What makes one group of people happy and another group sad by the very same situation?" The answer is found in our perception.

Perception is Reality to the Beholder

How you see life is real to you. How I see life is real to me. For a time, I was a counselor at the Utah State Prison. During one lesson, I told the inmates that they needed to get out of prison and get a job. I suggested getting a job that was 40 hours a week with a steady income. One inmate who was in prison for robbing a convenient store told me, "Webb, that might work in your world, but that's not the world I live in." His observation was certainly valid, but I helped him to understand that both worlds existed, and he had the power to choose which world he lived in. For him, reality consisted of getting up every morning and figuring out a plan to obtain money to meet his family's basic needs. In his heart, he did not believe he could hold down a job. He truly believed that his only chance at survival was stealing. He limited his options by his perception, which is something we are all guilty of at times.

This next quote is so crucial. **"Perception is reality to the beholder, but our perception does not make reality."** Just because you see life one way does not mean that life is actually that way. The above inmate's perception of life was not reality, but it was very real to him. I am certain I could find him a job that he could hold down and thereby obtain a steady income, but his limited perception did not allow him to find such a job on his own. To illustrate, it was like he was standing very close to a brick wall, and I was standing up on top of it. I yelled down and asked him what he saw, and naturally he replied that he saw a wall. I told him that just on the other side of the wall, there was a beautiful meadow with a pond in the middle and trees and flowers surrounding it. He could not see it, but that does not mean it was not there. Let me see if I can make this point more clear.

Policeman Turned Teacher

A former co-worker of mine was teaching 9th graders many years ago. He had previously been a police officer in California but decided to quit his job and move to Utah and become a schoolteacher. He was teaching the students about the law of witnesses. He explained that we need witnesses to convict a criminal and send him to prison. As he talked to the students, his wife walked into the classroom as previously arranged. None of the students knew his wife. She was wearing a long black overcoat. When she walked into the room, he asked her if he could help her. She mumbled, "Can I see so-and-so" (she made up a name). The teacher pretended he did not understand her and asked her to repeat herself. Just then, with fear in his voice, he yelled, "Don't I know you?" She pulled out a gun from under her coat and fired a couple of blank shots at him. He fell behind the desk as if he had been shot. His wife ran out of the classroom. The children naturally lost it. (It should be noted here that he never conducted this demonstration again due to the trauma to the students.) He quickly stood up and said, "You just witnessed a murder. I want you to write down all the details that you saw." Not surprisingly, the details spanned the spectrum. Some said that it was a man while others said it was a woman. Some said that the perpetrator had brown hair, others said blond hair, and still others were sure it was black hair. Not one student's description was exactly the same as another's.

To further illustrate, let's pretend you are one of the students and I'm the investigator.

"What did you see?" I ask you.

You reply, "I saw a man walk into our classroom."

I stop you in your remarks and say, "Well, let's get one thing straight - it was a woman not a man."

"No! You're wrong! I was there - I saw him with my own two eyes." You defend adamantly.

"Boys bring her in!" I yell as a woman is brought into the classroom. "We were just outside the door when she came running out, and we caught her."

Now for the first time you get to see her without all the emotions attached. You say to yourself, "I swear it was a man." Haven't you had any experiences like that before in your life where you saw something again and said to yourself, "I don't remember it that way?"

When my friend's wife, the "criminal" was brought back into the classroom, the students stared in awe. Some of them were positive it was a man, but now it was as clear as day that it was a female. We have all had experiences like that one before where we thought something was one way when it was actually the opposite. This is a good example of how our perception is reality to us, but our perception does not make reality.

Might Our Perceptions Be Wrong?

Might our perceptions be wrong? Yes, our perceptions can absolutely be wrong. Since this is the case, another look at perception is warranted, and we should be open to other people's perceptions.

I lived with five great guys while attending college. One day Frank, one of my roommates, and I argued on the couch for an entire hour. After an hour, I specifically remember Frank making a particular comment, and I said incredulously, "That's exactly what I've been trying to tell you for the last hour." Frank responded, "That's exactly what I've been trying to tell you for the last hour." We had been arguing on the exact same side of an issue for a very long time, but we were not listening to each other. Both of us were set in our perception of "I am right and he is wrong." As humans, we tend to think that in order for us to be right, someone else must be wrong.

Why must one person be wrong for another person to be right? Can we both be right? In fact, as illustrated in this example, both sides are right. We just see it from different angles. The perception of society is that in order for us to be right, someone else must be wrong. This results in an atmosphere of competition. There is another perception out there - cooperation.

In marriage counseling sessions, I typically start by flipping two milk crates over. I take out a rope and lay it down with the middle of the rope between the two milk crates. I ask each person to step up onto a milk crate. The setup seems to imply that a tug-of-war is about to start. I lift the rope up and hand a side to each of them and give them just two rules: 1) If you let go of the rope, you lose, and 2) If you fall off your crate, you lose. Then I yell, "Go!" They immediately begin a tug of war. When one person falls off, I allow them to get back on and try it again. After two or three rounds of this, I ask the one still standing why they pulled their spouse off the crate. That person usually says something like "I thought that is what I was supposed to do to win." So I inquire, "What were the two rules of this game?" They reply, "Not to let go of the rope and not to fall off the crate." I then ask, "Could you both have been winners?" They stand in awe as they realize they did not have to pull their partner off in order to win. They could have both won. Why did they not realize this? Because we have been brain washed by society with a perception that says in order for us to win the other guy has to lose. And that is simply not true!

I truly believe that the majority of all fights are due to the fact that both sides have different perceptions rather than because one person is right and another is wrong. They may very well both be right and can realize such if they would just take the time to consider another perception.

Might our perception be wrong? The answer is a resounding "Yes!" And so we should be willing to take a look at things from another point of view. This allows us to see things more as they really are because we can see things from all sides. Of course, if we do not like the other point of view, we are likely to become even more set in our own perception;

and that's O.K. However, if we do like the other point of view, our perception can change; and that's O.K. too.

Section II: How Perception Affects Moods

Depression Derived From Perception

Depression is heavily derived from a person's perception. There are people in the world who have a chemical imbalance in their brain, and they need medication to help treat legitimate chemical depression. But even these people can control the depth of their depression (to an extent) if they can change their perceptions. Studies conflict in outcomes with some demonstrating that cognitive therapy is more favorable than medication in the treatment of depression while others show that medications are the most effective. However, most agree that using medication and cognitive therapy together produces the best results. My purpose here is not to convince you of any of the findings but rather to show how cognitive therapy is about changing perceptions. I firmly believe that a change in perception is the best way to overcome depression. It is not easy, and in fact often proves to be extremely difficult. But, if treatment is easy, then you are doing it wrong, and likewise, if it is hard, you are probably doing it right. So, if you find yourself saying, "This is hard!" then celebrate, you are right on track.

Cognitive Therapy

Cognitive therapy deals with cognitions or thoughts. It helps change perceptions, and its real goal is to help us see life more realistically. There are two underlying principles of cognitive therapy. The first is that our thoughts control our feelings. I believe that all feelings are valid and that we should never fight feelings. However, I also believe that we need to find out what thoughts trigger those feelings of depression and fight those thoughts. If thoughts control feelings, then a negative thought will create a negative feeling. When we start to feel depressed, we naturally entertain more negative thoughts which create more negative feelings and thus deepen our depression. Whether depression lasts for a minute or days or longer, depression is caused by and/or exacerbated by negative thoughts.

The second principle is that all negative thoughts are illogical, irrational, and absolutely false. If you want to read more about fighting depression with cognitive therapy, please refer to Dr. David Burns' book, "Feeling Good[6]." I wish to give credit to men who have helped so much in this field particularly Dr. Albert Ellis, Dr. Aaron Beck, and Dr. David Burns.

The good news is there is hope. The truth or rational thoughts can help overcome depression because rational thoughts cause rational feelings. I will explain more throughout this chapter. I want to share a list of categories into which most negative thoughts fall. Included with each category, I will provide examples of how to change one's negative thought into a rational response, or in other words change one's perception.

Dichotomous Thinking

The first negative thought category is 'Dichotomous Thinking.' This is when life is seen in all-or-nothing terms or black-and-white terms. We are either perfect or worthless. You may think you are a bad mom or a good mom but nothing in between. Or you might see yourself as a total failure or a complete success but nothing in between the two. For example, I have a close friend who has to get straight A's in school or he thinks he is a failure. Even if he gets an A-, he feels compelled to take the class over to get a perfect grade. This is 'Dichotomous' thinking.

This kind of thinking is illogical, irrational and absolutely false. No one is a success at everything and likewise no one is a failure at everything. The truth is that we all succeed at some things and fail at other things. This is a rational response; rational meaning "the way life really is." We all succeed sometimes and fail sometimes. We all have strengths in some areas and weaknesses in other areas. This is what keeps the world spinning. We have some people who know how to grow rice. Some people know how to make cars. Some know how to make computers. Some know how to make clothes. None of us can do all these things to perfection therefore we need each other. As we all specialize in particular areas we can help each other. Together we can go a long way and achieve a lot, but no one can do everything alone. Therefore we should not think that we are failures because we can not succeed at something—that's just the way life is.

If you change this Dichotomous perception to seeing life on a continuum and not as an on/off switch, then you will begin to see life the way it really is. If you can change your perception then you would not be so harsh on yourself with the Dichotomous thinking and succumb to the feelings of depression that accompany it. Most everything in life can be seen on a continuum. For example, the success continuum has "Complete Failure" on one side and "Perfect Success" on the other side. To state it again, we all fail at some things and we all succeed at some things. Nobody is a complete failure. Some would say that Thomas Edison had reasons to feel like a failure because he had failed in making the light bulb 1000 times. However, he had a different perception and said that he did not fail 1000 times but learned 1000 ways how not to do it--success. He understood that failing is part of succeeding. We too, all of us, fail and succeed so we must stop beating others and ourselves up because we fall short of perfection.

My dad once told me of a friend of his who had straight A's all through high school. She went to college and got her first B grade and it so depressed her and ruined her self-image she ended up being institutionalized. That is 'Dichotomous' thinking to the extreme. How sad is it that she believed she had to get straight A's or she had no worth? I work with many, many clients who were raised to believe they can be nothing less than perfect. I tell them that perfection is simply not achievable in this life. We must stop the unhealthy thought process that we have to be perfect. What we do need to do is work to achieve our best, but this 'Dichotomous' thought process will destroy our happiness and possibly our lives.

I heard a story that I suspect is not true, but it illustrates the Dichotomous concept. There was a young man who really wanted to buy a BMW. He wanted to pay for it with cash, so he started saving all of his money. When he got into high school, he got a job and put all his money into the bank all the while keeping his eye on the prize of the BMW. He saved all of his money and would not spend a dime on anything else. At first his friends were willing to pay for him to go to the movies with them or chip in for his half of the pizza, but that did not last long. He lost a lot of friends and was not invited to go anywhere. Finally the day arrived when he had all the money he needed to pay cash for his precious BMW. He walked onto the car lot and picked out the car he wanted. He paid the man cash and hopped in his new car with excitement. He was so thrilled and had anticipated this day for so long. As he drove the car off the lot, he ran over a nail and got a flat tire. He got out of his car and looked at the tire and was so mad that he grabbed a can of gasoline and poured it on his car, lit it on fire, and walked away

Your first response is probably, "What?!! That is ridiculous!" But now let me ask this question, "Have you ever worked so hard on a relationship just to throw it away because of something small like a flat tire?" It happens all the time. If we do not see things eye to eye or we have a different perception than our spouse, we sometimes throw the relationship all away.

Some people give up on their marriage over a minor disagreement. If their marriage is not perfect and completely free of contention, then it is perceived as a failure. No marriage relationship is so perfect that it cannot be improved, and no marriage is so bad it could not get worse. All marriages fall somewhere in between the two extremes. The healthy approach would be to take a look at what is good in the marriage and keep it and then take a look at what is bad in the marriage and work on it.

So when we have a Dichotomous thought we need to recognize it first. Then we need to replace it with a rational response. A rational response is another way of saying the same thing but in a way that is real to life. For example, if I think I am a bad dad then I should recognize that as Dichotomous Thinking. Then I need to replace it with a rational thought like, "I have some good parenting skills and bad parenting skills." Isn't this true? Isn't this reality? If I say that I'm a bad dad then that simply isn't true. What is one good quality about me as a dad if I say that? The answer may be that I feel some remorse simply because I said, "I'm a bad dad" and isn't that a good quality.

Here's another example, "I'm a loser." Here again, I am going to 'Dichotomous' thinking by thinking that I am either a winner or a loser. Reality teaches me that, "Sometimes I win and sometimes I lose." This is rational, logical and absolutely true. Do you know anyone who has failed at everything in life? No. Take a look at their shirt and pants. Are they where they are supposed to be? In other words is the shirt on top and are the pants on bottom. Then in that particular moment they were a winner. Therefore it would be irrational, illogical and absolutely false to say, "I'm a total loser" which is what we mean when we say, "I'm a loser."

Overgeneralization
The next category of negative thought distortions is 'Overgeneralization.' This is when we use words that exaggerates a single event and generalizes it. It is when we use words like everybody, nobody, always, and never. For example, we might say to our spouse, "You never listen to me." Is that really true? Remember all negative thoughts are illogical, irrational, and absolutely false. Therefore, that statement is not true. If it was true then we probably would never have married that person. Who would marry someone

who never listens to him or her? A rational statement would be, "Sometimes you listen to me and sometimes you don't." That is more logical and truthful. What we are really meaning to say is, "I want you to listen to me now." But instead of the other person listening to us they begin to argue about the word, "never". They might respond with, "What do you mean I never listen to you? I listened to you the other night. Remember?" 'Overgeneralization' leads to arguments about what is real rather than opening up dialogue that might help a relationship.

Remember the song that starts out with, "Nobody likes me. Everybody hates me. I'm going to eat some worms."? Well, that simply isn't true. One time the Pope stood up and expressed his love for everyone in the whole world. Because of that alone, we can never say, "Nobody loves me" because that simply is not true, the Pope does, and it is likely that many others do as well. The rational thought is, "Some people like me and some don't." I like to remember that, "Hitler had friends and Jesus had enemies." It does not matter how you live your life, some will like you and some will not. That is reality.

Just because one person does not like you this does not mean that nobody likes you. But often times our thought process leads us to believe just that. We need to say, "Okay. I'll put you on the list of people who don't like me, and I'll spend my time with those on the list of people who do like me." Would this thought cause me to feel depressed? I do not believe so.

I had a client once who was convinced he was *always* messing up. I asked him to look down at his shoes and tell me if his right shoe was on the right foot and the left shoe on the left foot. Luckily for both of us, he got it right that morning. I then cheered and gave him a high five for getting it right. I also pointed out that because he did something right, he could never say that he *always* messed up because we found an exception (and there were likely many more).

The point I am trying to make is that the feeling attached to the comment, "I'm always messing up" is negative and triggers depressed feelings. On the other hand, the feeling attached to the comment, "Sometimes I mess up and sometimes I don't" is not negative but is rather neutral. It does not bring us down and thus allows us to put things in perspective. It helps us see life the way it really is and gives us confidence in dealing with difficult situations.

If you change your perception and see life as it really is rather than in the context of the extremes that accompany 'Overgeneralization,' then your perspective is more accurate and more rational which will combat depressive thoughts.

Negative Filter

Imagine a funnel with a filter in it. The filter traps all of the good and only the bad comes out the bottom. This falls into the category of Negative Filter. A Negative Filter works in this way and only focuses on the bad in a situation.

A prisoner in a state penitentiary might say, "This place stinks!" He is only focusing on the bad or the negative. So, is there any good in prison? I worked in the Utah State prison for two years as a drug counselor, and I can tell you, there are several positive things about prison. For example, a college education is offered to the inmates free of charge. They have a roof over their heads that does not leak, and they are fed three meals a day. Medical treatment was offered to them free of charge, they got to go to the gym without paying a membership fee, and I could go on and on. (Don't let me convince you though that prison is a great place to go; it isn't.)

The point is that every situation has some good in it, and when we choose to see only the bad, we do not see life completely. Our perception needs to open up a little to enable us to see the good as well as the bad. There is a story of a president of a company who went out to see a newly constructed building for the first time. At the building site, there was a pile of dirt still in the parking lot. A member of the construction team made the comment that they needed to clear away the dirt before the president's arrival. Upon hearing that, another workman said, "The president will never even notice the dirt. He only sees the good." What about you? What about me? Would we have seen the dirt, or would we have chosen to focus only on the good?

Do we choose to see the good as well as the bad? Or do we only see the bad? Do we quickly look for the weaknesses in other people when we meet them for the first time? It all comes down to perception. When I teach about Negative Filter in class, I usually have a student ask me, "What if I only see the good?" I tell him that Negative Filter is a category of negative thought distortions. If he only sees the good then it is not negative. And I personally would recommend he keep it up but to be aware so that he is not naïve.

A professor in my Master's program changed a perception of mine when he told me, "I believe everyone is trying to do their best. They do the best they can with the upbringing they received, their experience, their knowledge, their current state of mind, and their perception." As I heard this, I realized that it was true. My perception now is that people are doing their best, and this is very liberating for me.

If our perception was that everyone is trying to do their best, would we see the world differently? I knew a man whose approach to life was, "Screw them before they screw me." Not surprisingly, he was miserable and did not have any friends. Yet his perception was very real to him. He had been hurt in the past and believed everyone was out to get him. My perception is that people are generally good and are not out to get me. As a result, I have a lot of friends and enjoy much happiness in my life. Both worlds exist because of perception and it is up to us to choose which one we will live in. Would you rather choose to live in misery or happiness?

Let me give you two examples. Joe was at the park with his family for a family reunion. There were a lot of different activities going on, and most of the people were having a great time. Some people were sitting at the picnic table catching up on the latest; others were playing volleyball. Some were playing Frisbee while others were playing horseshoes. Suddenly, his little boy ran up to him crying and screaming and having a fit. His first impression was anger, and he thought, "Stop it! You're ruining everyone's fun with your tantrum." At that moment, he did not see the good going on all around him and was only focused on the negative. He believed that his son's behavior turned the reunion into a disaster. His perception was real to him, but his wife later explained that she had a wonderful day. Her perception was real to her, and because she chose that perception, she had a wonderful day.

For the next example, Sam was in church in the back row trying to listen to the preacher. There was a small child on the pew in front of him who was trying to play with him or at least get his attention. He tried to concentrate and feel the spirit, but this child was distracting him. He started to focus on this annoying child who was throwing her toy at him and then asking for it back. At the end of the sermon, he walked out totally annoyed and thinking, "That whole meeting was a waste of time. I didn't get a thing out of it." At the same time, he heard others in the hall saying, "That was the best sermon I have ever heard." Why did he not hear the best sermon ever? His focus was on the negative even though the positive was also in the room, and as a result he was not uplifted and moved the way the others were.

The same principle applies when we only see the negative in ourselves. We tend to see only the negative things in ourselves, and we ignore or overlook the positive. We must realize that there is good as well as bad in all of us. There is good and bad all around us. A good example of this is thinking, "I'm so fat." If this is your thought then you are only focusing on the negative. Do you have a cute smile? Toes? Hair? Etc.? We must start seeing the good and the bad.

If I walk through life being depressed because I only see the negative then that will actually create a life of only negativity. I could actually reinforce the very tool that is destroying my life and making me depressed. What I find interesting is that often times when we are pessimistic we see the bad in everyone else except for ourselves. It is as if we have blinders on to our own bad qualities or our negativity. So often we want to find some outside source for our discomfort when in reality we are to blame for the majority of our own discomfort.

Let me give an example of the individual being the source of his own discomfort. There are many people who get married then divorced. They remarry then they get divorced again. Then I hear them say, "Women are all the same!" Or "Men are all the same!" I often say to them, "The one common denominator in all your dysfunctional relationships is you." But the sad thing is these people do not see their part in it.

There is good as well as bad in all of us and life in general has its ups and downs. Every situation has positive and negative elements to it. With this perception, we can keep the negative aspects in perspective and avoid the depressive tendencies that come with Negative Filter.

Disqualifying the Positive

The category 'Disqualifying the Positive' is when someone compliments you and you immediately discredit what they say. You reject the compliment. For example, I said to a new client one time, "You're a good person." His immediate response was, "You don't know me." That is 'Disqualifying the Positive.' Unfortunately we live in a society where it is easier to accept an insult than a compliment? If I called you a loser, you might say, "Yea, loser, that's me." But if I were to compliment you on your cooking, you might say, "Anyone could have added water to that box of noodles." We do it for a number of reasons. One reason might be that we are under the impression that accepting a compliment is prideful, which is not necessarily the case.

Have you ever heard that for every negative comment you tell a child, the child needs 10 positive comments to get him back up to a normal level? I believe that is true because we have taught children to accept the negatives and disregard the positives. How sad! For most of us, it is easier to take an insult than a compliment. What is wrong with us, or better said, what is wrong with our society?

Maybe we do it because we have a 'Negative Filter' negative thought and we only see the bad, so when someone compliments us we truly do not believe it. The rational response is that we all have good and bad qualities, and right now someone is pointing out one of our good qualities. That perception does not drag me down as this one does: "He's just saying that because he thinks he has to."

Another way we 'Disqualify the Positive' is we tell ourselves that we are not good enough. Maybe we have a job interview and we skip out on it because we tell ourselves we are not good enough to get the job so why waste the time. 'Disqualifying the Positive' would stop us from going to school, asking someone out, getting a better job, making friends, and reaching our dreams.

If we change our perception and see our good qualities as well as our bad qualities and learn to graciously accept a compliment, then we will feel less depressed and gain a healthy perception of what really is true. We will then be able to see the positive things around us because our vision will not be hindered by our attitude.

I would guess that the majority of all people have more good qualities than bad qualities. Thus, if we see a negative aspect about ourselves we should list 10 positive things about ourselves. It helps us stay rational. If you are too hard on yourself and you cannot see 10 positive things about yourself then ask a parent, sibling or friend what they like about you. Then believe them.

One of the problems with 'Disqualifying the Positive' is that when your parent, sibling or friend tells you what they like about you, you say to yourself, "They are just being nice. That is not what they really think." This thought falls into the next category, 'Mind Reading' but for now just believe them.

Mind Reading

As the name implies, Mind Reading is when you think you can read someone else's mind. "I just know they don't like me" is an example of this if those in question have never made such a statement. We often declare: "I can just tell because of how they looked at me." However, I remember a time when I was standing underneath a ceiling fan and the breeze was really bothering my contacts. I was talking to someone, and I really wanted to look him in the eyes, but I could not without blinking abnormally. Those of you with contacts can understand what I mean. What did that person think of me? Did my actions indicate that I did not like that person because I did not look him in the eye? When we mind read, we do not understand all the circumstances revolving around that person and have to assume information that we have not been given, which we often do inaccurately.

For example, if you told me a joke today about death, I might laugh. However, if my mother died last night and you told me that same joke, I would likely take offense and get upset because I am extra sensitive on that subject right now. Not knowing why I acted that way, you might think, "What a jerk!" Your mind reading might have concluded that I am too sensitive and cannot take a joke. So, you decide to never tell a joke to me again even though in reality I have a very healthy sense of humor.

The rational response to mind reading is, "I am not God. I can not read minds. If I want to know what someone is thinking, I'll ask." Asking allows us to see another person's perception and enables us to change ours if we so choose. If we think someone does not like us (for whatever reason), we should simply walk up to them and ask, "Do you not like me?" They can then explain their position. They may even ask, "No, why did you think that?" We can then explain where we are coming from, and they can too; and if we are open and honest with each other, perceptions are changed and conflict can be resolved.

Here is an example from the prison. An inmate was sitting in his section just looking around at all the other inmates when his eyes subconsciously focused on one particular inmate. As he stared unknowingly at this inmate, his mind started to daydream and before long he was sitting on the beach in San Diego feeling the sand and smelling the ocean. The other inmate suddenly noticed the guy staring at him. He looked away and then looked back, and of course the first guy (still daydreaming about the beach) was still looking at him. The second inmate started pointing out this unwelcome stare to his buddies and finally went over and asked, "Do you have a problem with me?" Now in the prison setting, if asked that question, one can say, "Yes" and fight, or one can say, "No" and look like a punk which is the second worst thing you can be called in prison. So the first inmate was startled off the beach by an angry fellow inmate right in his face asking, "Do you have a problem with me? You want to take it to the closet?" (They fought in the closet to hide from the guards.) These two went into the closet and fought and someone got hurt. The second inmate was fighting because he perceived that the first inmate was challenging him to a fight by starring him down. The first inmate's perception was that he needed to save face, but in reality he did not have a clue why they were even fighting. So their perceptions become reality to them and they acted on them, even though neither perception was reality.

Mind reading rears its ugly head most often in marriage/love relationships. For example, one night I walked into my house after a long day at work. My wife, of course, had been working hard at home all day. As I walked in, she expected me to recognize that even though she had a long hard day, she made a special effort to get cleaned up to look nice for me. Being too tired to notice, I simply said, "Hi" and walked into the bedroom to change. Her mind reading told her that I did not care about her (and in turn love her) enough to recognize her efforts. My perception was, "It's great to be home and not have all the chaos like I do at work." She was mad. I was oblivious to her state of mind. If I had any idea of the amount of work she had done, I would have recognized it and made her feel good for it, but my mind was somewhere else. Her perception was not reality although to her it was. We will further address relationships later in the book.

Mind reading is rarely a positive thing. We must take the responsibility to ask others for their thoughts rather than assuming we already know. That way they can own their feelings and opinions and explain them, if necessary. We likewise will not be influenced by the negative feelings associated with mind reading.

Erroneously Predicting the Future

Erroneously Predicting the Future includes thoughts which predict the future turning out poorly. This could occur by simply using an, "I can't" statement. How do you know you can't unless you try? The perception of the outcome of a situation is automatically negative before the situation has been given a chance to play out. These negative thoughts set us up for failure or what is called a self-fulfilling prophecy. For example, a young man was sitting in a park with a friend and a pretty woman walked by. The young man told his friend that he wanted to ask her out, but every time (overgeneralization) he asked anyone out, they turned him down. The friend gave him a nice pep talk and built up his self-esteem until he finally said, "I'll do it." He walked up to this woman and said, "Excuse me; I was wondering if you would like to go out with me sometime? I know I just got out of rehab, and I know I have a codependent relationship with my parents. I don't have a job yet but I am on unemployment. My probation officer said I can stay out until 8pm now. I have some financial problems but my bankruptcy is about done. If you could look past all that, would you consider going out with me please?" She responded with a quick, "No" and walked away. The young man returned to his friend and said, "See! I told you she would say no!" Do you see how he set himself up for failure by thinking the future (asking her out) was going to end up with a rejection?

We often set ourselves up for failure because of our perceptions. The rational perception is, "I'm not God. I can't predict the future. If I want to know, I'll hope for the best and wait and see what happens." This way we are not entering the situation with a negative outcome already in mind.

Another example occurred at a park where a group of people were playing volleyball, and they invited a young woman standing nearby to play. She told them she was not any good at volleyball and did not want to play. They proceeded to encourage and even beg her because they needed just one more player to have a game. The young woman gave into peer pressure and joined them in the volleyball pit. The game got started and the young lady thought over and over again in her mind, "I sure hope the ball doesn't come to me because if it does I'll hit it out of bounds. I always (overgeneralization) hit the ball out of bounds." The ball eventually came to her. Where do you think she hit it? She hit it out of bounds, of course. Why? She hit it out of bounds because she told herself, "If the ball comes to me, I'm going to hit it out of bounds." That is what her brain was saying. The brain controls the body. Let us pretend that she "accidentally" hit the ball over the net and scored a point for her team. She most likely would have jumped to disqualifying the positive and said, "That was lucky. I hope the ball doesn't come back to me."

None of us can predict the future, and if you want to know what will happen, just do your best and wait and see. Do not waste your energy worrying about things that may never exist. Do not subject yourself to the depressive feelings accompanied by predicting a negative outcome or future.

Comparison

Comparison is a category where we compare ourselves with others. When we compare ourselves to other people, we tend to exaggerate other people's strengths and understate their weaknesses. At the same time, we understate our own strengths and exaggerate our weaknesses. Then we compare the two things we have just magnified. In other words we compare our weaknesses to the other people's strengths. For example, we look at a great basketball player and say, "What a great basketball player." We are then reminded that he has a gambling problem. We persist, "Yea, but what a great basketball player." Focusing on the negative, we observe, "I am a terrible basketball player." A friend then reminds us, "But you are great at public speaking," and our thoughts drift back to, "Yea, but I am a terrible basketball player." We are comparing our weakness (playing basketball) to someone else's strength (playing basketball).

Women oftentimes say with disgust, "She is so pretty" or "She is so thin." What they are not saying out loud is, "I am ugly." They are comparing someone else's strength (perceived beauty) to their perceived weakness (ugliness). Sadly enough, the one we are often comparing ourselves to is not a person at all but rather an airbrushed edited version of a model in a magazine. They edit the pictures to chop away a few pounds here and there, remove a few wrinkles, add a nice bronze tone, and place each hair in the perfect place. Women then compare themselves to this fake image, and their perception tells them this is how they should be.

We may sit in church and see another family whose children sit quietly each week and listen to the preacher. We then look at our children who are restless and embarrassing us with their wiggles and noise. Naturally we wonder, "Why can't our children be more like the Johnson children?" Our perception is that the Johnson children are behaving because they love church and they possess a maturity far beyond what our children demonstrate. We do not always have all the information however, and maybe there are dire consequences for the Johnson children at home if they do not behave at church. Again, we do not understand all the mitigating circumstances when we make comparisons; therefore, it is wise to avoid them all together.

If you have not seen it first hand, certainly you have heard about the next example. There were two children sitting at the dinner table doing their homework when dad arrived home from work. Mom handed over the children's report cards which arrived in the mail that afternoon. He read the first report card with pride and said, "Good job Julie, you got straight A's." Dad read the second report card and saw a "C" in Math. He frowned at Timmy and scolded, "Timmy you got a 'C' in math. Why can't you be more like your sister?" How sad! Maybe Timmy's strength is not Math and instead he excels in Art. His dad compared his weakness (Math) to his sister's strength (Math). This is also a good example of a negative filter in which the father saw only the bad and disregarded the good in his son. He never complimented Timmy for his other grades which happened to be all A's.

The rational response and reality is, "We all have strengths, and we all have weaknesses." Some are good at basketball; others are good at building cars. Some are good at math and some are good at pottery. This is how we can all live together much better than living alone. We share our strengths but there is no reason to compare our weakness with another person's strength. This is not comparing apples to apples. When we compare ourselves to others, we are hurting ourselves by setting unrealistic expectations which can lead to depressive feelings. Just do your best and stop using other people's yardsticks to measure your life.

I have a yardstick that I flipped over and on the backside made it a two-yard stick. Each inch now represents two inches. I give it to my clients and ask them if it really is a two-yard stick. They answer, "Of course not." I then ask, "Why do you measure your life with a different yardstick than you measure others' lives with?" If another person made the same mistake you did, you would easily forgive them. But you will not forgive yourself. Why? You measure their lives differently than you do your own. Stop it. See the good in you (your strength) and do not compare your weaknesses with anyone else's strength. Just do your best and be happy with that. God does not grade us on a curve so neither should we grade ourselves on a curve.

Catastrophizing and Minimizing

A catastrophe is an extremely large-scale disaster, a horrible event. Catastrophizing then, is when a person takes an issue and blows it up into a large-scale disaster or a horrible event. When a person does this, we often say they are seeking attention or are drama queens. This behavior tends to annoy us and we wish they would live in reality. Some people have done this for so long they do not recognize it nor are they doing it consciously. If they are not doing it consciously then it is a bigger issue than they think. It has become in-part who they are.

I had a client once who found a bump on her arm. She immediately started telling people she might have cancer. She started preparing for her death. She set up a doctor's appointment and found out it was an allergic reaction to something and it went away the next week. Sometimes we "make mountains out of mole hills." Wayne W. Dyer put it this way, "Don't "pole-vault over mouse turds" - by the time you've discussed the many options available to you, the problem itself could have been long behind you had you simply disposed of those rodent droppings with a simple tissue and dumped them into the garbage!"

Minimizing then goes in the opposite direction and minimizes or shrinks something of great importance. When a person does this to themselves they typically do not think they deserve better. They believe life is out to get them. They have given up on the fight and have surrendered to a hopeless state of being. They minimize their accomplishments, skills, talents and anything that might give them an emotional boost. For these people they can never do enough.

This could be directed towards others by stating, "I don't judge others." For example, a woman dating a man who was recently charged with child molestation who states, "He said he will never do it again." She has minimized his behavior and put her children at risk by bringing him into their home. She justifies her behaviors by saying she is a forgiving person.

Another example of minimizing is when a child is taken away from her parents and the parents say, "She is better off with someone else." That might be true or not, but here it is being used to not feel or deal with the natural emotions of longing and wanting to be with their child. This is achieved by convincing the parents it's not that big of a deal.

We must be willing to see life (which includes our feelings) as it really is. We must feel the bad as well as the good. We must not exaggerate or minimize the hand life has dealt us.

Emotional Reasoning

I mentioned at the beginning of this chapter that our thoughts control our feelings. Emotional Reasoning is when we believe our emotions control our thoughts. For example, "I feel stupid, therefore I am stupid" or "I feel like a jerk, therefore I am a jerk." Since we know that feelings come after thoughts we should be saying, "I feel stupid. Why? What thought preceded this feeling?"

Sometimes we feel things about other people and assume it must be true. I had a client who was convinced that his lover had cheated on him. "I feel that he cheated on me therefore I know he did." But after asking him, his lover told him that he had not cheated on him. But my client wanted to continue to hold the resentment even though there was no proof that his feeling was correct.

I actually know of another person who went through the exact same scenario. It turned out the reason she was pointing the finger at her husband for cheating on her was because she was cheating on him. She couldn't believe that he was not cheating on her if she could not be faithful to him.

The rational response is a little different than the other categories. What we should do is go backwards and figure out what thought preceded the feeling. With this process of backtracking, we can isolate and combat the negative thought. After identifying the previous negative thought, we can place it in one of the other eleven negative thought distortion categories and fight it. For example, if I had the thought, "I feel like a loser, therefore I am a loser" then I would ask myself why? My next answer might be, "Because I lost the basketball game for everyone." Is this true? Was I the only player that missed at least one shot in the entire game? No. I would also ask myself what my definition of loser is and then switch over to the Labeling category. (This category will be explained below) If we do not go backwards on our emotional reasoning and fight the negative thought that preceded our feelings then we are more likely to continue to entertain negative thoughts which can lead to depression.

We must realize that feelings do not create thoughts but rather thoughts create feelings. With an understanding of that principle, we can avoid the helplessness and depression that comes from emotional reasoning. Emotional reasoning is an important category to understand. It also plays a big part in anxiety which will be discussed later in the book.

I would like to make a quick comment on inspiration. Sometimes inspiration comes our way and we feel something is wrong with our children (or something else) and we need to learn the difference between inspiration and emotional reasoning. Both are real. One we need to give heed to and the other we need to replace with a rational response.

Must/Should Statements

A Must/Should Statement is a statement which uses words like: must, should, should not, and ought. This is a negative thought category because we punish ourselves for what we must or should have done or must or should not have done when there is nothing we can do about that now. Who writes our must/should statements? We do of course. So why not rewrite them?

There is a purpose to must/should statements. They are to get us back on track. But once we are back on track, the must/should statement has to stop. The psychologist Clayton Barbeau came up with the term "shoulding yourself" to describe this cognitive distortion. Another psychologist, Albert Ellis, calls it "musterbation." Many of my clients beat themselves up for past behaviors. They repeat over and over again: "I should have never used drugs." I ask them, "Are you using today?" Their reply is "No." I question further, "Are you planning on using tomorrow?" Their response again is a resounding "No." Then what is the purpose of saying, "I should not have ever used?"

The rational response would suggest that the must/should statement be rewritten into a goal like this: "I'm not going to use today." This goal inspires confidence, as they realize they are back on track. Now they have set it as a productive and attainable goal to not abuse substances, and they can work on that goal each and every day. Otherwise they are constantly kicking themselves down and living with regret for what they should not have done. They feel so much shame and guilt that they actually go out and use again to dull the pain. It is counterproductive.

Family members do the same thing thinking they are helping. A family member might say, "You should have hit your brakes faster and not caused the accident." That may be true but is this family member really teaching a lesson or are they putting the other person down? Then there are family members who will never get over an issue but choose to hold on to their resentments forever. This is the family member's issue and you can read about resentments later in the book to learn how to let go of them. But it does not help to knock a person down when they are back on track. We need to help those who are trying to get up and stay up.

Do not waste your time beating yourself up for what you did or did not do. Decide today to learn from your past and set goals for the present and the future. Do not fall into the depressive trap that comes from living in the past by entertaining a must/should statement. Learn from the past, live in the present, and prepare for the future.

Labeling

Labeling is basically name-calling. Whether you call someone else a name or call yourself a name, it is the same – labeling. To demonstrate why labeling is illogical, irrational, and absolutely false, I will share a conversation I had with a client:

Jason: "Tell me a name you have called someone else before?"

Client: "Jerk."

Jason: "Will you define that for me? Someone who…"

Client: "Someone who is mean."

Jason: "Someone who is mean sometimes or all the time?"

Client: "Sometimes because no one is mean all of the time."

Jason: "Hasn't everyone been mean sometime in their life?"

Client: "I suppose so."

Jason: "Then according to your definition, everyone is a jerk."

Client: "Well I don't believe everyone is a jerk."

Jason: "Then you need to redefine jerk."

And so the conversation continues in a cycle of definition, then application to everyone, and then redefining. A rational response would have you define your label then apply it to everyone (including yourself). The same applies if you label yourself. Define the word and then apply it to everyone else. My clients who call themselves names often defend their position by saying that their definition does not apply to everyone - just to themselves. I logically respond by saying, "I never knew there was a Webster Dictionary just for you." We cannot just make up words and assign their meaning to certain people and things.

That is why labeling is illogical, irrational, and absolutely false. If a label applies to everyone, then it is the norm, and if it is the norm, it should not be labeled. The other problem with labeling is that labels are absolute. If I say, "Jason is a loser," then I am really saying that from the time I was born until the time I die, I was and am and will be a loser. This means that I am the problem. If my perception is that I really am the problem, then there is only one way to solve the problem and that is by eliminating me. But, I am not the problem. You are not the problem. I have problems, but I am not the problem. You have problems, but you are not the problem. If I can identify my problems, then I can solve them. I would then have something to work on. For example, instead of saying, "I'm a bad dad," I would identify that I have problems with communication skills, parenting skills, conflict resolution, and controlling my temper. Now that I have identified these areas, I can work on improving them and making changes where they are needed. If I am walking down the street and someone calls me a loser, what am I supposed to do? What do I need to work on? They have not given me anything but a label.

We all have problems and we all have things we need to work on. If we can identify the problems and concentrate on those areas for improvement, then we can make progress. However, if we just label ourselves then we cannot do anything but get depressed. Labels are completely unproductive in that they do not provide us with any constructive feedback on what needs work. Be kind to yourself and stop labeling yourself or others. It is illogical, irrational, and absolutely false.

Personalization

Personalization is when you blame yourself for something that went wrong around you. I'm not talking about breaking a window and claiming to have done so. Here's an example of what I mean: One day I was talking to my mom, and she said that she felt like a bad mom because of something my sister had done (as an adult). I asked my mom if she blamed herself for all the bad choices her children have made, and she said she did. I asked her if she would accept all the credit for the good choices her children have made. She said, "Of course not, that is their doing." My siblings are all adults with their own lives and if they make a bad choice, my mom feels like it is her fault. She takes the blame but none of the credit. Does that make sense? That is personalization, and it makes no sense. Even if my mom was a perfect mother, that does not mean her children would accept everything they have been taught and make good decisions their entire life.

One day I was teaching a class, and I wrote the following on the board:

Mom + dad + siblings + friends + media + church + society + individual = individual's decision

When a child does something wrong, moms see: Mom = individual's decision.

When a child does something good, moms see: individual = individual's decision.

I said to the class, "My mom feels like it is all her fault when her children mess up. What about society's influence and what about individual choice? And when her children do something right, she quickly takes herself out of the equation and says it must be because of individual choice. This perception often leaves my mom with depressive feelings, and it stands in need of change."

Looking at the above equation it is easy to see how the decision of one person is not solely based upon his mother's teaching. Life would be a lot easier if the children always did what their mothers taught them but unfortunately that is not how life works. The equation above is even simplified. What if we were to break down "society's influence" into its smallest parts? We would include billboards, television, radio, church, brand names and fads, and friends such as John, Mike and Mary.

Now seeing the equation with all its parts makes the idea that my mother is responsible for her children's behavior absurd. We do our best as parents and then we do what is taught in Alcoholics Anonymous, "Let go and let God."

The best example I have of personalization comes from a 40-year-old man I counseled in prison. I taught him these negative thought distortion categories, ending with personalization as we have here. He turned to me and tearfully said, "Are you telling me I didn't kill my sister?" When he was 10 years old, he was living with his dad and stepmother. His stepmother asked him to go into the backyard and play with his stepbrother and stepsister (her biological children).

53

His biological mother showed up and asked him if he would like to go to lunch with her. Of course he jumped at the chance and left with her. While they were off eating lunch and enjoying their time together, his little stepsister fell out of a tree and landed on her head and died. When he got home, his stepmother angrily accused him of killing his sister. She believed that if he had stayed home, he would have been keeping an eye on his stepsister and she would not have fallen and died. At age 10, he accepted her accusations as fact and blamed himself for killing his stepsister. This was his perception and he hated himself for it. Is it any wonder why he rode with the Hell's Angels and turned to a life of drugs and alcohol? It makes perfect sense to me.

So when he asked me, "Are you telling me I didn't kill my sister?" I responded with, "Are you telling me that if you were there that day and saw your sister fall out of the tree, you would have ripped your shirt off and shown the 'S' on your chest and flew over to her and caught her in your arms and saved her life rather than have been another witness to her death?" He broke down and sobbed. "Why did she do that to me?" He begged for an answer with more feelings than he had ever felt in his life before. I said, "My best guess is that she felt guilty for her daughter's death and if she could pass the buck on to you and get you to believe it, then she wouldn't have to own it herself." He just continued to sob in my office as he began to let go of all the shame and guilt that had destroyed his life for so many years. That is personalization.

Have you ever heard someone say, "Wherever I go bad things happen?" As if God is following that person around and making His decisions based upon this one person. The rational response or perception to personalization is, "I am not God. The world does not revolve around me." Some things break while new, and some things wait until they are old to break. When I was looking for a home, my realtor said, "The difference between new homes and old homes is new problems verses old problems." Some people die young, and some people die of old age. If you think you are so important that everything revolves around you, just put your fist into a bucket of water and pull it out and see what kind of hole you left. To the world as a whole, we mean nothing, and by that I mean that we are replaceable. If we died today, our loved ones would gather to mourn, but the world would definitely go on without us even if we were the president of the United States of America. In fact, his replacement is already in place in case he does die. Now on the other hand, if you want to know how important you are to God, the answer is infinitely important. We have worth to Him beyond our greatest comprehension but even so, life does not revolve around us.

Assignment

The following exercise is recommended by Dr. Burns and I agree. Make three columns on a piece of paper. In the first column, write down all your negative thoughts. I can hear some of you saying, "All of them? That will take a long time." The answer is, "Yes, all of them." In the second column, identify which of the above categories the negative thoughts fall into. They may actually fall into more than one column. In the last column, write a rational response to each of the negative thoughts. This is a process by which we can stop entertaining negative thoughts because we can clearly see just how illogical, irrational, and absolutely false our negative thoughts are. I recommend doing this on paper until you have all the categories memorized, and the process becomes automatic in your head.

One day after studying the book, "Feeling Good,"[7] I was driving down the street in Orem, Utah. I was in the right lane as I pulled up to a red light. Normally as a person in the right lane drives up to a red light but intends to drive straight through the intersection, he pulls over to the far left of that lane to enable cars turning right to make their turn without waiting for the green light. This was my situation. However, an accident had occurred in my lane on the opposite side of the intersection that blocked me from proceeding through the intersection. I decided to turn right, and I started to creep forward looking for a break in the traffic to turn right. As I was trying to merge in, the car to my right pulled up right next to me and did not allow me to enter that turning lane. My first thought was, "What a jerk!" I then remembered that I was labeling. I then defined "jerk" as "someone who cuts other people off." I then asked myself if I had ever cut someone off. I realized that all people have at one time or another cut another person off whether or not it was intentional or unintentional. I quickly realized that the person next to me was not actually a jerk. I then began to see the whole picture, and I actually encouraged him to go into that turn lane by moving over to the far left of my lane. That day by thinking about the rational response I did not let the other driver or the situation get to me. My life was okay, and I went on without further interruption.

Summary

I know this may seem too easy, but it works and it is definitely not easy, especially at first. We become depressed because of the thoughts we choose to entertain. The world around us is painted in such a negative light that we begin to believe that is the way life really is. On the evening news, how often do you see a Boy Scout helping an elderly woman cross the road? Not often, if ever. Instead we see murders, fighting, wars, and destruction, and we come to believe that there is nothing positive happening in our world. How much of a 30-minute sitcom is negative? Almost all of it is negative. Many believe the days of sitting on the lake shore fishing with our boys, like we saw on The Andy Griffith Show[8], are over. They certainly do not have to be. They still exist for those who choose to see it and believe it and live it.

I was invited to a dinner some time ago with a speaker named Neil Cavuto[9]. He anchors a segment on Fox News called "Common Sense." He said that when he reports a bad news story, he also tries to report a good news story along with it. He told us that the New York Times staff got angry with him when he reported an employment rate of 96% instead of reporting the unemployment rate at 4%. What is wrong with that? Unfortunately I believe it all has to do with politics. That is what is wrong with that. The political environment in our country is less than fair, and things are constantly being painted into a negative light to make others look bad. How pitiful! The negativity and constant bickering is a drain on all of us.

We can choose to open up our perception and see life for what it really is. I am not suggesting that we ignore the bad, but rather that we choose to see the good with the bad. Both are all around us. In fact, I would bet that we are surrounded far more by good than bad. Most people are good people. Unfortunately, those that are bad often make the most noise and are given more of a voice than they deserve. Do not buy into it! Let good people's actions speak louder than bad people's verbal comments.

Here is how we do our part. We recognize that most things are not black and white. We do not overgeneralize when we speak or think. We see the good as well as the bad. We accept compliments. We stop comparing ourselves. We stop exaggerating or minimizing life's events. We stop mind reading. We stop predicting the future will be bad. We rewrite our "should" statements. We stop labeling others and ourselves. We stop personalizing everything that goes wrong. And we understand that our feelings are created by our thoughts not the other way around.

Anger Derived From Perception

Jason's Anger Transformation

When I was younger, I was hyperactive and had a very bad temper. Now for those of you who know me, I know that it will be a stretch of your imagination to comprehend such a picture. I remember the boys in the neighborhood coming over to my house in Concord, California, and taunting me, sometimes by hitting me, and saying, "Let's see the Incredible Hulk come out." I would get very mad and pick up rocks to throw at them. They would laugh and grab the metal garbage can lids (in those days the lids came off the garbage cans). I would throw the rocks and yell at them. Before long, my mom would come out of the house and grab hold of me and scold, "Control yourself!" I remember twisting in her arms to break loose saying (which I truly believed), "I can't control myself." She would then take me into my bedroom. My grandma, "the witch doctor," had an herb for everything, so my mom would give me one of her herbs called "Lady Slipper." I believe it was taken off the market because they did not like the results of this guinea pig. Nevertheless, my mom would put me in my room and tell me not to come out until I was calm. It did not take even five minutes before all the energy was drained out of me, and I would walk out of my room with my head down, walking slowly. My mom would ask, "Are you better now?" I would nod my head and respond sleepily, "Yea."

I know this situation did not play out every day, but my memory (or perception) of my childhood says that it did. I knew the routine and started telling my mom that I wanted to take the "medicine" with milk or juice because if I took it with water I could taste it when the capsule opened up inside of me.

A friend who knew of my story asked me for help with her child's out-of-control behavior. I explained to her that I used to say "I can't control myself," and even looking back on it today, I do not believe that I could. First of all, no one taught me what to do when I got mad. All I was taught was what not to do. My perception was limited to: if I get slapped in the face, then I get mad and throw rocks. I was little, and I felt the need to protect myself. Maybe I took the Bible story of David and Goliath a little too literally.

So everyone wants to know what happened. Frankly, I want to know what happened too. I have looked at my behavior over and over again, and the only answer I have is that I scared myself so much with my uncontrolled anger that I began to be afraid of me, and I did not like who I was becoming. When I was 12 years old, my family moved from Concord, California, to Phoenix, Arizona. I thought, "I don't like who I am." I consciously planned to make a change in my personality so Arizona would be a fresh start.

I stopped throwing rocks and fighting with my fists. Instead, I became good at arguing. I would argue any side of any issue just for the sake of argument. I would argue to make other people mad. I would argue just to have the final word. I remember my mom arguing with me (she was my favorite target) and pointing out, "You always have to have the last word!" "No I don't," was my reply. My mom at times was at the end of her rope and she would yell, "See you're doing it again. Now shut up!" "Okay mom," was my last attempt to push her buttons. It worked, and she yelled, "Don't even agree with me! Just shut up!"

I do not share this story to make my mom look bad because she is a great mom. I share this story to show how ruthless I became with my words. I convinced myself, however, that I was much improved just because I had stopped fighting physically. Interestingly enough, I only exhibited this argumentative behavior at home. My teachers and friends, as well as their families, thought I was a delight to be around. I literally took out my anger on my family, specifically my mom.

Just prior to my 19th birthday, I had a dream. I dreamt my mom and two sisters were in a bank when a robber entered and held up the bank. I remember standing on the outside of the bank with my dad and a lot of policemen. Finally the door opened and my sisters walked out of the bank and up to my dad and me. I asked them where mom was. They told me that the bank robber killed her to let the police know that he was serious. I then started to cry in my dream as well as in real life on my pillow. I woke up and my pillow was soaked. I ran into my mom's room and told her of the dream I just had. Since that day I have never been disrespectful to my mom. I never knew what I had (a great mom) until I lost her (in my dream).

At this point in my life, it was time to move again, this time at age 19. I served a mission for my church in Santiago, Chile. I remember consciously thinking, "I still don't like who I am." I did not like arguing with people just to argue. Something my parents used to tell me returned to my mind: "If you don't run, your brothers can't chase you." That made no sense to me because if I did not run, they would catch me and beat me up. But that thought crossed my mind, and I thought, "If I don't argue with people, then they can't argue with me." It was at least worth a try. I was going to a new area where no one knew me, and I could be whoever I wanted to be, and they would not know either way. I chose to be someone who did not argue.

One day my senior companion was arguing with a bishop in his office. It was a silly argument. We had changed the location of some baptisms to a different church building where there was hot water. We forgot to notify the bishop, and he thought we should have asked him for permission. My companion (full of pride) told the bishop that we did not need his permission and stood up to leave. He said to me in English, "Come on Elder Webb. Let's go." I looked at my companion and then the bishop and said, "This is silly. We are talking about the salvation of souls. Can we have your permission to baptize them in the other building?" My companion got even angrier, as his temper got the best of him. He retorted to me in English, "Speak for yourself!" I turned back to the bishop and said, "Can I please have your permission to baptize them in the other building?" The bishop consented. All he wanted was for us to recognize his leadership role as the bishop in the area, but my companion was too prideful at that moment to give the bishop the proper respect.

On the way home, while walking through a dirt field, he turned to me and yelled, "I'm your senior companion! When I tell you to come, you come!" Guess what I did? I did not do anything. I did not want to argue because of my new rule, so I just stared ahead and kept walking. It took me another year to learn that people become even more upset if you ignore them than if you argue with them. I was 20 years old by then, and I realized that both extremes of fighting and remaining quiet were not productive. I knew there had to be a happy medium, and I was actively searching for it.

I believe I have my answer now. Today when I am in a staff meeting, if I feel that my voice is heard, I am satisfied, and I can move on. The staff does not have to agree with me or go along with my ideas. As long as I feel heard, I am okay. My perception changed several times before it got to where it is today. It took me many years, but today I am happy with my temper, or the lack thereof. Today I can honestly say that no one sees my "Incredible Hulk" temper. I still get upset with people now and then, but my reaction is under control. I am not perfect and I have many faults, but I do not argue just to argue. I told my wife early on in our relationship, "I will never say anything to you with the intent to hurt you. I might say something that does hurt you, and I would ask that you simply ask me to clarify what I meant by it. I will never say anything to you or anyone else with the intent to hurt." That is not my style anymore. It used to be, and I did not like it, and it did not work for me.

Here is one more example of being okay once I feel heard. I was driving home from work one day and I was thinking about taking 14 children to a Utah Jazz basketball game. I thought about taking the Utah train system known as Trax. I called up the company and asked how long their tickets were good for. The answer was two hours. I told them that they should really consider making it three hours because I was going to watch the Jazz play basketball, and a game would last more than two hours. The person on the other end transferred me to their "Customer Service" department. A man asked me what he could help me with and I explained my three-hour proposal. He then said that they have meetings to discuss policy changes and advised me that he had written down my request and would present it in their next meeting.

I hung up the phone and wanted to scream for joy. I was not going to get what I wanted by the time I took the children. He did not even say it would happen. He just made me feel that my voice was heard. I was so excited that I called my wife and enthusiastically told her what happened. That is not common anymore. Usually we get answers like, "That's just our policy sir." But not this man, he made me feel like a thousand dollars. He respected me, and you will see in the next few pages why that made all the difference in the world. We did ride Trax to the game and bought a ticket both ways. They will continue to get my business because of that one man.

Suppressing Anger

Suppressing anger is just as unhealthy as violently exploding. These two extremes are on opposite ends of the spectrum, and some middle ground is needed here. When we see people who are not outwardly angry, we have a tendency to think that they do not have an anger problem. That is not necessarily the case. They may just be stuffing their feelings and not expressing them.

I will liken "stuffing our feelings" to building a dam. Back in the 1980's, the state of Utah had some flooding in the spring. One particular Sunday people left church early to help fill sandbags and place them in the streets to divert the water. In essence, they built little dams to contain the water and then redirect it. A dam must have an outlet for the water, and if there is not one, the water continues to rise, and at a certain point, the strength of the water is greater than the strength of the dam. At this point, the dam will break, and all the water will come flowing out and cause great damage.

We build emotional dams inside of us. It is sometimes called "sandbagging." Every time our feelings are hurt and we become angry, we just add another emotional sandbag to this dam inside. By doing this, we do not explode on people and we do not embarrass ourselves or have unwanted confrontation. The problem occurs when we do not have an outlet for our anger. Instead we continue to build this emotional dam higher and higher until at a certain point the strength of the built-up emotions is greater than the strength of the emotional dam. At this point, the dam breaks and all our feelings come flowing out of us and wreak havoc in our life. The sad part is that it is usually released upon an innocent bystander and sometimes even a child. They do not only get our anger for what they are doing, but they also get all the anger that has been building up behind our emotional dam and this is how abuse occurs.

For example, a woman woke up a little late in the morning. She was immediately frustrated because she did not have enough time to get ready for work. She quickly hopped in the shower, and to her dismay the hot water was gone because her husband just got out of the shower. She took a quick and cold shower. She got out and quickly got dressed. She tried to get breakfast ready and ended up burning it in her frantic rush. Her husband yelled at her over this, but she did not want to argue, so she stuffed her feelings. She drove to work and of course the traffic was horrible. She was late, and her supervisor noticed and reprimanded her. She did not want to lose her job, so she stuffed her feelings. She drove home a little too quickly and got a ticket. She did not want to get thrown in jail, so she bit her tongue and stuffed her feelings. When she got home, her children were fighting. She did not want to be a "bad mom," so she stuffed her feelings again and calmly settled things at home. She then ran to the grocery store to buy candy bars that she knew were on sale three for one dollar.

Now let me take a break from the story to explain the grocery store checkout cashier's job. I know I am greatly oversimplifying the job, but for the purposes of this story, the cashier essentially takes each item and swipes it over a laser beam which reads the price and puts it up on the screen. After all the items are scanned, the price is totaled and she announces the price to the customer. That is their job.

Now let's go back to the story. The woman in our story put her three candy bars on the conveyor belt, and the clerk scanned each one. The candy bars mistakenly came up at $.50 each. After all three were rung up, the cashier looked at the screen and said, "That will be $1.50 please." The lady buying the candy bars suddenly freaked out and yelled at the clerk, "The price said 3 for $1.00." Her anger continued to escalate, and she had a fit right there in the store.

Have you ever seen this happen before? You may have even been behind her in line and offered to pay the $.50 just so she will calm down and leave quicker. Of course she would not take it because she had clearly been wronged by the thoughtless cashier, or at least that is the case in her perception. From an outside point of view, this lady is completely off her rocker. But if we were to go back and follow her throughout her day and see how many times she has stuffed her feelings, then it becomes abundantly clear that the dam was full and broke over fifty cents. All of the woman's pent-up emotions had come out - unfortunately at an innocent person.

We must learn to express our anger appropriately. We should not suppress our feelings, and likewise we should not violently strike out at others. Here are a few ideas we can do.

- We can talk about how we are feeling. Talking is great therapy.

- We could write in a journal. Just getting it out of us is great therapy.

- We could exercise. This helps burn some of the energy and helps us think more clearly.

- We could write a letter and then burn it. This is a good idea if we do not want to confront the person we are mad at.

- We could hit a broken down junk car with a sledgehammer (I recommend it be a car you own).

- We could change our perceptions. Let me explain how this last one works.

Formula for Anger

I have learned that there is a formula for anger. It should not surprise you that perception is part of the formula. Here it is:

1) Situation

2) Perception

3) Want

4) If perception does not equal what we want, then anger occurs

5) If perception does equal what we want, then life goes on

When a situation occurs, we have a perception of that situation. We also have a want regarding that situation. If our perception is different from what we want to have happen, then we get angry. If our perception and our want are in sync, then life goes on.

In this exercise, when describing a situation, do not put your bias or opinions into the description. Just state exactly what happened (which can be very difficult to do). We often think we are being objective in our stories when we are not, so be careful. Do not incorporate what you thought about the situation, including a translation of what was meant by a certain gesture, or interpretation of any kind. Just state the facts.

However, when describing your perception, say whatever you want. This is where your bias, opinions, and interpretations can be included. You can include your mind reading and erroneously predicting the future in this column. This is where you get to say, "*I know* that is what they meant!"

When figuring out your "want," dig deep. This means that your want in the situation is not that someone do something for you or that you receive something. It is something much deeper than that. The majority of the time, what we want is respect, but it can also be love, value, validation, or something else. This concept is easier explained with an example.

Situation: There was a car in the left lane on the freeway driving just ahead of me as I drove in the middle lane. The driver pulled into the middle lane in front of me.

Perception: She cut me off.

Want: Respect.

Is there a difference between my perception and my want? Yes. I felt she was being disrespectful by cutting me off. She does not care about me.

Thus: I am angry.

This scenario, by the way, is the very reason that road rage occurs. This is very important: **Situations cannot make us mad, only our perceptions can.** Why did I get mad in the above example? Was it because of the situation itself or my perception of what happened? It is because of my perception. Let us look at the same situation accompanied by a different perception and see how my reaction differs.

Situation: There was a car in the left lane on the freeway driving just ahead of me. The driver pulled into my lane in front of me.

Perception: Maybe the lady in the car was having a baby and needed to get off the freeway very quickly.

Want: Respect.

Is there a difference between my perception and my want? No, they are the same. I did not see her as being disrespectful to me. I considered her situation and that changed how I felt. In fact, I would likely have further assisted this woman by motioning for the car next to me to back off and let her in so she could get off the freeway.

Thus: Life goes on.

Notice the situation did not change at all. Only my perception changed. Since my new perception and my want were in sync with each other, I did not have any anger and was able to go on with my life.

A few questions may be coming to mind: "But what if she wasn't having a baby? How would you know?" Let me answer by asking this question, "How do I know she is cutting me off <u>intentionally</u>?" For that is what we mean when we say "cut me off." The answer is that I do not know. Have you and I ever "cut" someone off just to look in our rear view mirror and say, "Oh, sorry. I didn't know you were that close?" Without knowing what is really happening, why would I entertain a thought that makes me upset versus choosing a perception that allows my life to go on without any hard feelings?

We need to understand that **no person or thing can make us mad. Only we have the power to choose to be mad or not.** When we choose to be mad, it is because of our perception of a situation. I cannot truthfully say, "He made me mad" as young boys (and not-so-young boys) do when they are quarreling. This is simply not true. I can choose to be mad or choose not to be mad and that is solely my decision. If it was my choice, I would make everyone happy. Wouldn't you do the same? Below is another example.

Situation: A man walked up to me and hit me in the arm and said, "How's it going?"

Perception: This man was my worst enemy. I have not seen him in a year and he is sizing me up and challenging me.

Want: Respect.

Is there a difference between my perception and my want? Yes, I feel he is being disrespectful to me by hitting me.

Thus: I get angry.

When you get angry it is because there is a difference between your perception and what you want. I challenge you to change your perception or ask yourself, "Might there be another perception for this situation?" The good news is that the answer to that question will always be, "Yes." Try to discover a perception that fits what you want, and you will not get angry. The above example might look like this with a changed perception:

Situation: A man walked up to me and hit me in the arm and said, "How's it going?"

Perception: This man was my worst enemy. I have not seen him in a year. Maybe he has cleaned up his life and wants to make amends with me. He's giving me a friendly punch on the shoulder.

Want: Respect.

Is there a difference between my perception and my want? No. He is trying to make things right between us.

Thus: Life goes on.

Are you beginning to see how situations do not make us mad, only our perceptions do? Our perceptions are derived from every experience we have ever had, every moment in our lives put together to give us our current view of what is happening right now. When we experience something new, our perception is likely to change a little bit as we take into account the new information. Here is an embarrassing story to illustrate:

Years ago I was sitting in the waiting room of a dermatologist's office. I had what I considered to be a bad case of acne. When I was a teenager, I was told that my acne would likely go away by the time I was in my twenties. When that did not happen, I was assured that it would likely be gone by the time I was in my thirties. Well, you get the picture, it still has not gone away completely, and maybe it never will. Anyway, I made an appointment during my lunch break. At the time, I was working and I only had one hour for lunch. I sat there in the waiting room and waited and waited and waited. I started to become inpatient (even though I was a patient). I kept asking the receptionist how much longer it was going to be. She seemed to be exhibiting an unusual amount of patience, and kept reassuring me that they were doing the best they could and would see me as soon as possible. Finally my name was called and I was escorted back to a room. I was livid by that point and fully intended to give the doctor a piece of my mind. I am convinced that the receptionist forewarned the doctor about my long wait and increasing agitation before he came into the room. When the doctor walked in, the first thing he said to me was, "I'm sorry I took so long. I just had to tell my last patient that she had skin cancer and is going to die." Boy, did I feel stupid. Do you think I had a change of perception? Let us look at it:

Situation: I sat in a waiting room for 45 minutes.

70

Perception: My time is not valued. The doctor should not schedule more people than he can actually see in a given time period. He is obviously only in this business to make money and is trying to squeeze as many people in as possible.

Want: To be valued.

Is there a difference between my perception and my want? Yes.

Thus: I get angry.

And afterwards it looked like this:

Situation: I sat in a waiting room for 45 minutes.

Perception: The last patient was dying of cancer. The doctor values our time and realizes she does not have much time left to live. He will give me the time I deserve too.

Want: To be valued.

Is there a difference between my perception and my want? No. The doctor is giving her the respect and value she deserves, and he will do the same for me.

Thus: Life goes on.

I felt bad that my original perception was all about me. As I have been able to take a look at the perceptions of others and see the world from their eyes, it has truly given me peace of mind and happiness. I know that the world is not out to get me and that everyone has his or her own struggles. By understanding that it is only perception that leads to anger, I have been able to free myself of many wasted moments spent in anger simply by choosing a different perception. How wonderful it is to know this secret!

Teaching about Anger

I worked at a boys' ranch as an intern one summer and was assigned to teach a class about anger. My class consisted of about 10 teenage boys with antisocial behaviors. I approached the boy who misbehaved perhaps the most and asked him if he would help me teach a lesson to the class. I told him I wanted him to be disruptive in class just like he always was. I told him that I would also act consistent with the past and ask him to be quiet like I always did. I told him to then start playing around with the overhead projector and assured him that I would ask him to stop. I asked him to ignore my request, just like always. His assignment was essentially to be himself.

The class began, and it went just according to plan. This young man began to talk and then to play with the projector and then ignored my requests that he stop. At that point in the class, I intentionally "lost it." I yelled at him to "Stop!" I opened the outside door of the classroom (we were on the second floor of a building with an outdoor stairwell leading down to the sidewalk). I grabbed the projector and threw the projector over the railing and shattered it on the sidewalk below. I then screamed at him to get down there and clean it up. He left the classroom obediently. I shut the door and regained my composure. I then addressed the remainder of the class, "Sorry, was that inappropriate?" The other boys in the classroom quickly responded with some fear, "No, no, of course not." I assured them that it absolutely was inappropriate. I opened the outside door again and invited the student back into the classroom to process what had happened. The boys were shocked to find out that it was all a set-up.

Is getting angry a bad thing? No. But we have to understand that it is always our choice. *No one can make us mad.* We should all have a point at which we do get angry. For example, if I went home and found a man abusing my wife, then I would get very angry. I would not say, "Hey, when you're done, can I talk to you in the other room." No way! I would get angry and justifiably so. But it would still be my choice.

So the question is, "At what point are you willing to get angry?" Are you willing to get angry over spilled milk? Have you ever seen the movie, "Regarding Henry[10]" with Harrison Ford? In the beginning his character is a wealthy high society man. His daughter spills her juice at the table, and he yells at her. Then he is badly injured in an accident and he goes through the rehabilitation process. His daughter spills her juice at the table again and looks at him with terror in her eyes and quickly says, "I'm sorry." He says to her, "That's okay I do that all the time." She is puzzled by his response and asks, "You do?" He says, "Yea" then knocks his juice over and says, "See." I find that scene to be so tender and such a great learning opportunity for all of us.

So what are you willing to get angry over? When I was first married, my brother-in-law made my wife and me a decaffeinated coffee table. My wife really treasured this gift. She would not let me put my cups on it and there were definitely no feet allowed on it. I told her that the day would come when we would have children; and I promised her that they would write on the table and leave little dings in it with their toys. We talked about how she would handle that situation and the message it would send to our children and what she valued more – them or the table. I do not disagree that children should be disciplined and taught to properly care for things. In fact, it is our utmost responsibility to teach and discipline our children. However, what is the message we send to our children? Is it a message of discipline or are we sending a message that we love an object more than we love them.

Here is an example: Some families have a special room in their house that is reserved for guests, and children are often not allowed in that room. What is the message a child hears when the parent says, "Don't go in that room! That room is just for our friends." How sad! The child must think, "I'm not your friend. Don't you love me? My parents love their friends more than they love me." It is wise to remember that, "No thing (nothing) is worth a relationship." So, what are you willing to get angry over? Things? Unkind words? Someone looking at you? Someone looking at your girlfriend or boyfriend?

That last question is one of my favorites. I had a client get mad because someone looked at his girlfriend while they were walking together in the mall. I asked him, what does that mean when someone looks at your girlfriend? It means your girlfriend is attractive. Would you rather be dating someone so ugly that people turn their heads the other way to avoid looking at her? Do you see how his perception was getting in the way? We should feel proud, not threatened, if people are looking at our significant others. I just say, "That's right buddy, she's mine!"

Transference Issues

Part of our perceptions (and anger) is made up of what is known as transference issues. Transference issues are preconceived notions taken from our past and transferred onto someone else. We might treat someone differently according to how he walks, or talks, or just by how he looks based upon

74

our past experiences with someone who walked, talked, or looked like them.

The way a little boy picks on another little boy might remind me of a boy that made fun of me when I was a child and felt picked on and defenseless. I might hear that boy say something mean to another little child, and I find myself snapping at him because he took me back to another time, and I associated strong feelings with that. This is a transference issue.

Let me illustrate further with a true story but I'll change a couple of details to protect the innocent. There was a boy who grew up in New York. Let us just say his name was Larry. Larry was an only child and he did not know his father. His mother worked two jobs just to make ends meet. Larry did not have very many toys and appreciated any toy he received from his mother. He knew how hard she was working. For his 10th birthday his mom gave him a brand new bicycle. He not only cherished it because it was a bike but also because he knew his mom had to work extra hours just so she could give it to him. A week after his birthday he was out riding his bike. A car pulled over and a man jumped out and held a gun to his 10-year-old head and took his bike. He felt hopeless and did not feel he could do anything about it. As he watched the car drive away that day with his bike in it he made a promise to himself that "I will never let anyone steal from me again."

When Larry was an adult, he was working as a school teacher. One day he discovered that he was missing a $20 bill. He became outraged. He locked the classroom door and would not let any of the students leave the room and even threatened them. He taught on the 2nd floor of a school building and he opened the window and threatened to throw each student out the window one at a time unless someone gave him back his $20. The principal showed up pounding on the door to get in. Finally he used his keys and opened the door. He asked Larry what was wrong and after learning about his missing $20 the principal offered him $20 from his own wallet. Larry said, "I don't want your money, I want my $20." Finally a student pointed to a bookshelf and Larry saw his $20 bill. The principal sent the students home. Larry was put on administrative leave for his actions. He was required to see a psychologist. As he was explaining what happened, it occurred to him that he had experienced a transference issue with his students because of the man that had stolen his bike as a 10-year-old child. He reflected his anger onto his students not only for the lost $20 bill but also for the bike stolen from him many, many years earlier. He held his students accountable, in a sense, for what the man had done to him.

Transference issues can be good as well as bad. I love my grandmother; unfortunately she passed away several years ago. If I went to a retirement home and saw a woman who reminded me of my grandmother, who I loved dearly, then I would treat her extra kindly. That is a transference issue. I counseled a young man one time who reminded me very much of my brother. I am sure I treated him with extra kindness just because he reminded me of my brother. We all have transference issues, and we need to recognize that fact.

A long time ago, a little boy watched as the police entered his house and took his father into custody which eventually led to time in prison. The boy was too young to understand what was happening or why it was happening. All he understood was that a policeman came into his house and took his loved one and friend away. Since that day, this boy, now a grown man has had a problem with the police. Today he despises them and does not exactly understand why. This is an example of a transference issue that has affected this man's perception. This perception does not equal his want of respect and therefore, he is angry with policemen in general.

We all have transference issues. When my wife and I were trying to decide on a name for one of our children, we sat down and discussed several names. She would say a name she liked and I would say something like, "No, I knew a boy named that in my past, and I didn't like him too much." Likewise, I would suggest a boy's name, and she would say something similar about an acquaintance in her past. These are transference issues. If I named my child one of those names that she mentioned, does that mean my son would turn out to be a jerk like the mean little boy I knew in my elementary school? Of course not, that is not how it works. But upon hearing a particular name, we relive a particular emotion and time in our past that may be unfavorable to us. So we chose to not name our child that name and relive that unpleasant memory over and over again.

Transference issues affect the way we treat other people. Transference issues also affect the way we perceive situations. If we do not want transference issues to control us, the first step we need to take is to admit that we have them. Take a look at who you know in your classroom, neighborhood, or church. Ask yourself, "Which of these people reminds me of somebody I knew in the past?" As the names come to mind - that is someone with whom you have a transference issue and it may be either good or bad.

Be honest in your assessment of this next situation. Let us say you are driving down a one-lane road, and you come up behind a car driving 10 mph below the speed limit. There is no passing lane in sight. So answer honestly about who you think is driving that slow car in front of you. Your answer reflects your past experiences. My answer was, "An old woman who can barely see over the steering wheel." So I have biases and one of them is, "Elderly women who can barely see over the steering wheel drive slowly." Does this mean that all older women who can barely see over the steering wheel drive slowly? No, but my perception is reality to me, and it says, "Yes, all of them." And when I finally pass the slow car and look inside it and see an elderly woman, I think to myself, "See I was right. That explains it." This response only furthers my perception and my biases and possibly my transference issues.

Our transference issues often times are the reason we do not get along with people around us. If there is someone in your life you do not get along with, then I would suggest the following assignment. Sit down for one hour with this person and just share each other's life stories. I find that when you hear another person's life story, you simply cannot help but love that person. You also get to know them for who they are and any transference issues you may have simply fade away. This also helps to change your perception so that your want is being met which prevents you from getting angry. I have never seen this assignment completed without the two parties coming back as friends.

Angry at God?

In my line of work, I meet a lot of people who are angry with God. They cannot understand why God, who is all-powerful, would allow such heinous things to happen to them. They cannot understand why a loved one had to die. They cannot understand why a child had to suffer so much because of another person's actions.

These are all understandable thoughts and feelings from one's perception. The problem is the perception. When God sent us here to live on earth, He gave us the ability to choose and act for ourselves. By giving me the ability to act and you the ability to act, we have the freedom to treat others unkindly if we choose.

Some people say, "Everything happens for a reason." What I believe they mean by this statement is that everything that happens is God's will. That is an interesting perception. I do not agree with it. That takes away my responsibility to own my feelings and my actions. In effect, I could rob a bank or kill someone and then just say that it was God's will. That would really be a universal scapegoat for everyone. Say I walked up to you and hit you in the face. If God did not want that to happen, he would have stopped me from hitting you – right? Do you really buy that?

Not everything that happens in life is God's will. Here is my perception:

God understands that there are two paths; one is a path to happiness, and the other is a path to misery. He has told us, through His servants and through our conscience, what we should and should not do. These are not rules that God is making up while He sits in heaven wondering how He might punish us. Rather as a loving Father who sees all, He tells us, "If you go down this path, you will suffer, and I don't want that for you." He kindly tries to direct us down the path to happiness. Do you want to know the secret to happiness? **Line up your actions with God's values.** That is it! I thought about making a lot of money by putting quarter machines in grocery stores that say, "The secret to happiness for just $.25." People would then put a quarter in the machine and get a piece of paper out that reads, "Line up your actions with God's values."

I have had people come through treatment who lie to themselves and try to line up their values with their actions. It does not work that way. We must line up our actions with our values. Do you think it is okay to hit your neighbor? If not, then if you hit your neighbor, you will venture away from God's value system, and have jeopardized your happiness. Is it okay to cheat on your spouse? No. You cannot find happiness going down that path. Is it okay to use drugs? No. Then you cannot find happiness by taking drugs. It is such a simple rule, yet we struggle on a daily basis to conduct our lives according to God's values.

So God has laid down the path to happiness. Unfortunately we choose to leave it at times. We try it our way. When our way does not work, we get angry and mad at God. Does that make sense to you? That is like me hitting myself with a hammer and getting mad at God because He did not stop my pain. Yet people blame God for dumb choices in their life that have caused them so much pain and sorrow.

I have learned that most of my pain is caused by me and my own dumb choices. I learned this on a smaller level after being in pain for a week many years ago. One night as I was working as a custodian, I was cleaning up while a dance was going on. One of the treats they provided at the dance was Popsicles. I thought, "Who deserves a Popsicle more than the custodian?" I walked inside the dance room and grabbed a Popsicle and walked back out to the hall to eat it. I quickly opened it and proceeded to lick it. My tongue got stuck to the Popsicle. I ripped my tongue off the Popsicle and thought, "I must need to lick it faster." I licked it faster, but my tongue got stuck again. I ripped it off again and thought, "I must need to lick it really fast" (this was truly a sign of intelligence). I licked that Popsicle incredibly fast, but my tongue again got stuck. This time when I pulled my tongue off, my tongue was bleeding. I went into the bathroom and put the Popsicle under some water from the sink. When I lifted it back up out of the water, it froze up instantaneously. Do you know why? They had the Popsicles sitting in dry ice! I wanted so badly to walk back into the dance hall to see if everyone had their tongues stuck to their Popsicles, but I was too embarrassed about it.

The next day I was eating some jalapeños out of the refrigerator. I put my fingers into the jar and got them out one at a time and popped them into my mouth. After a few jalapeños, I noticed that it was time for me to go to work. I quickly put the jar back in the refrigerator and ran into the bathroom. I got out my contacts and put them in my eyes. OOOOWWWW!!!! You do not need to wear contacts to try this experiment. Just simply put your fingers into some jalapeño juice and then touch them to your eye.

The next day I was cleaning out my refrigerator and decided I needed some space. Instead of throwing out the jar of jalapeños, I dumped them all out onto the table. Then I said "One, two, three!" and I ate them all as fast as I could. I did not want to waste them. I started sweating, my nose was running faster than I could wipe it, I was crying, and my mouth was burning. Needless to say, the next day I had more pain.

My point in sharing this particular week with you is to show you that often times we cause ourselves significant pain. Yet there are people who still have a tendency to blame God. It does not make sense.

Some people blame God for allowing other people to hurt them or abuse them. Why are they not blaming the person who hurt them? Do we really want God to stop all of us from making dumb choices? So, who is to say which dumb acts He stops and which ones He allows? I believe if God stopped us from doing stupid things, then we would get mad at Him for not allowing us the agency to choose for ourselves. He would say, "That is a dumb choice" and stop it from happening, and we would disagree and say, "Let me try it and see if it is dumb." So, if we want God to allow us to choose for ourselves, then we must allow others to choose for themselves too even if it means someone could get hurt. I have often wished He would take away everyone's agency but mine. Can you relate to that thought?

I believe God is in heaven watching all of us. I believe He has a time table that is not my time table or your time table. I believe that as He watches a little child being abused, He is up there weeping tears of sorrow and doing everything in His might not to come down and destroy that perpetrator. I believe He tells Himself, "Not yet. My day will come." He understands that some people do change their lives, and He is willing to give all of us that opportunity. I am grateful He has not struck me down for any of my dumb choices (at least not yet).

So God sits in heaven watching all these terrible things happening to His children, and he cries because He knows now is not the time to intervene, but it must be horrible for him to watch. The victim then blames God for what happened to him or her. I am sure that is just adding salt to God's open wound. There is a song called, "Water into Wine"[11] by T. Graham Brown. In one verse he sings, "I shook my fist at heaven for all the hell that I've been through, now I'm praying for forgiveness and a miracle from You." Let me ask you this question: **Why do we shake our fist at heaven for all the hell we go through? Have we ever thanked hell for all the heaven we went through?** It is just a change of perception. I choose to shake my fist at hell for all the hell I go through, and

I choose to thank heaven for all the heaven I go through. It just seems to be more logical that way.

This is just another change of perception that helps us see who is to blame and who is not.

Anxiety & Panic Attacks Derived From Perception

I believe that if I can teach my clients about anxiety and panic attacks, they will never again need medication to control their panic attacks. Anxiety is caused by our thoughts. **Anxiety's job is to predict that the future is going to be worse than it is.** Anxiety dwells upon the worst and magnifies it to the extent that we allow. Panic attacks come from our magnification of a negative thought to the extreme. I will explain panic attacks a little later in this chapter.

Imagine you are inside a metal box that is completely sealed. There is a little hole towards the bottom of one wall. You have one match and a stick of dynamite. How do you get out? Think about it for a minute. Then read the next line which has the answer.

The answer is: stop imagining. Can you make the connection between that riddle and anxiety?

Stress

Stress is normal. According to Hans Selye, M.D.,[12] stress can be defined as, "A nonspecific response of the body to a demand." Stress is then any feeling outside our comfort zone. Stress can be a good thing or a bad thing depending on how much we have and how we use it. Stress often gives the body extra energy and manifests itself in a pulse rate increase, blood pressure increase, and sometimes excess sweat. Stress is caused by one's perception of what might happen. Our thoughts send signals to the body which then responds accordingly.

How stress is perceived is also different from one person to another. Some people, like me, find it stressful to not have anything to do. We have so much energy that we must always be doing something. Otherwise the inactivity itself causes stress. One client said, "I am stressed out because I have no stress. Something must be wrong." In the introduction, I talked about the cruise I went on. I literally spent the first half of the cruise learning how to relax. I woke up in the mornings and looked frantically for something to do. I had nothing to do except what I wanted to do. My cell phone did not work, and I did not bring any work with me. Notice the cruise only became relaxing for me when I found something to do - write this book. I eventually learned to relax even beyond that, to the point that I could just watch the waves and feel the peace.

In the book, "Don't Sweat the Small Stuff"[13] by Richard Carlson, I learned that the difference between peace and boredom is that peace is embraced while boredom is fought against. In other words, to turn boredom into peace, we must embrace it. It is all about our perception. Some might find a night at home all alone to be very boring. On the other hand, someone who has had a very chaotic day would cherish a night at home all alone and find it be very peaceful. A co-worker of mine said (sarcastically) she would love to be put in jail for 30 days with nothing to do but just sit there. Yet that scenario would obviously cause extreme anxiety for others.

Some people work better under stress while others collapse due to the stress. I am the type of person that needs to be working on at least four or five projects at a time or I go stir crazy. I am always thinking about what I can do next. Others I know must focus on just one thing at a time or they go crazy. Some friends have told me that I have Attention Deficit/Hyperactivity Disorder (ADHD). I disagreed with them and presented to them that I actually have Attention Surplus/Hyperactivity Disorder (ASHD). There is no deficit in my attention span. In fact, I can pay attention to several things at the exact same time.

The point is that it is difficult to pinpoint exactly what stress is because it is different for everyone. It can be caused by different things in all of us. Stress is liked by some and disliked by others. Stress causes some to have more energy and others to lie in bed and become almost catatonic. But this much we do know - everyone experiences stress. We live in a very stressful world. I often ask, "Why can't we go back to the days of sitting on the front porch swing and drinking lemonade?" I believe the answer is, "We can if we choose to."

Anxiety

The Merriam-Webster dictionary,[14] defines anxiety as: 1 painful or apprehensive uneasiness **of mind** usually over an impending or anticipated ill; 2 **fearful** concern or interest; 3 an abnormal and overwhelming sense of apprehension and fear often marked by physiological signs (as sweating, tension, and increased pulse), **by doubt concerning the reality** and nature of the threat, and **by self-doubt** about one's capacity to cope with it. As was mentioned in the chapter on depression, our thoughts control our feelings or emotions. Therefore, our perception causes our anxiety.

If you notice, the main difference between stress and anxiety is the intensity of what they are feeling due to their perception. Some people feel so much stress they get scared about the future. It could be standing up in front of a crowd and speaking. This can be scary and intimidating, so much so that people avoid it due to the stress it causes. My advice is that **it is okay to feel scared; but DO NOT allow your decisions to be based upon fear. Do not let fear run your life.** See your fear for what it really is, and then move forward. When I find myself in these intimidating situations I force myself into doing what I know I should and then when I step back and think about it and really get nervous, I say to myself, "Oh well. It is too late to leave now."

If you have read the chapter on depression, then this will seem a lot like the negative perception called, "Erroneously Predicting the Future." It is predicting that the future will turn out badly. Anxiety disorders are divided into several categories. I have listed each one with a very simplified definition. In actuality, they are much more complicated than the description implies.

1. Panic Disorder-When you have panic attacks for no reason.

2. Generalized Anxiety Disorder-When you are always worried about something.

3. Anxiety Disorder with Depression-When you are feeling down and sad and worried about the future.

4. Panic Disorder with Agoraphobia-When you fear leaving your home and have panic attacks because of it.

5. Social Phobia-When you are fearful of being in public.

6. Simple Phobia-When you are fearful of a particular object.

7. Obsessive Compulsive Disorder (OCD)-When you have obsessions or compulsions or both to prevent your fears from occurring.

8. Post-Traumatic Stress Disorder (PTSD)-When you can exactly recall the stress from a past traumatic event and bring that stress to the present moment.

All these disorders are a result of perception. I wish to say a word or two about panic attacks, phobias, PTSD, and OCD.

Panic Attacks
Panic attacks are caused by having a catastrophic thought which creates a bodily reaction. We then interpret the

bodily reaction with another catastrophic thought. This in turn causes another bodily reaction. This cycle continues until a full-blown panic attack is experienced. The point when anxiety becomes a mild panic is when fear of loss of control enters the scene. Notice that the beginning is a thought or a perception. If the perception was different, the panic attack would not happen.

An example of this would be when a person is anxious about meeting someone new for the first time. His perception may be that the person will not like him. His perception may be that the person will think he is crazy. He gets nervous and his hands start to sweat. As he starts to sweat, he thinks, "This person really isn't going to like me. After shaking my hand, they will know I'm nervous. My heart is even starting to pound harder." Then the heart actually starts to beat a little harder. The next thought escalates the anxiety a bit with, "What if I have a heart attack? My heart feels like it's going to beat right out of my chest." The heart naturally starts to beat harder with that thought. "I am having a heart attack! I can't breathe!" The body reacts to this thought, and the person has more difficulty breathing. "I'm going to pass out! I think I'm going crazy!" And the cycle continues.

Fortunately the cycle cannot last forever. It is impossible. It is impossible for the body to maintain such a state of panic forever. In fact, most panic attacks last about five minutes. Rarely do they last beyond 20 minutes. At the end of the above example, this person was afraid of passing out. Do you know what the best outcome of the immediate situation would be? It would be great if he would actually pass out. Why? Because then the mind would break free of the vicious cycle and the mind would get completely out of the picture. The body would take over and homeostasis would be achieved again. In other words, the perception would stop. The perception is what aggravates the bodily symptoms.

Now the bad news (or maybe it is actually good news).

- <u>Panic attacks cannot cause a person to pass out.</u> If the person does pass out, it is due to some other medical problem.

- <u>Panic attacks cannot cause a person to have a heart attack.</u>

- <u>Panic attacks also cannot cause a person to stop breathing.</u>

- <u>Panic attacks cannot cause someone to go crazy.</u>

Why? Because panic attacks are caused by our perceptions, and our perceptions cannot cause these medical conditions. We may think that these symptoms are occurring at the time, and there is no doubt that they feel very real. But in reality, they are not happening. It is just our perception.

Do you see how powerful our perceptions are? They can actually convince us that we are having a heart attack, and we rush off to the hospital just for the doctor to tell us that nothing came up on the EKG and our heart is just fine.

So the next time you start to have a panic attack, you can change your perception and stop the panic from happening. Use this statement for encouragement: "I've been through this before, and I can do it again." Do you think that the body is going to respond negatively to this statement? No, it will not.

The worse thing you can do when feeling the anxiety and panic is to fight against the panic and anxiety. It will only make it worse. Just ride the wave as the anxiety goes up, knowing that it is coming back down. You can find more examples and greater details about panic attacks in a book called <u>The Anxiety and Phobia Workbook</u> by Edmund J. Bourne, Ph.D.[15]. I found this book to be extremely helpful and practical.

When I meet with someone who has a history of panic attacks, I ask them if they can have one for me in my office so that we can work on some coping techniques together. Obviously they cannot oblige me because no one can force a panic attack. I give them the homework assignment to have one sometime over the next week and then practice the techniques we talked about and see if at least one works well for them. Most of the time, they report back that they did not have any panic attacks. One of my previous clients reported daily panic attacks prior to learning of the above techniques. He has not had one since. We only met for a few weeks. He did not see the need to meet any longer, and neither did I.

Viktor Frankl

Viktor Frankl is one of my favorite people. I am saddened that I never had the chance to meet him in person. If you ever get the chance, read his autobiographical book, Man's Search for Meaning.[16] He was a Jewish Austrian neurologist and psychiatrist who was taken to a concentration camp during World War II, and he survived. The first half of the book details his experiences in the camp as perceived by him. The second half of the book is written from a psychological perception as to what happened and why. It is a fascinating and inspiring book.

Sigmund Freud, Alfred Adler, Carl Jung, and Viktor Frankl are known as the four Viennese psychologists. They all studied in Vienna, and they all emerged with their own philosophies or perceptions, each very different from the other.

Sigmund Freud's theory was based around our will to pleasure.

Alfred Adler's theory was based around our will to power.

Carl Jung's theory was based around our will to live.

Viktor Frankl's theory was based around our will to meaning.

Dr. Frankl taught logotherapy which is a type of existential analysis. Logo means "meaning." He taught that everything we do is motivated by our will to find or live our meaning in life. He explained that everyone has a meaning in life even if they do not know what it is. He believed that addictions, aggression, and depression were all caused by not knowing what our meaning in life was. He called these three the neurotic triad. Certainly we can see the stress in all three of these tragic conditions.

Paradoxical Intentions

I bring up Viktor Frankl in this chapter because of his teaching of Paradoxical Intentions in his book, The Doctor and The Soul.[17] The word paradoxical is derived from the word paradox which means, "A statement that contradicts itself." Intention is something that is "deliberate" or intentional. Paradoxical intentions are things we deliberately do which are the opposite of what we want but in the end what we want is created instead. This principle only applies with things that are natural. Let me see if I can shed some light with some examples.

One example was already given. If you do not want to have a panic attack, then say to yourself, "I'm going to have a panic attack right here in front of everyone. I'm going to go so crazy that they will have to lock me up in the state hospital forever. Come on and panic!" You deliberately try to have a panic attack (something you do not want) and in doing so, you actually cannot have a panic attack (something you do want). It is just a change in perception.

Say that you do not want to sweat when you meet someone for the first time, but based on your history, you typically do. As you are about to meet that new person, you would say in your mind, "I'm going to sweat so much that after we shake hands, she will need a towel to wipe herself off. Come on and sweat!" You cannot force nature. You cannot force yourself to sweat. By trying to force yourself to sweat (something you do not want), you actually stop sweating (something you do want). Try it right now - can you make yourself sweat? Sweating is a natural phenomenon.

Some people are afraid of elevators. They are afraid if they go into one, they will be so overcome with fear that they will faint and cause a scene. You can probably guess what I would suggest you say to yourself if you are one of these people. "I'm going to go into the elevator and I'm going to panic to the point that I pass out. I'm going to cause such a big scene that they will need to call 911. It will be so big that I'll end up on the evening news." By trying to force yourself to pass out (something you don't want), you will not pass out (something you do want). Passing out would be the natural occurrence in this case.

I have given plenty of examples, but let me give you just one more that is very common. When we have a difficult time sleeping, we often lay in bed thinking, "I can't sleep! I can't sleep!" By thinking these thoughts, we actually make it so that we cannot sleep. What Dr. Frankl suggests is that we lay in bed with our eyes closed and we think, "I'm not going to sleep tonight. I'm just going to lay here all night thinking about whatever (do not think about things that cause you stress, think about a favorite get away spot), but I'm not going to fall asleep." By thinking these thoughts, nature takes over and we fall asleep. Try it for yourself and see if it works.

Phobias

The point at which a person will do anything and everything to avoid a stimulus then it becomes a phobia. They avoid the thing that is causing them anxiety. Some people are afraid of traffic jams on the freeway. There is a fear of not being able to escape because they cannot move in any direction. When people stop using the freeway and drive 100 extra miles on side roads to avoid freeway traffic, this would then be considered a phobia.

I once worked with a man who had a phobia of wheelchairs. He reported that when he saw someone in a wheelchair, he felt the need to get out of the situation as quickly as possible. He reported an incident in a cafeteria one time when he got his tray and turned around to find a table and suddenly saw someone sitting in a wheelchair. He set his tray back down on the counter and quickly fled the cafeteria. He really did not understand why he had such a great fear. His phobia was a direct result of his perception. In counseling, I took him through some baby steps to break this phobia. The worst possible thing a person with a phobia can do is to avoid the anxiety-causing object or event. Why? Just by doing so, the anxiety intensifies and the stimulus is reinforced. By facing the fear head on, they come to realize it was not as they had perceived.

The approach we took to his wheelchair phobia was for him to picture in his mind driving to a hospital where many people inside were in wheelchairs. With this picture in his mind, I asked him where his anxiety level was on a scale of 1 to 10. It was a low number, so we went on. I asked him to imagine that he was getting out of the car at the hospital and just standing in the parking lot. He was still okay, so I asked him to imagine seeing someone through the window who was sitting in a wheelchair. I then had him step inside the building, not looking at anyone, and come back outside the building. All this was just imagined in his head. I then had him walk into the hallway where he saw someone sitting in a wheelchair. He would not say anything to the person but just turn around and walk back outside. He then would go into the building walk up to someone in a wheelchair and say, "Hi" and then walk back out. When we could arrive at that point and maintain his anxiety at a low level, we carried out this experiment in reality. If his anxiety peaked during any one of those steps, I would simply take him back a step and help him to calm himself and then again move on to the next step. We followed the exact same baby steps in real life. He finally got to the point where he was able to walk inside the building, talk to someone in a wheelchair, and walk back out. He was so proud of himself. He also had a change of perception and realized that his fear of wheelchairs was not rational.

When working with people with phobias, it is important to have patience. This exercise illustrated in the above paragraph could take literally weeks or longer to successfully complete. If the person's anxiety is increased just as he is imagining the scenario in his mind, then stop right there. Help them to work on some relaxation techniques, and then go back and try it again. Do not rush them. If a person is afraid of snakes, then do not start off by bringing a snake right up to his face and demanding, "You need to face your fears." It simply will not work that way. The person needs to be willing to follow the process and do the work. They must have a desire to overcome the phobia.

Post-traumatic Stress Disorder (PTSD)

As I write about some of these things, I can already hear people saying that I am oversimplifying it. By saying that PTSD is all about perception, I am by no means trying to say that PTSD is not real. Of course it is real, to the holder of the perception. My intent is not to make light of it or to say, "Just get over it." Instead, my message is one of hope and encouragement by saying, "You can change your perception and not be haunted by the trauma anymore." It will take time and effort, but **I believe if it is hard, it must be worth it.** Like I said before, **if the treatment is easy, you are doing it wrong, and if it is hard, you are probably doing it right.**

PTSD is a disorder wherein a person is haunted by a past traumatic experience. It may be an assault, a car accident, or watching someone die. The experience involves actual or threatened death or serious injury, or a threat to the physical integrity of self or others. The person's response involves intense fear, helplessness, or even horror. The person persistently re-experiences the event. The person religiously avoids the stimuli associated with the event. The person consistently experiences symptoms of increased arousal, which may include: difficulty falling asleep, anger, concentration problems, hyper vigilance, and exaggerated startle response (see Diagnostic and Statistical Manual IV[18]).

I choose to not list the entire criteria here because one of the rules of diagnosing is that a person cannot self-diagnose. We have all experienced bad things in our lives, but thankfully we do not all have PTSD. Even people who experience a traumatic event may not have PTSD, while someone with whom they shared the traumatic event may have it. What is the difference? The difference lies in their perception.

We do not all have the same brain. We do not all have the same background. Yet at times we expect everyone to see the world the way we see it. That is just not going to happen. We need to be sensitive to all people but especially to people with PTSD. My neighbor once asked me to never slam the trunk of my car down when he was around. He had returned from war and said the sound put him back at war. If we are aware of these things then it is easier for us to be sensitive to their needs.

One of the things we can do is help the person relive the experience with a different perception. Sometimes we can relive the situation and change the outcome in our minds and view it as real. The mind is a powerful tool. **Yesterday's experiences, thoughts, ideas, dreams are nothing more than today's memories.** Therefore if we change our "Yesterday's experiences, thoughts and ideas" in our minds, then today's memories are not so hard to live with.

Change Your Past

I met a man who was paralyzed and lay dying in bed when he was 18-years-old. His father asked him to meet with a psychologist. He told his father that he was not crazy; he was dying. After some gentle prodding, he reluctantly agreed to meet with the psychologist. The psychologist taught him about today's memories being so strong that we believe they are reality. He taught this man to imagine playing soccer like he used to do. He taught him to feel the wind in his hair, smell the freshly cut grass, hear the crowd cheering him on, and feel his foot kick the ball and watch it fly through the air and into the goal. If he could imagine all of that really happening, then it will be implanted into his brain as though it really happened.

This young man also liked to play the guitar. If he could imagine playing the guitar and feeling the strings against his fingers and hearing the beautiful music then it would become real to him. Even though he was paralyzed he could still enjoy the things he once did.

This young man reported to me that in the beginning, it was difficult to meditate for even a short period of time. Then he was able to do it for about 10 minutes at a time. But, with nothing else to do, he practiced a lot and became very good at it. He was able to meditate, or in other words, play soccer, for eight hours straight. Most of us do not have that kind of time, but he certainly did. It brought him so much joy.

His story is even more incredible because he went on to imagine that he was living in the time period of the Bible. He told me about Jesus healing the sick from his own firsthand experience. He told me who was there, the kind of day it was, where people were standing, and their expressions of joy as they watched the lame rise to walk, the blind open their eyes to see, and the deaf hear for the first time. He said it was so real to him that he determined to get in line for the Savior to heal him. He had someone carry him to meet Jesus because he could not move on his own. As he approached Jesus, the Savior reached out and touched him and he was healed. After reliving this joyous scene over and over again, he asked himself, "If this is so real to me, why don't I believe it and get up out of my bed and walk?" Following the next time he relived this scenario, he stood up out of his bed and walked for the first time in a very long time. He shared documents with me from his doctors stating that he was dying. He now has documents in his possession stating that he no longer has even a trace of the disease. I wish you all could have heard his story straight from him. It was incredible to say the least.

Are you getting the picture? Our memories can be changed. We can figuratively go into our brain, pull out a few wires, make a few extra connections, and create a past that we never had. We can rewrite the past despite what some people may think. Have you known people who tell a lie and believe it so strongly that it is true to them? That is the same idea.

A woman who was attacked in the past and now suffers from PTSD can picture the tragic event and put herself back into that exact situation. She can be the one to chase away the perpetrator. She can have her adult-self give her a hug and tell her she loves her and that it is not her fault. She can watch herself fight the perpetrator with everything she has. She can picture herself as a savior to other girls by preventing the abuse from occurring to them. She can watch as her dad busts down the door and lets the perpetrator have it. The options are limitless, and she can choose whatever she wants.

Memories Increase with Emotions

Memories that are attached to emotions are the strongest memories we have. That is why we can remember a heated argument we had much easier than we can remember a subject we studied from a book. Life's experiences that have emotions attached to them are recollected easier than ones without an emotion. This creates a little problem with the solution mentioned above when dealing with PTSD. How can we recreate a scenario in our heads and believe it will overpower the other perception that is already attached to an emotion? In order for it to be effective the traumatic experience must be relived over and over again and in great detail. It cannot just be scattered related thoughts going through the mind.

As in the case of the young man mentioned above, he was playing soccer in his mind so much that all the details were alive and vivid. He was not just casually thinking about it. He was actually reliving the moments, including the emotions. It is so hard, but it is so worth it.

Abuse

One of the things I cannot explain is why our society frowns upon expressing anger at the deceased. I work with many abuse victims and when their perpetrator is dead, they do not believe it is okay to be mad at them. Yes it is! Expressing anger appropriately is a great tool for victims. At the facility where I work, we have an old car on site that we allow our clients to hit with a sledge hammer to help release anger. They say out loud the cause of their anger and then let the car have it. After a while, they become physically tired and emotionally satisfied.

Expressing anger inappropriately is not good. For example, cutting or burning yourself in an effort to relieve guilt or shame is not okay. It does not solve the problem or address the real issue. It may be an escape from the immediate emotional problem, but we want to heal the soul and not just put a Band-Aid on the open wound. Many adolescents turn to violence as a release of their frustrations because they report that it feels better to perpetrate than to be perpetrated upon. But as you can see by their repeated behaviors, this form of expression does not heal the soul.

Do you remember the scene in the Star Wars[19] series where Luke Skywalker is working with Yoda, and he walks into a cave and sees Darth Vader. They fight with Light Sabers, and Luke cuts off Darth Vader's head. His mask falls to the ground and flips over. The face burns out of the mask, and Luke sees his own face inside the mask. Yoda then teaches him that he cannot fight the enemy by becoming the enemy. Yet this is the reasoning that some victims employ because in their mind it is the only way to not become a victim again. That is dichotomous thinking. We do not have to become the enemy to beat the enemy, and that was Yoda's message to Luke.

My suggestion is to become a transitional character. This is someone who says, "The abuse stops here." They stop the cycle of abuse by not passing it on to the next generation. They talk about it and share their experiences so others do not have to feel alone in what has happened to them. They become an advocate for victims.

Here is a quote from a book called, "The Uses of Adversity" by Carlfred Broderick.[20] A man is giving a female victim of family abuse a new perception.

"But the Lord inspired me to tell her, and I believe with all my heart that it applies to many…that she…volunteered to come to earth and suffer innocently to purify a lineage. She volunteered to absorb the poisoning of sin, anger, anguish, and violence, to take it into herself and not to pass it on; to purify a lineage so that downstream from her it ran pure and clean, full of love and the Spirit of the Lord and self-worth. I believed truly that her calling was to…suffer innocently that others might not suffer."

I hope that helps. Some victims will not come forth and share their story until they understand that it might protect and save another innocent person. If a victim can help another person and prevent further suffering, their pain and suffering would not have been in vain.

My friend was molested when she was a teenager. Before it happened, she was the most beautiful girl in high school. She was outgoing and fun to be with. She was full of light and love and excitement for life. Afterwards, her self-worth was diminished to the point that she did not believe she deserved to be loved. She blamed herself for what had happened. She lost the light and excitement she had. She was not allowed to have her "day in court" when the perpetrator was sentenced to prison. Every victim (who wants to) deserves a chance to speak out against their perpetrator in a court of law.

About 10 years later, she made plans to meet with the perpetrator. She had been in two abusive relationships as an adult because she simply did not think she deserved any better. She met her perpetrator in a park in Arizona. She brought her boyfriend with her, and the perpetrator showed up with a mutual friend. My friend asked the perpetrator if she could speak with him alone, and they walked together to the middle of the park. She had just one question to ask him: "Why me?" He had served time in prison and had completed sex offender classes. His response that day should be heard by every victim of a sex crime. His reply was simply, "It had nothing to do with you. It wasn't the way you walked or the way you talked or what you looked like. It didn't have anything to do with you. You were just there. I am a perpetrator. I will always be a perpetrator though I'm not acting on it now. You were there and I abused you." After that response, she hugged him. She is a better person than I am. She called me soon after that meeting and was happier than I could ever remember her being since those high school days. She learned a valuable truth that all victims need to hear, "It had nothing to do with you."

There is nothing a victim can say or do to justify the abuse. The law does not allow it. I have never heard of a court case being thrown out because the victim deserved the abuse (for whatever reason). Court cases have been thrown out for other stupid reasons, and perpetrators have gone free, but this is where we must take comfort in the scriptures where it says, "Vengeance is mine; I will repay, saith the Lord" (Romans 12:19). The day will come when every perpetrator will pay the ultimate price for their wrongdoings. I believe God counts every tear a man causes a woman to shed, and that is not good news for some people.

The change of perception I recommend is from, "It was my fault" to "It was not my fault" because it wasn't. Change the perception of "He got away with it" to "He'll pay the price eventually, and God can punish him a lot worse than the legal system can." Change the perception of "I'm embarrassed about what happened to me" to "Maybe I can help another person who has been abused or maybe even prevent another person from suffering as I have."

Visualization Therapy

Visualization Therapy is new to me but I have found that it brings a lot of relief to abuse victims. I saw Dr. Jeffrey K. Zeig[21] do the following which I have used since to help victims.

"I want you to imagine that you work with clay; you are a potter. As you stand there in front of me I want you to mold out of clay your perpetrator. I want you to describe out loud what it is you are seeing so that I too can see the same thing. Just go ahead and mold him now."

The client then molds her perpetrator and describes how tall he is, how broad his shoulders are, his eyes, nose, mouth, etc. Usually this is extremely hard and many clients do not want to accomplish this task to which I say, "Just trust me on this one. It will get better." They continue until they finish molding the perpetrator.

"As you stand there and look into your perpetrator's eyes tell me which part of you feels?"

She then describes which parts of her feels. For example, it is common for her to say, "My head, my eyes, my throat, my chest, my stomach, my legs."

"What I want you to do is make rays of clay going from the parts of your body that feel to the same parts of your perpetrator's body."

She then proceeds to make rays of clay from his head to her head, from his eyes to her eyes, from his mouth to her mouth, from his throat to her throat, from his chest to her chest, and from his legs to her legs.

"Tell me how that feels?"

She does not like it one bit. I ask her to take a step back. She does so and I say, "He follows you doesn't he? That is because you are connected. This is how you have been living your life."

"Let us take a break from this scene for a moment. I want you to turn yourself around (180°). Now mold for me your Higher Power and describe to me what you see so I can see what you see."

She then molds her Higher Power and describes what she sees to me.

"Now turn 90° and mold your Higher Power one more time. This time you do not need to describe for me what you see just mold your Higher Power."

She then molds her Higher Power again but this time in silence.

"Now let us go back (turn 90°) to when you were connected to your perpetrator. Remember wherever you go he goes. Now I want you to pretend you have a knife in your hand. You will start at the tip of your head and go down the length of your body cutting him out of you according to how deep the rays go into you. If the rays go all the way through you then your knife will need to cut all the way through you to get it all out."

She then cuts him out.

"Now you are filleted open. You are in a very vulnerable spot right now. So what I want you to do is turn around (180°) and connect yourself to your Higher Power. Fill in all the spaces that you just cut out."

She then connects herself with rays of clay to her Higher Power.

"How does that feel?"

She responds, "I like that feeling."

"Take a step back. Your Higher Power follows you. Does that bother you?"

"No" is her answer.

"Now take a break from this scene for a minute. Turn around again (180°) and now take your perpetrator and turn him so he is facing your other Higher Power. Now connect him to your Higher Power."

She begins to do this.

"Is he getting mad?"

Some say yes and some do not.

"Now I want you to turn around again (180°) and remember being connected to your Higher Power. Now I want you to look over your shoulder and imagine your other Higher Power walking away from you while being connected to your perpetrator. I want you to hear your perpetrator yelling because he is mad but he can't do anything about it. I want you to see as they disappear into the horizon until you can't see them any longer."

She then does that.

"How does that feel?"

"I like it" she responds.

"Now look your Higher Power in His eyes and feel His love. I want you to hear Him say to you, 'I've got you now.

You don't need to be afraid any longer. I will take care of you. I love you…'"

I allow a little bit of silence. Then I say, "Whenever you start to get upset feelings because you are thinking about your perpetrator, "El Dingdong," I want you to put yourself back into this scenario and find the peace that accompanies you now."

This is a powerful experience. I usually go into a little more detail and allow time to feel it but you can get the idea behind it. All I am doing is changing the client's perception and seeing it in a new light.

Trauma

I do not want to leave out people with PTSD who suffered a traumatic event other than abuse. However, some of the same tools discussed above can be effective for them a well. For example, reliving the event but changing the outcome in their mind. Maybe some of them blame themselves because they were driving the car but not paying attention. What if his perception changed to: "No one pays attention 100% of the time to everything going on around them. I was doing the best I could." That is probably true. We can all do better, but if we spend our time beating ourselves up over our past mistakes we stop ourselves from experiencing the present and the future to the fullest. Will we beat ourselves up tomorrow for the things we did today? Or will we learn from what we did today and change tomorrow because of it?

Some images are very hard to get out of your mind. I worked with a man who had discovered a disassembled body, and the image was so vivid to him years after the incident it was still very difficult for him to deal with. In some situations, we can only do our best and then ask God to take care of the rest for us. One perception might focus on the horror of the initial discovery while another perception might be, "I'm glad I found him so that justice could be served and those who did this punished." Another perception of that situation could be, "I'm glad this happened to me so another person didn't have to suffer this pain." Would you be willing to do it again if it stopped another person's pain?

The hardest experience for me as a therapist occurred on a Saturday morning a few years ago. My boys brought my phone into me while I was still in bed. The message alert was beeping. I listened to the message from a former client of mine. She left a suicide message on my phone and asked me to tell her husband and children that she loved them. She apologized for leaving it on my phone but knew I could handle it. As difficult as it was, I suppose I am grateful that I heard the message and not her children so that they would not have to suffer the pain as I did. It is all about perception. My perception today is that she is indebted to me for the pain she caused and in the hereafter she will have to wave a palm leaf over me and serve me lemonade while I bask in the sun on a beach.

Let me share another experience I went through. I used to work for BYU and was provided with a university vehicle. I was responsible to lock up all the BYU-owned buildings that were off campus. If you are familiar with Provo, Utah, I was driving north on 900 East just past the Missionary Training Center where the road turns west. I had turned the corner and was now a couple blocks west of that corner. I was going about 40 mph. It was dark, and the light on North Canyon Road had just turned green for the cars driving east. A college student was jogging south with headphones on and saw the light turn green and thought, "I can cross the road before they get to me." He darted out right in front of my truck. I slammed on my breaks but still hit him. He flew into the other lane of the oncoming traffic as I came to a stop. He hit the pavement and rolled a few times. He then stood up and walked very unsteadily to my side of the road. I jumped out of the truck and grabbed him and someone yelled, "Get him to the hospital!" I put him into my passenger seat, quickly gathered a few eye witnesses' names and numbers, and raced off to the hospital.

On the way to the hospital he was cupping the blood in his hands as it fell off his face. I asked him, "Why did you cut in front of me?" He responded, "I saw the cars coming at me as the light turned green and I figured I could run across the street before they got to me. I didn't even think about looking behind me." I then asked, "Why did you get up so fast after being hit?" He said, "As I was flying through the air, I saw the headlights coming at me from the other direction and I did not want to get hit again."

When I pulled into Utah Valley Regional Center, I was not sure where the Emergency Room was, so we just went in the nearest door and found an information desk. When I asked the lady where the emergency room was, she pointed down the hall and yelled, "Get him down the hall now!" We hustled down the hall with him still cupping the blood in his hands as it ran off his face. We got to the emergency room and stood in line. When the lady at the desk looked up and saw him and all the blood, she yelled, "Get him around the corner now!" A nurse was waiting for us around the corner and started cleaning up his face. She asked, "What happened?" He said, "I was hit by a truck." And I responded by saying, "Yea, I hit him." Unbeknown to me, there was a policeman right behind me, and he said, "I think we need to talk."

We walked out to the parking lot and I pointed out the truck. The man I hit was probably 6'2'' tall and very well-conditioned. I hit him about where his waist was so his whole upper body slammed against my hood and crushed the hood so badly that BYU had to replace the truck. The policeman reprimanded me for leaving the scene of an accident. Someone had apparently called 911, and when the paramedics arrived, there was no one in sight. I told him, "Logic said that I could get him to the hospital quicker than waiting for paramedics to arrive." He agreed but pointed out, "If he would have had a seizure in your truck on the way to the hospital and died, then you would have spent the rest of your life at the point of the mountain" (where the Utah State Prison is located). My unspoken thought was that the Good Samaritan Act would have hopefully saved me, but who knows.

The policeman asked if I was in shock. I told him that I did not believe that I was. His answer was, "Some people don't know it when they are in shock." I could not help but wonder then what the purpose of asking me that was. I believe this is why I did not go into shock. First, I knew the accident was not my fault (luckily this was the victim's perception too) and second, he stood right up after I hit him. I likely would have gone into shock if he had just laid there in the street. But this much I can say, when I witness an accident and stop to help, I usually go into a more focused mode in order to be helpful in the situation. Some people lose their minds and panic; I seem to find my mind. I believe it is because my perception is, "I need to help these people."

Now that story I know does not compare with a lot of your traumatic stories. Some of you have stared death in the face or seen horrific things. To me, it was a horrific thing to watch a human body slam into my hood. I was with my friend one time when he hit a deer with his car. That was awful, but hitting a human is much worse. Fortunately for him (and me), the man I hit was okay and did not suffer any serious injuries. My initial perception at the accident scene helped me a lot: "The accident wasn't my fault." And again, luckily, the victim agreed with that.

If you want a good reference for working through PTSD issues, then I would suggest The PTSD Workbook[22] by Mary Beth Williams, Ph.D., LCSW, CTS, and Soili Poijula, Ph.D. It is a wonderful and helpful book with hundreds of activities that will help change your perception on your past traumatic event.

Obsessive-Compulsive Disorder

Obsessive-compulsive disorder (OCD) involves either obsessions or compulsions or both. A person might obsess over something in their head. Can we say that it is a perception that they have? Compulsions are essentially a ritual that is enacted to reduce the stress caused by an obsession. Little rituals are performed to meet the requirements of perceptions. One criterion for OCD is that the person knows that his thoughts are not real and are rather a product of his own mind. I want to emphasize here again that I do not intend to oversimplify OCD. I hope this book generates thoughts and ideas to further the work along in this field.

Two common obsessions or perceptions displayed in OCD are thoughts about suicide (not that they want to but that they are afraid one day they will) and homosexuality (not that they are homosexuals, but that they might be). Obsessions obviously do not stop with those two thoughts and can really be about anything. I worked with a client one time who was convinced that if he had bad thoughts about his wife, then she would die. I went into his room one night and said, "Let's kill your wife tonight by thinking bad thoughts." He responded, "Jason, I know it's not real." That was important for him to recognize because if he did not know it was not real then he would not have OCD. He could possibly have OCPD (you can read more about this towards the back of the book).

I had another client who would not answer a question until he counted to a certain number in his head. He was not just trying to calm himself down but truly believed he had to get to a certain number before he could speak. A common thing I see with people who have OCD is perfectionism gone too far. Their shirts have to be hung up two inches apart (like the military does), or their bed has to be perfectly made before they can leave their room. The socks have to be in the sock drawer, and the pants have to be in the pants drawer. Now, most of us like order. The difference is that they cannot leave their room if something is out of place. They cannot function if something is out of place. It must make one's life unmanageable. The movie "What About Bob"[23] is an example of a person with OCD, but it is important to note that Hollywood shows an extreme case to make us laugh. Of course, one does not have to exhibit the extremes in behavior that Bob does in order to have OCD.

Even in cases of OCD, we can change perceptions. You must have a sense of humor when combating your OCD. I have walked into a client's room before and taken a pair of socks out of his sock drawer and placed them into his pants drawer. I then shut the drawers so he could not even see it. But he knew it was messed up, and it was like the socks were yelling at him to put them back in order. I asked him, "Who decides order?" His response was, "I do." I told him, "I hope you do. But if your choices are based upon what things are telling you, then things dictate order in your life and not you. In other words, those socks are trying to tell you right now what order is and what it isn't. If you chose to put a sock in the pants' drawer, is it in order? The answer is yes if you chose it to be order." Order is defined as, "A condition of regular or proper arrangement." Who decides what is regular and proper? You decide for you, and you can decide where the socks go. Decide that the socks are in order in the pants drawer and walk out of the room. The socks will scream at you again, and I want you to say, 'You sure look dumb but guess what? I chose you to be that way. Ha!" Then just walk away. Remember, a sense of humor is vital to this exercise.

Start with something small. Maybe it is breaking free of having to have your shoes matched up in pairs in the closet. Maybe it is not cleaning a little corner of the living room when you vacuum. You must find something that will bug you but that you can handle for a week or maybe just a day. Start small and then work your way up to bigger and harder things. **Remember, you choose order; things do not.** Take control of your life by changing your perception. The book I recommend for more information on OCD is Too Perfect: When Being in Control Gets out of Control[24] by Allan Mallinger, M.D., and Jeannette Dewyze.

Approval from Others

One source of stress and anxiety is caring too much about what others think of us. We are often our own worst critics and judge ourselves harsher than anyone else ever would (unless of course you are in junior high school). We worry too much about being a part of the "in crowd." This would include how we speak, who we spend time with, what we drive, and what we wear. We are too worried about our self-esteem and do not care at all about our self-worth.

I lived in Brandon, Florida, during the summer prior to college. I worked at a pants factory and also at the Sheraton Hotel as a bell-hop. My job at the pants factory was to pick the list of pants that a particular store wanted. I would walk down the aisles of pants, pick the pants the store was requesting, and put them in my grocery cart. I would then take the pants over to the sewing section where the labels would be sewn into the pants. Then I would take them to the packaging department, and the pants would be boxed up and shipped out (I will spare you all the little details). Sometimes we would get a package of pants back from a store requesting that we send them a different brand of pants. We would simply unstitch the old patch and stitch the patch they wanted (with the desired brand name) back into the same pair of pants. Again we would package them up and send them back to the store. This way the store could sell the exact same pair of pants for a different price just because of the different patch.

Teenagers think they have to have the cool pants; otherwise, they are not cool. It is merely a game that the retail market is playing with our minds. Guess who the suckers are? That is right, we are. As if the clothes we wear really makes us who we are. Unfortunately, it does not just stop with clothes.

I have always wanted to own a Lexus. One day my wife and I bought one. I quickly realized that not only do people compare themselves to others based upon which car they drive, but people who drive Lexus vehicles also compare themselves according to which model of Lexus they drive. My pride went sky high as I drove my Lexus. I would cut people off on the road and think, "I can - I'm a Lexus." I told my wife I did not like who I was becoming, and I wanted to trade the car in for something else. My wife is so patient with me. She said that if that was what I needed to do, then go ahead. So I drove into a little mechanic shop in Provo, Utah. I had already done my homework and found that the car with the best gas mileage on the market was a 1997 Geo Metro. The mechanic happened to have a 1997 Geo Metro out back. I went inside and asked him if his car was for sale. He said he had bought it for his friend, but his friend was currently driving a Geo that was working just fine, so the car had been sitting in the backyard for a couple of months now. He was waiting for his friend's other car to die. He said he would sell it to me if I wanted it. I asked him if he would trade the Geo for my Lexus straight across, and I would keep the Lexus payments. He asked me if I was serious, and I assured him that I was. It was crazy I know, but it was a lesson I really needed to learn at that time in my life. So we traded straight across. Then when I would cut people off I would think, "I can't help it. I would go faster, but I only have three cylinders."

So often we base our self esteem upon the approval of other people. We care too much about what people think and not enough about what God thinks. I thought I looked good in that Lexus, but I did not like who I was on the inside when I drove that car. When we care so much about being in the "in crowd," we end up doing things that go against our core values. We abandon our values system and it is then impossible to find happiness. We might end up using drugs and alcohol as an escape from how we feel about ourselves.

There are many differing opinions on the definitions of self-esteem and self-worth. I agree with the side that says self-esteem comes from man and fluctuates. It comes from our perception of what others think of us. If I wear the right pants, others will admire me, and my self-esteem seems to go up. Self-worth on the other hand comes from God. We get it at birth, and we have the exact same amount our entire life. Self-worth does not change based upon what we do or say. Self-worth is constant and consistent. If we were to focus more on self-worth, which is infinite worth, more than we focus on self-esteem, which is man-made, then our lives would be filled with so much love and joy. If people were more focused on their God-given self-worth, then they would understand their infinite value and never lower their standards.

Jason's Theory

My theory was not developed from scientific studies. It comes from the actual therapy I have conducted in individual and group settings. After fourteen years in this field, I am convinced that my theory is accurate. I saw an article in a magazine affirming my belief wherein another person shared a very similar theory.

I believe that every one of us is a child of God. We come to earth as a baby knowing who we are. Some say that the reason babies cry is because they miss being with God. As we grow, we experience life - the good and the bad. We look to our parents as gods who can do no wrong. As we experience abuse, neglect, or we see our parents or other adults do things that are not right, we begin to doubt God. We also sin and make mistakes. When we sin or make mistakes, we are punished and sometimes even led to believe that God does not love people who sin. Sometimes we are even taught that abuse was our fault and that if we were not so cute, or insolent, or mean then it never would have happened. We are told that if our parents ever find out about the abuse, they will not love us anymore. We believe that we are horrible people and that God certainly cannot love us anymore.

Because of our belief that God does not love us, we turn away from God until we no longer feel His love. Once we no longer feel God's love, there is a key puzzle piece within us that is now missing from our life. Let us say that the puzzle piece is in the shape of an octagon. With that puzzle piece missing, we look to fill the void with another puzzle piece, perhaps a rectangle shaped piece. There are two directions we seek out to fill this void.

The first avenue is to deny love from outside as well as inside. We feel so badly that we do not believe we are worthy of anyone's love. This is displayed through behaviors (or square puzzle pieces) such as: drinking, using drugs, self-mutilation, isolation, and ultimately suicide. We believe these actions (puzzle pieces) will fill the void left by the octagon-shaped piece only to be disappointed that the pieces just do not fill the void. As a result, we feel more shame and guilt and continue to look in the same direction towards destructive behaviors. This is insanity, but we are now caught up in this vicious cycle.

The other misfit puzzle piece is seeking love from others to fill the void. These behaviors (or square puzzle pieces) are things like: popularity, sex, gangs, gambling, crimes, money, cosmetic surgeries or other extreme makeovers. We believe these behaviors will give us what we have been missing for so long. We think that they will bring happiness back to us. But in reality, it is the feeling of God's love that is missing. So, once again we come up short-handed and continue that vicious cycle, still not really understanding what the void is. The reason I use the analogy of a puzzle can be summarized as follows: The puzzle pieces that we are using are not the correct puzzle pieces to fill the void. The only way to fill the void is to come to feel God's love again.

But what happens instead is that people lie to themselves and try to convince the rest of us of the same lie. They say they are just expressing themselves. They say they are just finding out who they are. They truly believe they will find that happiness they are looking for in the next tattoo or the next piercing. Others tell us it is just a phase they are going through. Some have cleverly disguised it as, "diversity." In the end, it is what it is—the wrong puzzle piece.

Finding God

Finding God is the only solution. The widely used 12-Step program is ultimately a vehicle by which a person finds God. In the Alcoholics Anonymous[25] book (The Big Book) the first two steps talk about being powerless and then finding a higher power. In Step 3 and beyond, this Higher Power is referred to as God. But in the beginning, it is important that people who feel so lost and ashamed can grasp on to any higher power. Through the process and over time, they are led to God. I have worked with people who have attempted to go through the entire 12-Step process claiming that their higher power is something other than God. One man told me that his higher power was the mountains. I asked him, "If I was really wealthy and bought your mountain and tore it down to build a subdivision, what would happen to your higher power?" He stumbled for a moment and said, "It's the spirit that revolves around the mountain." Well, sobriety did not work for him, and he relapsed and went to jail. Thankfully, in jail he found God, and it has changed his life.

The 12-Steps do not ask us to create a higher power of our liking. We do not create a higher power that agrees with how we are living. No! We _find_ our Higher Power. He already exists, and we have to come to Him. Our Higher Power is God. We then line up our actions with God's values, and therein is found happiness.

There are three questions that I advise all my clients to ask of God in prayer. Before they ask these questions, they must understand something - there are no prerequisites for praying. God loves us because of who we are. We are a part of Him. I loved my children right when they were born because they were a part of me. It was not because they had done anything for me. It was simply because they were mine. People tell me all the time they cannot pray because they do not feel worthy. There is no requirement of worthiness to pray. In fact, the best time to pray and get reconnected to God is when we feel unworthy or disconnected from him.

So with no prerequisites for praying, here are the three questions to ask God: 1) Do you know who I am? 2) Do you know where I am? 3) Do I really matter to You? An answer to one of these questions is an answer to all three. I want my clients to pray until they receive an answer that comes from God specifically to them. They are looking for an answer that they cannot rationalize or explain away, an answer that encompasses the entire soul. They say to me, "I know that God's love is all around us," but that is not the answer I want them to experience. I do not care if they <u>know</u> He loves them; I want them to <u>feel</u> His love for them personally. If you have not asked these three questions of God, then I would invite you to do so as well. You will get the answer when you want it badly enough. You will not get a response if you are just doing it to say you did it. Once you get your answer, your life will change forever because the void is filled. I got my answer long ago, and it sustains me through all my trials and afflictions.

Now you may ask yourself why I went into a lengthy discussion about God when the topic is stress and anxiety. The reason is simple and logical. Our stress and anxiety is greatly magnified when all that we experience is about this life and has no eternal significance. Logo therapy teaches that when we have meaning in our life, anxiety and stress are reduced because it is given proper perspective.

Section III: How Perception Affects Our Relationships

Marital Discord or Bliss Derived From Perception

Below are the lyrics to the song, "Imagine That" by Diamond Rio.

Imagine That[26]

(Derek George/John Tirro/Bryan White)

What is the world comin' to
When lovers can't believe
They got a love comin' true
Then they up and leave
They say they will when they won't
They say I do and then they don't
That ain't the way it's got to be
With you and me

Imagine that, a love that lasts forever
Imagine that, for all the world to see
That two people stay together
The way it ought to be
Oh imagine that

I don't intend to change the world
I couldn't if I tried
As long as I've got you with me girl
I'll be satisfied
Let's do what we can, mean what we say
We'll just take it day by day
'Cause I want to prove to everyone

That it can be done

Imagine that, a love that lasts forever
Imagine that, for all the world to see
That two people stay together
The way it ought to be
Oh imagine that

Do you believe in love enough to go the distance
Do you believe in love enough to make a stand
Do you believe enough to handle the resistance
I believe we can

Imagine that, a love that lasts forever
Imagine that, for all the world to see
That two people stay together
The way it ought to be
Oh imagine that
Oh imagine that
Imagine that
Oh imagine that

You have probably heard that the divorce rate is now over 50%. Have you ever had someone explain to you how they arrived at that number? Let us say that in Los Angeles County in the year 2006, there were 5,000 marriages. For us to know exactly what the divorce rate is for those 5,000 marriages, we would need to do a longitudinal study and follow those same couples for 50+ years. This is not convenient since we would not get the results until the year 2056. In the year 2056, people will not care about what the divorce rate was for the people who got married in 2006. So the statistics are calculated in a different way.

First, they calculate how many marriages occurred in 2006 in Los Angeles County – in this case 5,000. They then calculate how many divorces occurred in Los Angeles County during the same year – in this case 2,500. The statement then follows: "Half of all marriages will end in divorce." Is that true? Not necessarily, and not if that is the method by which the statistics are contrived. Who knows, maybe our children will be smarter than we are and will recognize the value of honoring their word to each other, and the divorce rate will actually decline.

If the perception going into a marriage is that there is a 50/50 chance of either staying married or getting divorced, then divorce automatically becomes an option when things get rough. If I enter a marriage, like I did with my wife, where divorce is not an option, then I am bound to find another option when we do not see eye to eye.

For example, my brother got married, and they elected to have his' and hers' bank accounts. That is not uncommon these days. But in my opinion, that is just preparing oneself for divorce. I have even heard a client say, "We need separate accounts. What if we get divorced?" Have you ever heard of a self-fulfilling prophesy?! This is definitely one if I have ever heard one. You predict the future will turn out in divorce, and amazingly it does just that.

I have seen people get divorced over the smallest issues, and I have seen people stay together through the most difficult situations. What is the difference between the two groups? The answer is perception. Some couples' perception does not allow for any flaws. They say to themselves, "I hate my spouse because of his flaws and he can't change." While other couples' perceptions led to "I love my spouse, and flaws are what we have, not who we are, so we can change."

Do you see how powerful our thoughts are? They become our reality and even our destiny. I have seen people get divorced, then remarried, then divorced, then remarried, and then divorced again, and then they say, "All women are alike." They have rationalized themselves into thinking that the reason they cannot seem to stay married is actually because of the other person. One of my favorite quotes states, "The one common denominator in all your dysfunctional relationships is you." But due to his perception, he believes it is always the other person's fault. Therefore, he does not change and carries that perception and all his baggage into the next relationship expecting different results.

Is that not the definition of insanity - doing the same thing over and over again and expecting different results? I also came up with another definition of insanity: doing different things and expecting the same results. People think change (or treatment) won't work, but that is because they think they will end up where they once were. They will with that perception, but in order to get there they must go back to doing what they once did.

Care versus Worry

My wife and I had a different perception of the word "care" during our first year of marriage. One night she had been at the hospital with her sister. It got very late, and I decided to go to bed. I locked the front door, including the dead bolt for which we did not have a key. I went into our bedroom and got into bed. I had turned on the fan so I could not hear the people living upstairs from us, and I went to sleep. Luckily for me, as my wife left the hospital, her father followed her home due to the late hour. She got a flat tire, and he stopped and fixed it for her. When she arrived home and found the door locked, she proceeded to knock on the door. Of course, I could not hear her, so she knocked louder. She then walked around the house to where our bedroom window was and knocked on it until I finally woke up. I let her into the house. She then said to me, "You don't care about me." I said, "Of course I care about you." She responded by saying, "If you cared about me, you would have been worried about me." I responded, "I can care about you and not worry about you (every man knows I'm right and every woman knows I'm not). I had gone to bed and fell asleep, and her perception was that I did not worry nor care about her. After a few minutes of disagreeing, I told her that I would look up the word "care" in

118

the dictionary because it was obvious that our argument was about semantics. I then read to her the following definition of care: "Mind, be concerned, think about, heed, be bothered, attention, custody, caution, and treatment." Then I came to the last word in the definition which was "worry." I simply omitted that word, shut the dictionary, and told her, "See I can care about you and not worry about you." Alright, before you get too mad at me, I did tell her later ... after about a year. By the way, I do not think that people should have any type of heated discussion or argument in the middle of the night especially right after one of the parties has been woken out of a dead sleep. But the point of the story is that she wanted me to show her love (or care) by worrying about her, and that is not how I had showed love (or care) to her that night. That does not mean I was not showing her love, but it was being done in my way and not hers.

Love Given/Love Received

I heard a story once of a newlywed couple. In the man's family-of-origin, when someone got sick, the family left the house so the sick person could sleep all day in peace and quiet in order to get well. In the woman's family-of-origin, when a person got sick, the others stayed faithfully by her side and read her books or just kept her company and were available to wait upon her needs. This is not a conversation that would naturally cross one's mind before getting married. In this particular marriage, the man got sick first, and the woman stayed by his side the entire day. He thought, "Why doesn't she love me enough to leave me alone so I can sleep?" But he did not say anything to her. Some time later, she got sick, and he left the house so she could get some rest. She thought, "Why doesn't he love me enough to stay and keep me company?" It was finally brought out into the open when they came to treatment and they were able to discuss it. Was she showing him love when she stayed by his bedside? Yes. Was he showing her love when he left the house? Yes. But the problem was that the love given was not the love received.

My wife loves to get flowers. As an example, let us say one night before I get home from work, she thinks, "I want to show Jason that I love him. I know! I'll buy him some flowers because I like it when he buys me flowers." (My wife would like me to note that this particular example never actually happened.) So I come home, and she hands me the flowers and simply says, "Here you go Honey." I might respond to her by saying, "What did you buy these for? These are a waste of my money. They are going to die in a few days. Can't you see how hard I work for us to have money and you are wasting it on stuff like this?" If this were to happen, then the love given (the flowers) was not the love received. Why? Because of my perception of what love is and is not. In my perception, a gift of flowers does not equal love, but in her perception it does.

Here is a simple assignment that my college professor at Brigham Young University, Dr. Brent Barlow[27] gave to the class. Take a piece of paper and write on it, "How I show love to _____" (and fill in the blank with someone whom you want to improve your relationship with). Then number below that 1 through 5. Then write "How I receive love from _____" (and put the same person's name in this blank). Then number again below that 1 through 5. So if I were to do this assignment with my wife, it would look like this:

How I show Melanie love:

1)

2)

3)

4)

5)

How I receive love from Melanie:

1)

2)

3)

4)

5)

I would also ask my wife do the same thing for me. So her paper would look like this:

How I show Jason love:

1)

2)

3)

4)

5)

How I receive love from Jason:

1)

2)

3)

4)

5)

It is important to not exchange papers until both partners are done filling them out. Otherwise, you may be influenced by the other person's paper or vice versa. For the exercise to be helpful, both papers need to be completed before you swap.

Now, let us say that Melanie writes on her paper that she shows me love by giving me flowers, and I have now read that. Next time she gives me flowers, even if that is not how I receive love, I receive her love because now I know that is one of the ways she shows her love. Therefore, the love given is the love received. Or, let us say that she has said, "I want to show Jason love tonight." On my paper, I have written down that one way I receive love from her is when she makes me dinner. That night, she makes me dinner knowing that I will receive it as love because I have now told her that is one way I receive love from her. Therefore, the love given is the love received.

You can do this assignment with anyone with whom you want to improve your relationship. When I worked at the state prison, I told the inmates if they did not have anyone at home with whom to complete the exercise, they could participate with their cell mate because that relationship could always be improved. It is a great tool to utilize every couple of years or so in a marriage. We change as we grow older, and the ways we receive love today might be different than they were when we first got married. For example, a man might write in his first year of marriage that he receives love from his wife when she rubs his back. However, as he gets older he is injured in a car accident and his back must be surgically repaired. In the future, whenever his back is rubbed, it causes him severe pain. Therefore, he no longer likes it or receives it as love when his wife rubs his back. In fact, if she were to carelessly rub his back, he might think she is being insensitive to his needs and get upset with her, even though at one time he received the very same action as love. I think it is obvious why this exercise should be done often.

Piña Colada[28]

Have you ever heard the song, "Escape" by Rupert Holmes? Most people know the song as, "Piña Colada." When I first heard it on the radio, I listened to the first verse and was both shocked and offended. Luckily, I kept listening and found the song to be very insightful. Here are the words:

I was tired of my lady
We'd been together too long
Like a worn-out recording
Of a favorite song
So while she lay there sleeping
I read the paper in bed
And in the personal columns
There was this letter I read

If you like Piña Coladas
And getting caught in the rain
If you're not into yoga
If you have half a brain
If you'd like making love at midnight
In the dunes on the Cape
Then I'm the love that you've looked for
Write to me and escape.

I didn't think about my lady
I know that sounds kind of mean
But me and my old lady
Have fallen into the same old dull routine
So I wrote to the paper
Took out a personal ad
And though I'm nobody's poet
I thought it wasn't half bad

Yes I like Piña Coladas
And getting caught in the rain

I'm not much into health food
I am into champagne
I've got to meet you by tomorrow noon
And cut through all this red-tape
At a bar called O'Malley's
Where we'll plan our escape.

So I waited with high hopes
And she walked in the place
I knew her smile in an instant
I knew the curve of her face
It was my own lovely lady
And she said, "Oh it's you."
Then we laughed for a moment
And I said, "I never knew."

That you like Piña Coladas
Getting caught in the rain
And the feel of the ocean
And the taste of champagne
If you'd like making love at midnight
In the dunes of the Cape
You're the lady I've looked for
Come with me and escape

What is the problem with this relationship? They stopped discovering each other. He says in the second verse, "But me and my old lady have fallen into the same old dull routine." I would say this is more common than not in most marriages. We get so caught up in the day-to-day necessary things in life and raising our children and being so busy with work that we forget to nurture our marriage. We forget to continue discovering each other and fall "into the same old dull routine."

Based on our discussion above, do you think the woman in the song had shown her husband love and he just did not see it or receive it? And likewise did he show her love, and she not see it or receive it? Most likely the answer is yes.

Otherwise they could not have fallen in love so quickly. My English professor, Dr. Thayer, used to always say, "Love isn't a noun, it's a verb. You can't fall into it." On the other hand, a good friend of mine, James, teaches in his seminars, "Love isn't a noun, it's a verb. It's not something you have but something you do. So if you don't love your wife, then love her." Again it is all about perception.

Fiddler on the Roof

Here is a great example from a great movie: "Fiddler on the Roof."[29] Tevye is the father, and his daughter is getting married to someone she loves very much. Tevye's marriage, on the other hand, was arranged for him by a matchmaker. In one scene, he wants to know if his wife, Golde, loves him. If you have not seen this movie, these words go back and forth from talking to singing between the couple. The song is called, "Do You Love Me?"

Tevye: Golde, I have decided to give Perchik permission to become engaged to our daughter, Hodel.

Golde: What??? He's poor! He has nothing, absolutely nothing!

Tevye: He's a good man, Golde. I like him. And what's more important, Hodel likes him. Hodel loves him. So what can we do? It's a new world ...a new world. Love. Golde ...do you love me?

Golde: Do I what?

Tevye: Do you love me?

Golde: Do I love you?

Tevye: Well?

Golde: With our daughters getting married
And this trouble in the town
You're upset, you're worn out.
Go inside, go lie down!
Maybe it's indigestion ...

Tevye: Golde, I'm asking you a question...
Do you love me?

Golde: You're a fool.

Tevye: I know...
But do you love me?

Golde: Do I love you?

Tevye: Well?

Golde: For twenty-five years I've washed your clothes
Cooked your meals, cleaned your house
Given you children, milked the cow.
After twenty-five years, why talk about love right now?

Tevye: Golde, the first time I met you
Was on our wedding day
I was scared.

Golde: I was shy.

Tevye: I was nervous.

Golde: So was I.

Tevye: But my father and my mother
Said we'd learn to love each other.
And now I'm asking, Golde,
Do you love me?

Golde: I'm your wife.

Tevye: I know...
         But do you love me?

Golde: Do I love him?

Tevye: Well?

Golde: For twenty-five years I've lived with him
         Fought him, starved with him.
         Twenty-five years my bed is his
         If that's not love, what is?

Tevye: Then you love me?

Golde: I suppose I do.

Tevye: And I suppose I love you too.

Both: It doesn't change a thing,
         But even so
         After twenty-five years
         It's nice to know.

In this song, Tevye kept asking his wife if she loved him. Was she answering his question? In her own way, she was telling him that she loved him, but he was not receiving it because she did not say the exact words he wanted to hear. Sometimes my wife and I will do the same thing in the sense that one of us will try and show love to the other and the other does not receive it. For example, she might clean the kitchen and I might not notice even that it is clean. We have learned now to stop each other and just say, "Receive the love being given." That helps us both to recognize the love in the air and to receive it.

Own Your Expectations

This idea of telling each other to "receive the love" is what we call owning our expectations. We heard this first from

Dr. John Lund.[30] The idea is that instead of my wife getting mad at me for not noticing how clean the kitchen is, she simply tells me that she needs me to recognize how clean the kitchen is on the day she has worked extra hard on it. I then walk into the kitchen and say, "Wow! Look at the counters, they are all cleared off, and the table is clean too." Then I ask my wife if that is sufficient recognition for her efforts, and if she says "no," then I go on: "Look at the cupboards. They are all so neat and organized. Is that enough?" At that point, she is satisfied. Now some people feel that if you have to ask for it, then it does not count. Which is more logical: Asking for recognition or praise and getting it and feeling appreciated or getting mad that your spouse cannot read your mind and give you the praise you deserve?

I have told my wife that I want to give her the praise she deserves. Unfortunately men are not equipped to see things that are not right in front of their face or specifically pointed out. I heard a joke once where a young man asked a young woman out on a date. She accepted his invitation. The young man went to his friend and said, "I've got a date with this girl, and I want to show her that I like her, but I don't want to do too much. I don't want to scare her off. What should I do?" His friend thinks about it for a minute and says, "At the end of the date, take her to the doorstep and shake her hand and tell her you really had a nice night." This is exactly what the young man did. He asked the young woman out again, and she accepted. He went back to this same friend and said, "Okay, we're on for a second date. I want to show her that I like her, so I've got to do more than just shake her hand, but I can't do too much. I don't want to scare her off. What should I do?" His friend thinks about it for a minute then says, "At the end of the date, take her to the doorstep and give her a hug and tell her you really had a nice night." The young man did just that. He asked the young woman out again, and she accepted. He went back to his friend and said, "Our third date is tomorrow night. I've got to show her that I like her by more than giving her a hug, but I don't want to scare her off. What should I do?" His friend thinks about it for a minute and says, "At the end of the date, take her to the doorstep and give her a kiss on her forehead and tell her you really had a nice night." So at the end of the date, the young man took the young woman to the doorstep and gave her a kiss on her forehead and said, "I really had a nice night." To this she replied, "Can you do that a little lower?" So in a nice deep voice, he responded, "I really had a nice night." The point of this joke, ladies, is that sometimes men are a little slow, and we need your help. In order to get her point across, she would probably have to point to her lips when she said, "Can you do that lower?"

So men are not equipped to see things that are not right in front of our faces, and even if it is right in front of our face, there is only about a 50/50 chance that we will see it. I cannot stand it when my wife walks me into the living room and says, "What do you notice that is different?" Honestly, I panic inside. I wonder what is going to happen the rest of the night if I cannot tell what is different. I offer a guess: "You moved the pictures around?" Usually I am wrong. I would very much appreciate it if she would just tell me that she has painted the room red so I could thank her and give her the "Atta girl" she deserves.

In owning our expectations, we need to understand that the two most important things about communication are time and place. Let us say that I am watching the World Series, and my wife walks into the room and says, "Will you please take out the trash?" I might say, "Yes" and I might even nod in agreement, but of course I do not take out the garbage, and the next day, she is annoyed with me because of it. My response to her frustration is, "What? You never asked me to." She then says, "I did too. You were sitting on the couch last night, and you said you would." But I do not remember any such thing because the communication happened at the wrong time.

Sometimes we find ourselves in a public place and on the verge of a disagreement. My wife will say, "Not now." She is telling me that this particular place is not the right place nor is it the right time for this particular conversation. We wait until we get into the van or get home to talk about it.

When we were first married, I had to explain to my wife many times that when I climb into bed and my head hits the pillow; I am gone in a matter of seconds. I fall asleep so fast that it drives my wife crazy. She might be talking to me and I will fall asleep right in between sentences. Then as she begins the next sentence, I jump because it startles me. I finally told her that if she wanted to talk with me at night, we needed to talk on the couch. Lying in bed is neither the right time nor place to have a conversation with me. As I own my expectations and convey them to my wife, she can respect them and does not feel invalidated when I fall asleep while she is talking to me.

Differences in Marital Perceptions

There are several differences in our perceptions that make marriage harder than it needs to be. If we could just identify them and learn to compromise, marriage would be a lot easier.

For example, when we were first married my wife liked to cuddle in bed at night. I, on the other hand, really like my space. In fact, even before we got married I owned a king-size waterbed just for me. I rolled around so much during the night that I would joke that I felt like a gymnast and needed to touch all four corners of my bed before finishing my routine in the morning. So it was difficult for me to learn how to sleep with another person in my bed. She would try and cuddle with me, and I would tell her to scoot over. Then she would slide her foot over ever so gently and touch my foot. I would then tell her that I could feel her foot and that she needed to move it. Today we have compromised to cuddle for a few minutes after which I kiss her goodnight and roll over and go to sleep. I am getting better, but it has been almost 16 years. If we did not openly discuss this issue, then my wife's perception would likely be: "He doesn't love me because he never wants to cuddle with me." My perception may have been, "She doesn't respect me enough to give me my space when I'm trying to sleep." Both are far from the truth. In reality, she was simply trying to show me love, and I do love to cuddle with her, just not when going to bed.

Couples often argue over whether the toilet lid should be up or down. Women usually want it to be down, and men often do not care if it is up. Personally I believe it should be down because one time my toothbrush fell out of my cupboard and bounced off the counter and into the toilet. Now our toilet lids stay down. Anyway, my friend had this discussion with his wife, and they decided the toilet lid would be kept down. One night, his wife when leaving the bathroom decided to be nice and leave the toilet seat up for her husband. My friend walked into the bathroom a while later and neglected to turn the light on. He sat down and landed in the water inside the toilet. His perception could have been, "She's trying to prove a point. She's not being very nice." When in reality, she was trying to show him love by compromising a bit.

Are you in a relationship where one person snores and the other does not? Supposedly I snore. There is no proof of that, but hypothetically, I may possibly snore. When my wife wakes me up in the middle of the night and tells me to stop snoring, my perception could be, "She doesn't care if I get any sleep tonight. Why can't she love me enough to let me sleep?" She might simply want to fall asleep herself. Do I not care enough about her to be quiet while she is trying to sleep? What if those were my thoughts and perception? Would I get upset? Or could I try and respect her sleep as well? One night she finally owned her expectations and told me that I had to give her at least five minutes to fall asleep before I came to bed. I agreed and tried it, but it turns out that she cannot actually fall asleep that fast and was still awake when I came to bed.

Where do couples go for the holidays? My family grew up in Concord, California, and Phoenix, Arizona. My grandparents lived in Los Angeles, California, and Salt Lake City, Utah. I hardly ever saw my grandparents. On the other hand, my wife grew up in Pleasant Grove, Utah, and both sets of grandparents lived within one hour of her home. On nearly every holiday, my wife's family would visit her grandparents. When we got married, we naturally had very different perceptions as to what we would do on holidays. She wanted to visit her family-of-origin and her grandparents, and I wanted to stay home with my wife and children (once we had them). We discussed this at length so that I could gain a new perception and we could compromise.

These differences are sometimes small in nature. My professor in college called them "tremendous trifles." They truly are small conflicts, but we tend to blow them up into tremendous problems. If we could just take a step backwards and look at them from an objective point of view, we are likely to understand the big picture and the miniature nature of the problem. I sometimes stop myself from arguing about something by thinking, "This issue really doesn't matter."

When I was at home, I used to argue and fight over which television channel my brothers and sisters and I were going to watch. Sometimes my brothers and I even got into actual physical fights over who controlled the remote. I left home at 19 and spent two years in Chile away from my family. I can still remember sitting outside in Chile trying to think of anything that I had in common right then with my family. The only thing I could pinpoint was the sun. I felt so far away from them. I remember having the thought, "I will never fight over the television again. Relationships are more important than television, and if my brothers and sisters want to watch a different channel, then I'll let them." Remember, no thing (nothing) is worth more than a relationship.

I do not think it is true, but I heard a story of a couple where the wife kept a shoe box that she asked her husband to never look in. He honored her request and never touched the box. Many years later when they were both in their old age, she lay dying in the hospital. He thought of the box and grabbed it and took it to the hospital. He pleaded with her that he had honored her word all those years, but it was time that she allowed him to look inside the box. She agreed. He opened the box and found two crocheted doilies and $25,000.

He held the money and asked her what the two doilies were for. She said, "When I got married, my father told me to never argue with you but instead to bite my tongue and make a doily." The husband then said with delight and a bit of pride in his voice, "Since we've been married, you have only made two doilies. That is pretty good, but what's up with the $25,000?" She said, "That's how much money I've made by selling all the other doilies I made."

Her father's advice is good advice for the small tremendous trifles we face. Some things are not worth fighting over. Other things are certainly worth discussing. I have a cross-stitch hanging in my room of a quote from B.H. Roberts[31] that says, "In essentials, let there be unity, in non-essentials, liberty, and in all things, charity."

What is the Message We Are Sending?

What message was I sending to my family when I fought with them over television programming? Was the message, "What I watch is more important to me than you are?" When we fight over things, the message is that things are more important than the relationship we have with the person.

How about in a relationship? Do we often time send messages that are unintended and not true? When my wife is trying to share her feelings with me and rather than just listen and be sympathetic, I try to fix her problem, even though my intentions are pure and altruistic, the message she gets is, "He doesn't care because he is not listening. I can't share my feelings with him because he won't listen."

After watching the video, "Men Are from Mars, and Women Are from Venus[32]" by John Grey, I decided to practice what he preached and that was to just listen and not to try and solve her problems. I went home and sat on the front porch swing with my wife one night. She began to share her experiences that day. I did everything in my will power to not fix any of her problems. I just sat there and said things like,

"Really!" "What happened?" "Wow!" "Then what happened?" "That's terrible!" and even grunted a few times. When we finished talking, we went to walk in the house, and she asked "Can I tell you something?" I turned around and faced her and she said, "I just want to tell you - you did it perfect tonight." I was dying inside as I said, "Thank you." I sent the correct message that night, but it was so incredibly hard to do and it still is. Unless I am consciously thinking about it, I naturally fall back into old behaviors and attempt to fix her problems.

If you are ready to be humbled, then go ahead and ask your companion this question, "Are you okay with me?" Or "What could I do better in our relationship?" Then listen without debate and say, "I'll take a look at that" and then do just that.

Different Types of Love

There are different types of love. These different types warrant discussion because we interpret love in different ways. If we can understand the different types of love, then we can improve our relationships by focusing on which part needs the most work.

The types of love we will discuss here are: romantic, sexual, manic, egocentric, altruistic, companionate, and pragmatic. Romantic is love full of romance. How romance is defined is up to you and your partner. However, for you men out there who are not very romantic, let me share with you what some women consider to be romantic. Try giving a gift when it totally unexpected. I have learned that if I give her a gift on her birthday or Christmas, she appreciates it, but I do not get any extra bonus points because it was expected. If, on the other hand, I forgot to give her a gift on a special occasion, then I lose a lot of points. However, if I give her a gift just because I was thinking of her that day, then I score big-time extra points. Other romantic ideas include: candlelight, her favorite music, getting dressed up nice, cologne, opening the door for her, being a gentlemen, flowers, genuine praise, cuddling, and sensitivity.

Sexual love is self-explanatory.

Manic love is crazy love. It might be described as out-of-control love where one person is obsessed with another. This is definitely the kind of love that stalkers have. When we first fall in love with someone and we cannot get them out of our minds we sometimes call this manic love. We cannot sleep or eat or concentrate on anything. When I was in the 6th grade, I called up a girl named Kim and said, "Kim will you go out with me?" She said, "Go where?" I said, "You know, go out with me like boyfriend girlfriend going out." She then said, "I'll think about it." For the next couple of days I was on pins and needles. Then at last her friend approached me on the playground and said, "Kim says she'll go out with you." I was so thrilled! I told Kim, "Now that I'm your boyfriend, I need to walk you home because that is what boyfriends do." She said that would be fine if I walked on the other side of the street because she already walked home with a group of friends. I did that. I actually walked her home by walking on the opposite side of the street! Now that is manic love.

Egocentric love is love focused on oneself. Growing up in this Judeo-Christian society we are often taught to love one another and turn the other cheek. But we are rarely taught to love ourselves. Having love for one's self is just as much a part of Judaism and Christianity as loving others. Obviously we do not want to get too carried away with it, but we all need a healthy amount of self-love.

Altruistic love is focused on the other person. This includes loving others even when they have done us wrong. Two automobile accidents occurred many years ago here in Utah where two different drunk drivers killed many members of two different families. In both cases, the father and one child survived. Also in both cases, the fathers openly stated that they forgave the drunk driver. I've met both these men and they are great examples to us all. That is altruistic love, and it is to be admired.

Companionate love is having a companion to be with and talk to. An example would be when vintage people (a nice way of saying the elderly) marry in the very end of their lifetime just for companionship. My grandfather married a woman when he was older, and I believe it was because he wanted to have someone to talk to and play games with and just be with.

Pragmatic love is practical love. This could consist of getting married because we get a tax break. Maybe it is being together because it's easier to raise children with two parents instead of one. Maybe it is getting married so the other person can stay in the United States and become a citizen or at least have children who will be citizens. The love is based on logic and practicality rather than emotion.

Having a mixture of all seven of these love types can help a relationship. This is what I would suggest. Write the seven types of love down on a piece of paper with a scale ranging from 0-10 below each type (0=not at all; 10=totally satisfied). Make two copies and give one to your spouse. Each of you circle which number best describes your relationship with regards to that particular type of love. Repeat the exercise for where you would like to be in your relationship with regards to each of the types. Then share your answers with each other. So it would look like this:

Where I believe we are in our relationship:

Romantic

0—1—2—3—4—5—6—7—8—9—10

Sexual

0—1—2—3—4—5—6—7—8—9—10

Manic

0—1—2—3—4—5—6—7—8—9—10

Egocentric

0—1—2—3—4—5—6—7—8—9—10

Altruistic

0—1—2—3—4—5—6—7—8—9—10

Companionate

0—1—2—3—4—5—6—7—8—9—10

Pragmatic

0—1—2—3—4—5—6—7—8—9—10

Where I would like us to be in our relationship:

Romantic

0—1—2—3—4—5—6—7—8—9—10

Sexual

0—1—2—3—4—5—6—7—8—9—10

Manic

0—1—2—3—4—5—6—7—8—9—10

Egocentric

0—1—2—3—4—5—6—7—8—9—10

Altruistic

0—1—2—3—4—5—6—7—8—9—10

Companionate

0—1—2—3—4—5—6—7—8—9—10

Pragmatic

0—1—2—3—4—5—6—7—8—9—10

Share the responses to both exercises with your partner. If your spouse's answers are significantly different than yours on the two scales, then that is a concern. It is important to note that I am not at all concerned about *my* interpretation of where I am romantically - I am only concerned about where *she* thinks I am romantically. If I scored low on her chart in this or any other area and she wants it to be higher, then I would ask her what I could do to improve. This chart helps me to see her perception of our relationship, and likewise, she gets to see my perception.

It would be completely ridiculous for us to argue about where we are in our relationship. If we argue and I convince her that we are better off than she thinks, does that change the reality of our marriage? Most likely she has just given in and decided to keep quiet and make a doily rather than make me mad. The reality of marriage boils down to the perception of the husband and the perception of the wife – that is it. Some people, more often men than women, would rather live with their false fantasy than face the reality of the situation. But to improve a relationship, we must first find out where the relationship is at, and in order to do that, we have to see the relationship from both perceptions. Both perceptions in a marriage are reality to the beholder.

Once validated, both perceptions can be improved. If one is invalidated, change is nearly impossible. I am not speaking of what the relationship looks like from the outside but rather what it really is on the inside. Sure she might resolve to be even more submissive to her abusive husband, but her perception of the relationship is not improving just because

138

her actions appear to be. We must take the time to listen to each other's perception of our relationship. Often we do not share with each other until our resentment and anger have built up to a boiling point and we yell at each other and the whole laundry list of frustrations comes flowing out. Try asking your spouse, "What is one thing I could do to improve this relationship?" Everyone can handle working on one thing. It is when we are faced with many faults and complaints that we get overwhelmed and defensive and do nothing but make up excuses for our behavior.

I have a friend who was in an abusive relationship, but her husband's perception was that it was not abusive. He would drag her by her hair or throw her cat across the room, but he did not hit her. In his perception, as long as he did not hit her, he was not being abusive. Her perception, at least for a while, was that she deserved it and could not do any better. It took a while to change her perception and convince her that he was abusive and that she did deserve better. Once her perception was validated, only then could change be made.

Marriage has the potential to be the most rewarding of all institutions. Unfortunately, it also has the potential to be the most punishing if not properly nurtured and cared for.

Codependency

A definition of codependency is: 1) A relationship of mutual need; 2) a situation in which a person (such as the partner of an alcoholic or a parent of a drug-addicted child) needs to feel needed by the other person; 3) the dependence of two people on each other, especially when this reinforces mutually harmful behavior patterns. Codependency is not well understood by people who are in a codependent relationship even after people on the outside try to help them see it. As a drug and alcohol therapist, I often find my clients to be very easy to work with and their family members to be incredibly hard to work with. The family members drop off the client and expect us to fix them, but they refuse to accept their part of the equation.

I had one client who pawned off his own things, which happened to be gifts from others. His mother would then go and buy them back from the pawn shop. My client would then pawn them off again. This cycle repeated itself several times until the mother determined that she would never do it again. She never did buy his things back again - his father did. The parents did not understand how they were enabling their child in his drug abuse. They were providing him with money or a means by which to get money to purchase.

I heard an interesting statement made by a son in a codependent relationship with his mother. He said, "I finally got my mom to read the book on codependency ... well, I mean I read it to her." It is important to note that no one is in a codependent relationship unless they have great love for the other person. It is just that they love the other person too much and begin to hurt that person by enabling them. For example, a father loves his child very much. His child breaks the law and gets arrested. Instead of allowing natural consequences to take their course, the father quickly bails his son out of jail to prevent any suffering. An inmate I worked with many years ago told me, "The best thing my father ever did for me was refuse to bail me out of jail. It would have only cost him $60. Instead he put $10 into my account each week for seven weeks. He ended up paying $70 instead of $60, but I was kept in jail all that time which allowed me to face the consequences of my actions."

I have heard so many parents say, "I just can't let my child live on the streets." No, instead they allow their child to take advantage of their generosity and continue to use drugs, sometimes with their parents' money. If the mom and dad had a rule that no one living at their house could use drugs and as a result of the rule being violated, kicked the child out, then their child would be forced to face life and the decisions they are making. Then they may consider stopping the drug use. The problem comes when parents cannot face the fact that their child might end up dead on the streets. But who is to say that their child would not have died of an overdose in their own basement if they continued to tolerate a drug user living in their home? We must own our side of the street only and allow the other person to own their side of the street. If we own their side of the street too, then they never have to become responsible or accountable for their own actions and are not likely to change their behavior.

It is not just parents and children who are codependent, a lot of spouses are as well. When conducting therapy, my goal is to separate the two codependent people; it does not even have to be a physical separation. I teach each of them how to function independent of the other; then I bring the two independent individuals back together into an interdependent relationship. An interdependent relationship is where both parties do not have to have the other person in their life to survive, but by bringing these two together, they can accomplish so much more than the sum of their individual efforts added together. This is also known as synergism.

Synergism is often explained in the following equation: $1 + 1 = 3$. For example, if I have all the parts of a car engine on the ground separated from each other, they do not do me a whole lot of good. However, if I put them together, then I can make an engine that runs a car and is very useful. This is what is meant by the solution being more than the sum of its parts. Let us just say that I can lift 100 pounds on the bench press and so can you. If we both lift together, we could lift more than 200 pounds because there is something added to our strength as we work together.

Spouses and parents frequently get confused when we tell them to back off because they are hurting their substance abusing partner or child. They do not believe this person can make it on their own. I am telling you that they can. I have seen people who even I doubted could make it alone, and they got along just fine. Survival is possible for everyone. There are homeless shelters, food banks, and other charitable organizations that are willing to help people in even the direst circumstances.

I knew a 40 year-old man who lived at home with his parents. I told his parents they should kick him out. They said that they could not kick him out because he did not have a job. I said, "Of course he doesn't have a job. You give him money and a place to live. Why should he get a job? You're hurting him because he's not learning how to work and take care of himself. If you two ever die together in a car accident, what would happen to him? Who would take care of him? He won't know how to take care of himself, pay bills, hold down a job, etc."

As one of my clients begins to recover and get better and healthier, the parents ask if they can help their son find an apartment while he works on getting a job and getting back on his feet. I tell them to go ahead because this is not a codependent behavior. It is not enabling him to not take responsibility or reinforcing negative behaviors. I do suggest, however, that they have him sign a contract that he will pay them back and then hold him accountable just like they would anyone else with whom they had a contract. This is sometimes a difficult concept to get across. It seems that parents these days are more concerned with being their child's friend than they are teaching their child responsibility. This is hurting these children, and it needs to stop.

After learning about codependency, perceptions can be changed and family members usually say, "I didn't mean to hurt my child" or "I didn't know I was hurting my spouse." They experience a truly liberating feeling, as they come to understand that they do not have to take on the other person's feelings or responsibilities. They can each live their own life. I would highly recommend the book Codependent No More[33] by Melody Beattie. She also wrote Beyond Codependency.[34] Both books are helpful in changing perception and eliminating codependency from your life.

I would like to give you a new perception. Instead of thinking that you are being mean when you are holding your ground and give people boundaries, see it as loving yourself enough to not let people take advantage of you or walk all over you. I teach my clients this same principle. They know they cannot hang out with old "friends" now that they are sober, but they do not want to be mean either. I tell them to not see themselves as being mean to their "friends" but rather loving themselves enough to avoid relapse at all cost.

Victim vs. Survivor Derived From Perception

Choose To Be a Survivor

A <u>victim</u> is someone who says their actions today are a result of what has happened to them in the past. They may have been abused before and so today do not trust anyone. They may never leave their apartment building because they are afraid that someone will abuse them again. Their actions today are based upon what happened to them in the past, and unfortunately for this person, the past consisted of abuse. Thus they are a victim of their past, and the perpetrator still has power and control over them. It might be as much as 10 or 20 years later, and the victim is still being haunted by the abuse and continues to give the perpetrator power over their everyday life. Meanwhile, the perpetrator continues on with their life giving no thought to the victim at all.

Do you remember when the twin towers fell in New York in 2001? We were told at that time that we should not change our lives or become paranoid. Otherwise, the terrorists would be getting exactly what they want – power over our lives. So we did our best to go to school, work, and church and attend large gatherings without thinking about what had happened or what could happen. The same concept is true in this scenario.

A <u>survivor</u> is someone who acknowledges the abuse in the past, but makes their own decisions every day based upon what they want and not based upon what happened to them. By no means am I trying to ignore or push aside the horrific experiences in the past, but rather I am trying to take the power away from the perpetrator and put it back where it belongs, with the victim. The difference between the two scenarios is their perceptions.

I heard another client share a different perception about her abuse. She said, "I'm glad he only raped my body and not my soul. I am not my body and so he didn't get to me." I was very impressed when I heard her say that.

The victim mentality does not allow them to break away from what happened and move on. It convinces them that what we do or what happens to us is what makes us who we are. The survivor believes that what we do or what happens to us is just a part of our past and does not make us who we are. The survivor understands that the lessons learned from our experiences are more important than the experiences themselves.

Some victims like being victims. In their perception, it somehow takes away their responsibility. They do not have to succeed now because of what happened to them. They are free to take the easy road of laziness and failure. The failure can simply be blamed on what has happened to them in their past, and they have no ownership. They carry resentments around for the rest of their lives not realizing that they are only hurting themselves.

Resentment

Resentment is another factor that affects our perception. It has been said that resentments = re-sentiments. Sentiments are feelings, so re-sentiments would be feeling something again. When a person is hurt or abused, a certain feeling occurs at the time of the actual pain. This is normal. When we choose to hold onto our resentment about what has happened, we choose to relive those feelings again and again, and that is our choice. The good news is that we can choose to let it go and it will not continue to affect us.

When counseling abuse victims, I teach them that as long as they continue to hold on to their resentments, the perpetrator continues to have power over them. When Jesus taught us to forgive our enemies,[35] it was not for our enemies' sake, it was for our sake. When we hold on to our resentments, we are continually bothered by those negative feelings while

145

our enemy goes about their day not even giving us a second thought.

People who get sober from drugs and alcohol and then relapse tend to relapse for three main reasons: 1) overconfidence, 2) resentments, and 3) cross-dependency (using a different drug, thinking they would not be addicted to it). Resentments are strong negative forces that influence us for bad.

Have you ever listened to someone tell a story over and over about a resentment they have? The story gets embellished and exaggerated and more inflated the more times it is told. This is where our perception comes into play. We often do not remember exactly what happened but instead focus on one part and develop the story around it.

Another way our perceptions play a part is when we believe that not forgiving the other person somehow leaves them in debt to us. That is simply not true. We might also believe that to forgive the other person means that we condone what they did. That is not true either. I do not like the saying "forgive and forget." I do not think it is ever wise to forget. If we do, then we have not learned the lesson, and we might become naïve or vulnerable to that same situation again. I believe in forgiving other people while remembering the lesson learned so it does not ever happen again. I also believe as we forgive others we forget the pain attached to it.

A good example of this would be family members of addicts who want so badly to trust their child again that they do trust them and end up getting burned. They forgive their child again and eventually trust them again. They get burned again. So the cycle continues because the lessons are not being learned or remembered, and the mistakes are being made again and again.

Assignment

To help you get over any resentment you may have, try this exercise. I heard of this exercise from Joe & Charlie[36] from A.A. Make five columns on a piece of paper. Title the five columns going in order from left to right: Who/What, Why, How Did I Feel, My Part in It, and Do I Still Hold the Resentment (see the chart below). In the first column, list every person or institution that you resent. I mention institutions because that includes jails, schools, police departments, etc. In the second column, explain why you resent that person or institution in five words or less. Do not go into great detail as that is counterproductive to the purpose of this assignment which is not to have you relive the resentments but rather to help you get over them. In the third column, write down how you felt or still do feel because of what happened. In the fourth column, which is probably the most critical column, write down what your part was in the situation. Some situations you will not have had any part in (such as abuse), but most of the situations will have some part that is yours to own. Most of the resentments we have are because someone did something to us before or after we did something to them which means we did contribute to the situation. The last column is asking, "After looking at my part in the situation, do I still have resentments toward that person or institution, or can I understand why they did what they did?" The chart would look like this:

Who/What I resent?	Why? (4 or 5 words only)	What part of me was affected?	What was my part in it?	Do I still carry the resentment?

Now let me give three examples:

Who/What I resent?	Why? (4 or 5 words only)	What part of me was affected?	What was my part in it?	Do I still carry the resentment?
Mark	Abused me	Invalidated	Nothing	Yes
Larry	Hit me	Hurt, betrayed	I hit him too	No
Sherry	Dumped me	Abandoned	I dated her knowing she was a player	No

Your examples of course will vary according to your life experiences. As a side note, when a person has been abused, they have absolutely no part in it. No one can say anything or do anything that justifies another person abusing them. That is true despite what the perpetrator says. In fact, they do want you to feel responsible and will tell you that it is your fault or that you did something to provoke them. Do not believe them! They have already hurt you and are trying to hurt you again.

As you take a look at your chart, you will likely gain understanding for why the other person acted the way they did in 90% of the situations. However, there will probably be about 10% of your resentments remaining that you still hold on to and feel justified in doing so. Here is what you then do: Pray. You pray to God like this: "Please bless _____ (name the person) with the same joy and happiness I am looking for in life." You are not going to want to do this, and it will be difficult. Thankfully, wanting to do this is not a prerequisite for actually doing it. Just do it. Say it in every prayer whether you want to or not. After a few days or a couple of weeks, you will begin to see the miracle in your life as God takes your resentments away as you turn them over to Him.

I mentioned this several paragraphs before, but I am going to repeat it here. Christ taught us to pray for our enemies.[37] And why did He teach that? It was not for our enemy's sake. It was for our sake. Most likely our enemy is living his life without thinking twice about us. He is living his life as if nothing ever happened. But we carry the resentments around and they weigh us down. They ruin our days. They keep us from smiling. They only hurt us. So as we let go of our burdens, either by seeing them as nonsense or by turning them over to God, we become lighter. We can begin to enjoy life the way it was meant to be enjoyed. Too many people get offended too easily. We need to learn to relax and enjoy life for what it is. But first we must let go of our resentments.

Adversity in Life

Adversity comes continually to all of us throughout our lives. What is the purpose of adversity? It is not to knock us down but to make us stronger. If we face the challenges in life head on, then we become stronger as we overcome them. The body is made so that the muscles do not grow without work, the brain does not grow without work, and spirituality does not grow without work. So when we come across problems in life and we work out the problems and discover the solutions and work towards them, we become stronger. However, many people unfortunately buckle and collapse under the weight simply because they refuse to try and lift the weight. The problem with people committing suicide is that the answers to their problems may very well have surfaced the very next day, but they did not live long enough to find that out. It is important to remember that the light at the end of the tunnel is not always an oncoming train.

B. H. Roberts[38] once said, "Some of the lowliest walks in life, the paths which lead into the deepest valleys of sorrow and up to the most rugged steeps of adversity, are the ones which, if a man travel in, will best accomplish the object of his existence in this world....The conditions which place men where they may always walk on the unbroken plain of prosperity and seek for nothing but their own pleasure, are not the best within the gift of God. For in such circumstances men soon drop into a position analogous to the stagnant pool; while those who have to contend with difficulties, brave dangers, endure disappointments, struggle with sorrows, eat the bread of adversity and drink the water of affliction, develop a moral and spiritual strength, together with a purity of life and character, unknown to the heirs of ease and wealth and pleasure. With the English bard, therefore, I believe: Sweet are the uses of adversity!"

Some of the strongest people I have ever known have endured some very hard trials in their lives. Vicktor Frankl, in his book, The Doctor and the Soul,[39] talks about a client of P. L. Starck who was a nurse he worked with. The client had been shot and was now quadriplegic. Listen to P. L. Starck's story about this young woman's perception of adversity:

"I have a twenty-two-year-old female client who was injured at age eighteen by a gunshot as she walked to the grocery store. She can only accomplish tasks by use of a. mouthstick. She feels the purpose of her life is quite clear. She watches the newspapers and television for stories of people in trouble and writes to them (typing with her mouthstick) to give them words of comfort and encouragement" (The Doctor and the Soul, p. 300).

This young woman could have chosen to be bitter and angry at God, but she did not. She could have chosen to wallow in her sorrow, but she did not. She could have expected everyone around her to take care of her, but she did not. She chose to find her mission in life and fulfill it.

Dr. Frankl said,

"The way in which a man accepts his fate and all the suffering it entails, the way in which he takes up his cross, gives him ample opportunity - even under the most difficult circumstances - to add a deeper meaning to his life. It may remain brave, dignified, and unselfish. Or in the bitter fight for self-preservation, he may forget his human dignity and become no more than an animal. Here lies the chance for a man either to make use of or to forgo the opportunities of attaining the moral values that a difficult situation may afford him. And this decides whether he is worthy of his sufferings or not." (Man Search for Meaning, p. 88)

There are a number of reasons why we might suffer afflictions in life. Some suffering is simply due to bad choices we or others make. We must suffer afflictions to help us develop our character and to make us stronger. Maybe afflictions are to help us find our deeper meaning in life. Maybe they are a blessing in disguise. Maybe they prepare us to help others who suffer similar afflictions. This much I do know - if we get mad at God for the trials in our lives, then we do not understand His will for us.

Meaning of Life

We all have a meaning in life. In Dr. Frankl's book Man's Search for Meaning,[40] he states that we all have a meaning in life whether we know what it is or not. That meaning or not knowing that meaning controls what we do. He teaches that without a meaning in our lives, we turn to addiction, aggression, and depression.

As I taught about this concept one day, a client asked me the difference between the purpose of our lives and the meaning of our lives. I said that we might have a purpose in life that is put upon us by other people. If we adopt that purpose as our own, then it becomes the meaning of our life. If we do not, then there is no meaning to that purpose. For example, some might say that the purpose of our lives is to serve others. If I do not believe that, then that purpose is not the meaning of my life. Maybe the meaning of my life is to die with the most toys. Have you seen the bumper sticker that says that? I hope the driver of that vehicle is joking; otherwise they have seriously missed the point.

The meaning of our life comes from our perception of life. Going back to Dr. Frankl, he taught that the meaning of our life comes from one of three areas: creating something, experiencing something, or having a particular attitude towards something. If my mission in life is derived from creating something, I might write a book, paint a picture, make a scrapbook, have children, etc. If my mission is derived from experiencing something, it might be watching my children or grandchildren grow up, helping to feed the starving children in Africa, touring Europe, etc. If life throws at me the hardest of circumstances and I cannot create or experience anything because I am dying of cancer and have just a short time to live, then my mission in life can still exist. It would then be derived from my attitude. I still can help others to live their lives to the fullest by sharing my experiences with them. I can still be positive and set a good example for the nurses and doctors and thank them for all they do. The possibilities are limitless.

I would recommend asking yourself these questions to see if they help you to pinpoint a meaning for your life:

1. What do you like to do?

2. Who do you love?

3. Do you believe in God (or a Higher Power)?

4. What does He expect of you?

5. What does life expect of you?

6. Do you plan to have children?

7. What do you want for them?

8. What would you like to achieve in life?

9. Why do you want to achieve this?

If you can discover the meaning of your life, then when obstacles or challenges come along, and they surely will, they are nothing more than a hurdle to be jumped over and you can continue on with your life's meaning. For example, when a teenage boy falls in love with a teenage girl and is head over heels for her, he will do anything to see her. If his parents tell him he cannot see her that night, he might climb out his bedroom window and even risk getting caught and punished just to see her. He has a mission and nothing is going to stop him from achieving it. When we have a mission in life, it drives our daily actions.

If we struggle with finding our mission in life, it is okay to start out with finding a meaning for the here and now. What is my meaning for the next 30 days? What do I want to accomplish this year? When we find a meaning that will encompass our entire life, then it would be great if we could work towards it and feel success at it regularly but never achieve it completely, as that would eliminate it. My mission in life is to "Lift the heads that hang down." I can work towards this goal everyday but never really completely achieve it, as it would be impossible to reach everyone. I hope to achieve my mission in part by writing this book and lifting some of the heads that hang down.

Happiness Not Joy Derived From Perception

We discussed how our perceptions affect depression. Now we will discuss how our perceptions affect our happiness. First we must make a distinction between joy and happiness. We will refer to joy as happiness that is everlasting. Likewise, we will refer to happiness as the happiness that is in the moment. With that being said, joy does not come from our perceptions, as everlasting happiness comes from lining up our actions with God's values. This is not based upon our perception but upon the only reality we have - that God lives. God's existence is not dependent upon our perceptions. If we believe in God, then it is our privilege to understand Him and get to know Him. If we choose not to believe in God, then we pay the price of living in this world without understanding Him or getting to know Him. But either way we choose to believe, the fact remains the same - that God lives.

God wants us to be joyful. He loves us. He knows the path to joy. When we choose to do things our way and disregard God, then we follow the path of misery. When our perception and our pride take us away from God's way, we end up on the road to misery and we suffer.

Some of my clients tell me that they do not believe in God. I have watched them change who God is to them so that He matches their lifestyle. The key to joy is lining up your actions with God's values, and that does not mean lining up God's values with your actions. It does not work that way. One client of mine shared in group that his higher power says that he can sleep with as many women as he wants. This behavior did not work for him, and he ended up in prison. Maybe he needs to actually find God rather than trying to create God.

Happiness

Happiness comes from our perceptions. If our perception tells us that something is enjoyable or pleasurable, then we are happy. Someone might tell a funny joke and we laugh and find happiness. We might be sharing some memories with friends from our childhood and find happiness in reminiscing. Again, the difference between happiness and joy is that our happiness leaves when our friends leave and go home, and we are faced with the reality of our life if our life is not in accordance to God's values.

Happiness becomes a defense mechanism if we are not experiencing joy. We put this happy mask on not only to fool others but to fool ourselves as well. No one likes feeling hopeless or helpless or shameful, so we do things that we believe will make us happy – even turn to substance abuse. If we were to look in on a party, we might see people "having a good time." But watch as one of the young party goers returns home and sits in the corner of her bedroom crying because her family has left her, she has lost her job, she does not believe she is worth anything, and she is contemplating suicide. An hour earlier, she was "happy" but now death knocks at her door and she is about to open it.

A person who is full of joy does not think, "I wonder if drugs and alcohol could increase my joy?" Joyful people do not use mind altering substances to change or suppress the way they feel because they are everlastingly happy.

The problem with seeking happiness instead of joy is that we often do things that are contrary to God's values. In choosing this path, we make it impossible to find joy which is what we really want. If others tell us to do God's will, then we get upset and say that they are trying to push their morals on us. We get offended and say that we can do whatever we want. Maybe we should change our perception and see that they are trying to help us and not impose their will on us. Our perception can change.

There is nothing wrong with seeking happiness and joy simultaneously. Happiness can still be enjoyed, but only if it does not go against God's values. This might look like jumping out of a plane and enjoying the adrenaline rush and landing on the ground safely. Then going home that night and falling asleep with the peace of mind that if you were to die that night and meet your Maker, you could do so with a clear conscience.

Hugh B. Brown wrote, "Men are a thousand times more intent upon becoming rich than on acquiring culture, though it is quite certain that what a man *is* contributes more to his happiness than what he has; not wealth but wisdom is the way."[41] There is a quote that says, "You can never get enough of what you don't need because what you don't need will never satisfy you." People seek happiness through accumulating wealth, popularity, friends, and toys yet they do not find the joy they seek. Instead, they find temporary happiness, but what they want most is joy, and that can only be found within the individual as he lines up his actions with God's values.

Anticipatory Stimulus

A positive anticipatory stimulus is something we look forward to that brings us happiness. Have you ever looked forward to going on a vacation only to find that once you arrived at your destination, you were anxious to get home? The vacation plans were the positive anticipatory stimulus, and it brought happiness as you looked forward to going. Unfortunately not all the stimuli you encountered on vacation were enjoyed as the positive anticipatory stimuli were.

I bring this up because a positive anticipatory stimulus is nothing more than individual perception of what is going to happen. I feel happiness because of my perception. If I look forward to taking my family to Disneyland, then I enjoy the preparation and anticipation time much more than if I were to dread the trip because of the difficulties involved in taking six children to Disneyland. So instead I choose to look forward to seeing my children's faces as they ride the rides and see the characters. I enjoy the moments and make memories at the amusement park and do not think about the hot sun burning my face or my tired feet. My perception is focused on the good times.

In the beginning of the book, I mentioned that I started writing this book while on a cruise. I now have positive anticipatory stimuli as I look forward to going on another cruise. I mentioned to my wife that I would like to go on another cruise. She gave me a sympathetic, "Alright" and said, "It took us 10 years to go once we'll probably go after another 10 years." I then said, "Let me rephrase it, I'm going on another cruise, do you want to go?" Thankfully, my positive anticipatory stimulus was so intense that it did not take me ten years to go again.

Sometimes we call these positive anticipatory stimuli goals. Goals are good and should be used by all of us. We should set goals that we strive for because they help us to be happy and achieving goals provides a sense of accomplishment.

Negative anticipatory stimuli work the same way. Sometimes we dread things happening before the situation ever occurs. It is possible that we make the situation worse by dreading it. It is also possible that we enjoy the situation and thus suffer some negative feelings that were totally unnecessary.

All too often, fathers find work to be an escape from the crazy life at home. With this perception, as the end of the day nears we feel a sense of dread as we return home. Sometimes spouses are not getting along and they dread going home to be with each other. Do you think these perceptions help or hurt the relationship? Upon my arrival home from work, if I think to myself, "I'm too tired to do anything tonight," and my wife asks for my help, I will probably sigh and be annoyed at the request. She will get frustrated with me and likely angrily respond, "Fine - don't help!" I then get defensive and try to explain how hard my day has been with no thought as to how hard her day has been.

As a side note: I admire all of you women out there who stay home and raise the children. C.S. Lewis said, "Ships, railways, governments exist that people may be warm and safe in their own homes. The homemaker's is the job for which all others exist."[42] Thus, we work hard because you exist. You are so needed and not valued near enough. Caring for children has to be the hardest job in the world and then you have to deal with us men who come home from work and say, "I have had a hard day." I am not sure we even know what a hard day is.

I used to arrive at home after work exhausted and ready to relax. One day I had a change of perception. I have five sons with lots of energy. I was listening to the radio one day and heard the song, "The Dollar"[43] by Jamey Johnson. These are the words:

Daddy hugs his little man, says son I've got to go
And he pulls out of the drive and disappears
As they walk back in the house, the young boy asks his mama,
Where does daddy go when he leaves here

Mama tells her little man, your daddy's got a job
And when he goes to work they pay him for his time
Well the young boy gets to thinking and he heads up to his bedroom
And comes running back with a quarter and four dimes

And says mama how much time will this buy me
Is it enough to take me fishing or throw a football in the street
If I'm a little short then how much more does daddy need
To spend some time with me

The young boy tells his mama now I know daddy's busy
Cause most times when he gets home it's dark outside
But tell him I've got me some pennies saved up from the tooth

fairy
And I keep 'em in my piggy bank and I believe there's thirty-
five

And mama how much time will that buy me
Is it enough to take me camping in a tent down by the creek
If I'm a little short then how much more does daddy need
To spend some time with me

Mama how much time will this buy me
Is it enough for just an afternoon a day or a whole week
If I'm a little short then how much more does daddy need
To spend some time with me

Mama takes her little man sets him on her lap
And starts dialing up some numbers on the phone
She says daddy come home early, you don't have to chase that
dollar
Cause your little man has got one here at home

I called my wife on the phone crying after I heard that
song. She asked me what was wrong, and I asked her if she
had ever heard the song. She said she had and that the words
did not apply to me. She assured me that I was a good father
and spent time with my boys. I told her it did not matter. I
always want to spend more time with my boys. Since that day,
I have tried to go home from work with the energy to play with
my boys. I do not care anymore if I am tired. To me that is
just an excuse. My boys mean everything to me, and I need to
show them every day. What is the difference between how I
am today and how I was before I heard that song? The answer
is my perception.

Success Derived From Perception

What is success? And who defines success? The answer is found in your perception. Do you decide what success is? Do you allow society to tell you what success is? Or do you allow your partner to tell you what success is? My Grandpa Webb died in 1989. After he died, the family went through his things and found his General Educational Development (GED) from just a few years before. He obviously wanted to get his GED and worked very hard to get it, but he was apparently too embarrassed to tell anyone. I believe, had we known, we would have thrown him a party and celebrated his achievement. His perception might have been that he wanted to achieve this long-life goal but was worried others might have seen it differently. So who defines your success?

School

What if I told you your success in school is partly based upon your perception? If you believe you cannot make it through school, then you will not. If you believe that school is hard, then it is. If you believe that school is easy, then it is. Certainly your perception will be based somewhat on your intelligence and how hard or easy the material is for you. Let me give you an example from my life.

When I was in high school, I did not like to read. I could not read very well. I hated to read in front of people. Every time the teacher would tell us we were going to read a book together, I would put my head down so that our eyes would not meet. I dreaded being called upon to read out loud. Eventually she would call on me to read, and I would stumble over my words as I read slowly out loud in front of the class.

Now, you might wonder if I had a reading problem or disorder. That was not the case. When I went on my mission,

I had to learn Spanish. As I began to learn Spanish, I figured it was okay to mispronounce words and stumble over the words because I was a "gringo" and it was expected that I would mess up. I learned how to read Spanish out loud without a mental blocker. When I returned home, I did not think about my problem with reading out loud because I had not thought about it for two years. I just picked up English and began reading and was even reading it very fast and accurately – even when reading out loud in front of other people. The people who know me today cannot believe I ever had a problem with reading. I am even shocked at how well I can read now. What was stopping me in high school? My perception stopped me from excelling in reading because I believed I could not do it without messing up and embarrassing myself. So every time I tried, sure enough I messed up and embarrassed myself.

I am not trying to undermine any other factors involved in success at school. I am just pointing out that perception is a contributing factor and has an impact on our educational success or failure. As we treat students who have lower grades, let us not forget to help them with their perception as we focus on increasing their academic skills.

Our society is set up in such a way as to favor sciences over arts. Take a look at art. It seems like the only time an artist makes money is when they die. I know many artistic people, and they live in prison because their talent is not valued in society. They felt like less of a person because their strengths lie in undervalued areas and as a result chose a criminal lifestyle in order to support themselves and/or their family. Now do not take my words to the extreme on this one. I am not suggesting that they cannot make a living. I am suggesting that their perception is that they are not valued and that their talents are not valued in society.

Work

I work in the rehabilitation field, and the burnout rate in that line of work is huge. My burnout is caused by my perception of not only what is happening but also my perception of whether I can continue. In March of 2005, I was feeling burned out with my job. I even considered leaving my job and maybe my field. I did not say anything to my boss, but one day she walked into my office and said, "Are you thinking about leaving?" I told her that I had entertained the thought. I happened to be going on a vacation down to Phoenix the next day. She said, "Take the next few days and figure out what you need to stay." I did just that. I drove to Phoenix with my family and while on the road, my wife asked if I wanted to talk, or if I wanted her to read to me or something. I said that I just wanted to think. What I learned was this: If my voice could be heard in clinical meetings with the staff, then I would stay. I had spoken up for years, but for whatever reason I stopped speaking my mind, and I was not as happy at work as I once had been. My coworkers had not stopped me from speaking up - it was me. My perception and my resulting actions stopped me from succeeding in my workplace.

Our perceptions tell us if we can or cannot do a specific job. Our perceptions tell us to either speak out or keep quiet. Our perceptions stop us from making suggestions that could benefit the company. In my field, I have heard new counselors say they do not feel competent. They are scared. I believe anyone in the counseling field can relate to this. With time and experience our perceptions change and we become more effective; not only because we have experience but also because our perception of our own ability to help increases.

I want to go back to the topic of burnout. If you ever get the chance to listen to Chuck Jackson[44] from Oklahoma speak on burnout, I highly recommend it. He states that to be burned out would suggest that we were once on fire. That is a great change in perception. Can we get back to that fire? We should even know how if we once were there.

In the book, <u>Seven Habits of Highly Effective People</u>,[45] Stephen Covey teaches that the Seventh Habit is Sharpening the Saw which includes staying healthily balanced in all aspects of our lives. The story is told of a man sawing down a tree. Another man walks by and asks the first man what he is doing. The man responds with, "I'm sawing down a tree." The second man asks, "How long have you been out here?" The first man said, "All day." The second man then says, "Why don't you stop and sharpen your saw?" The first man responds, "I don't have time, I have to cut this tree down." I have clients come into my office and tell me how busy they are and ask what they can do to help themselves. I suggest they take care of themselves spiritually, physically, mentally, socially, and emotionally. They tell me that they do not have time. I then explain that as they take care of themselves they will actually have more time to do the things they like. If I am feeling good in these areas of my life, then I will accomplish the tasks at hand much quicker thus freeing up more time for other things that I enjoy.

This is true with being burned out too. Are we taking care of ourselves spiritually, physically, mentally, socially, and emotionally? If not, we will get burned out. We may think the best idea is to quit work and go somewhere else. But as you can see, the problems will go with us and we will still be burned out. We need to take care of ourselves. Do not allow your perception to tell you that you *cannot* take time for yourself for whatever reason. Try it and see what happens.

Home

Our perceptions at home are huge in determining how the family functions. Some people find no problem at all in yelling at each other, as long as they continue to love each other. Others do not want voices to be raised at all. Some families use a lot of sarcasm with each other. Others try to only speak kind words. It is not that the kind-word families do not have sarcastic things to say, but their family's perception of healthy communication does not allow for it. Some families feel strongly about eating dinner together at the dinner table every night just like they used to in the 1950s. Some families do not seem to care about this at all. All these family dynamics are chosen based upon the family's perception.

One day my wife was feeling like she was not a good mother. I decided to give her the day off, and I stayed home with our four boys. When she got home that night, I was relieved and told her that if she could make it through the day without killing the children, she was a fantastic mom. My perception was so different from my wife's. She felt she was not a good mom because she got frustrated with the children and maybe raised her voice at them, and maybe the children even manipulated her by telling her they wished she was not their mother. On the other hand, I felt that if she stopped at just being frustrated with the children instead of going on and abusing them or killing them, then she was a great mom.

When I was young, I remember manipulating my parents by telling them, "You don't love me!" I remember saying this once to my mother as I walked to my bedroom and slammed the door and hopped into the top bunk to sulk. My father walked in and waved his finger in my face and said, "Don't you ever talk to my wife like that again!" In an instant, my perception changed as I thought, "Now she's not my mother; she's your wife?" I knew he was serious.

These days I do that with my children. If they talk to their mother inappropriately or disrespectfully, I make it clear to them that they are not allowed to treat my sweetheart like that. If I hear them arguing with her and I say, "Don't talk to your mother that way," then I am a third party spectator. However, if I say, "Don't talk to my wife that way," then I have joined my wife's side of the issue and now I am part of the equation, and it takes on a whole new meaning for all of us.

Finances

I did not understand that perception played a role in how successful we are in our financial life until the last few years. The people I grew up with always said, "You have to have money to make money." I believed this too and used it as an excuse as to why my wife and I were not rich. I asked a co-worker of mine, "If I want to make money through real estate, what should I do first?" He told me to read the book, "Rich Dad, Poor Dad"[46] by Robert Kiyosaki. I read this book, and then his second book, and then I read every book he has written. I started to understand how I could get me some real estate without having much money.

To make a long story short, I changed my perception and got involved in real estate. I then got involved with an investment I did not understand fully. I lost a lot of money. I then started listening to Dave Ramsey[47] and working his plan. Here I just want to say, "Listen to Dave Ramsey." He changed my perception, and financial peace is now my goal and new perception. I want to say, "Thank you Dave."

Biases

Life is all about perception. Every aspect of our lives is impacted by our perceptions. Another word commonly used to describe our perceptions is bias. Our biases are what determine our first impressions. We all are biased, but we do not all act on our bias; therefore, we are not all prejudice. Blonde jokes are a great example of bias. Blonde jokes are not about blonde males, and they are not talking about smart people. We are talking about women who are dumb. When I was growing up, the same kind of jokes went around about Pollocks. In Chile, they tell Argentine jokes. Every country has their own group of people they make fun of, and these represent our biases.

In a group therapy session I conducted, I did an exercise that involved taking a lot of newspapers and tearing them up and throwing them all over the floor. I then said to the group, "I want you to do something with the newspapers that you would do if you were a two-year-old child." I then watched as the majority of the group got on their hands and knees and walked over to the newspapers and tore them up and threw them around the room. I then told the group to sit back down in their chairs and gave the next set of instructions, "Now I want you to do the exact same thing you just did, but this time I want you to do it as if you were an 80-year-old man." I then watched as they stood up slowly (maybe bent over a little) and walked as if they had a cane over to the newspapers and did the same thing they did before. I then invited them back to their chairs. I then said, "Now I want you to do the same thing as before, but this time I want you to do it as if you were a homosexual." I watched as they struggled with what to do. I pushed them a little and said, "Come on." Some of them got up and acted very feminine-like and walked with one arm up with the hand hanging down bent at the wrists.

You can choose whatever group you want to in this activity, but the results will be the same. I asked them, "How does a homosexual act?" We discussed this and then discussed how a 2-year-old and an 80-year-old act. I explain to them that there are 2-year-olds that do not crawl and 80-year-olds that are not hunched over and slow and homosexuals who are not feminine at all. I pointed out that the way they acted to my request showed them (and me) what their biases (or perceptions) are toward these three groups of people. There is no right or wrong answers; it is just how they see it. As we discuss these issues, they have the opportunity to change their perceptions if they want to.

Section IV: How perception affects personality disorders

Even though this section is about personality disorders, I believe we can all benefit from reading the different criteria and relating them to ourselves.

Let me start this section by saying that I do not think that it is helpful to diagnose someone and give them a label and be done with them. I think it is beneficial to diagnose someone and share with them the criteria for such a diagnosis and then work on each criterion together. In this manner, I believe people can have a change of perception and change their lives for the better. What I do is give my clients a chart that looks like this:

Daily Inventory

BENEFITS
Strive for these

Month _____

Year _____

DRAWBACKS
Avoid these

If this side--10

If this side--1

EVALUATE YOUR DAY

1	2	3	4	5	6	7	8	9	10	11	12	13	14	15	16	17	18	19	20	21	22	23	24	25	26	27	28	29	30	31

Every night compare the two sides

After giving them the chart, I either fill it out or they fill it out according to the diagnosis they are given. We list the criteria for their diagnosis on the left side and then the exact opposite of the criteria on the right side. Every night before my clients go to bed, they review their day by going down the chart line by line. They compare the first criteria on the left side to the opposite behavior or thought on the right side and then ask themselves, "Which side did I display today?" They then rate themselves on a scale from 10 to 0 on how they did that day. If they decide that they are completely on the left side, then they put a "10" in the box that corresponds to that date. If they decide that the opposite behavior or thought was totally what they displayed that day, then they put a "0" in the box. If they displayed both sides that day then they can rate themselves between 10 and 0 based on where they think they are for that day. After a few days, they can look at the chart and decide which area to focus on for the next day by seeing which line has the lowest numbers on it. Every week when I meet with them, they bring the chart so we can review together what they have done over the past week and where they will focus their energy over the next week. This puts all the accountability back on them. I find this chart to be very helpful to my clients.

I do not include this section so that you might diagnose yourself. In fact, you cannot diagnose yourself. The rules of diagnosing forbid it. I include this section to stir up thoughts about personality disorders. Once diagnosed with a personality disorder, there is a belief out there that says you have it forever and it is incurable. It was also once believed that there were not any medications that helped with personality disorders, particularly the Cluster B disorders. For a long time, there did not appear to be much hope in helping these individuals. I disagree, this is not the case. I believe we can change personality disorders with education and changing our perceptions. This is what I hope to show in this section.

Personality disorders are divided into three categories or clusters. (All the diagnostic information in this section comes from the <u>Diagnostic and Statistical Manual of Mental Disorders, Fourth Edition</u>.[48]) Cluster A includes Paranoid, Schizoid, and Schizotypal Personality Disorders. These occur in individuals who often appear odd or eccentric. Cluster B includes Antisocial, Borderline, Histrionic, and Narcissistic Personality Disorders. These are individuals who appear dramatic, emotional, or erratic. Cluster C includes Avoidant, Dependent and Obsessive-Compulsive Personality Disorders. These include people who appear anxious or fearful.

There are general diagnostic criterions for a personality disorder which are "An enduring pattern of inner experience and behavior that deviates markedly from the expectations of the individual's culture. This pattern is manifested in two (or more) of the following areas:

1. Cognition (i.e., ways of perceiving and interpreting self, other people, and events).

2. Affectivity (i.e., the range, intensity, lability, and appropriateness of emotional response).

3. Interpersonal functioning.

4. Impulse control.

The following are also noted:

1. The enduring pattern is inflexible and pervasive across a broad range of personal and social situations.

2. The enduring pattern leads to clinically significant distress or impairment in social, occupational, or other important areas of functioning.

3. The pattern is stable and of long duration and its onset can be traced back at least to adolescence or early adulthood.

4. The enduring pattern is not better accounted for as a manifestation or consequence of another mental disorder.

5. The enduring pattern is not due to the direct physiological effects of a substance (e.g., a drug of abuse, a medication) or a general medical condition (e.g., head trauma)."

Let us break it down one criterion at a time. First, it is an enduring pattern of inner experience and behavior that differs from society, meaning that a person's perception is different from society's perception. So if I do not think the way society thinks, then I meet the first criteria for a personality disorder. Put me in that category because I am weird. In fact, I tell myself that I am the only normal one in the world and everyone else is abnormal. I like how that feels.

What am I doing? I am diagnosing myself. I cannot do that, and neither can you. We will naturally see some of these criterions in ourselves, but in doing that, we cannot be objective and thus we should not diagnose ourselves. A fellow student in my Master's Degree program would say, "That's me" every time we studied a new diagnosis. I think she was in school more to learn about herself than to help others. Again I caution you not to say, "That's me" and diagnose yourself with a personality disorder. However, feel free to see the dysfunctions in your life and begin working on them. Okay, moving on.

The next part says that the "weirdness" can be seen in at least two ways. Maybe it can be seen in the thought process, meaning that one might perceive things differently than everyone else. It might be that one interprets himself differently or they interpret everyone else differently. It would also include seeing events differently than others.

I once took a client to a psychiatrist. Upon our arrival at the office, we walked up to the receptionist and told her that he had an appointment with "Doctor A." She looked at his chart and said, "You've been in here before and you met with 'Doctor B.' Maybe we should have you see him again since he already knows you." My client looked at her and very seriously said, "The dude has bad vibes." She looked at him strangely and said, "Okay, if you will take a seat, 'Doctor A' will be right with you." My client saw people differently than you or I do. But was his manner wrong? Would we be better off if we chose who we associated with by their "vibes?"

The "weirdness" might be seen in their affectivity or how they show and feel their emotions. It has to do with feelings, likes, pleasures, ideals, dislikes, annoyances, and values more than understanding. It includes a range of emotions. Is their range as broad as most people's? Can you see the intensity in their face when they are feeling very stressed out? Do they feel for others when they are hurting? Do they feel when they are hurt or have they been born with or learned how to completely shut out their feelings? There is also a dulling of emotions that is caused by computer games and television. We are exposed to people being murdered and because we do not know who they are and because they are not even humans [to us] we are calloused by it. Some see it as an everyday thing. When it happens to someone they know, do they have feelings or are they hurt by it? If not, this criterion would apply. One client said, "Everyone dies in my gang. It's just a matter of time. It's nothing to cry over. It's just life."

Their "weirdness" might include their interpersonal functioning or how well they get along with other people. Can they talk to others? Can they socialize with others? Or do they avoid people and not talk to them at all?

The last category that their pattern of "weirdness" might fall into is impulse control or actually a lack of impulse control. But I even find that to be a scapegoat. With this classification, if I do something wrong, could I not just say, "Well, I'm impulsive" and then society will accept that and maybe not punish me? The law does not see it that way – that is for sure. Sometimes we do act without thinking, but that would be called a habit or an addiction. It is a learned behavior, and it can be unlearned. When you reach for the dinner fork to eat with, which hand do you use? Is that impulsive since you did not think about it? What if you wanted to eat with the other hand, can you do it? Yes, it would take time and practice, but it can be done. In the same manner our impulses can be controlled and changed but it takes a lot of desire, time, and practice.

The above criterion is what distinguishes a personality disordered person from a "normal" person. We could argue the definition of "normal," which is why I just say, "Normal is me." Basically, the thing that separates someone who has a problem with something verses a disorder is that a disorder makes one's life unmanageable. The next chapters include the specific diagnoses and my perception of each. The purpose of this section is to see how our perceptions affect our personality disorders. Can we change our perceptions? I believe so. Can we change our personality disorders? I believe so.

Cluster A

Individuals who often appear odd or eccentric

Paranoid Personality Disorder

Paranoid Personality Disorder is "A pervasive distrust and suspiciousness of others such that their motives are interpreted as malevolent, beginning by early adulthood and present in a variety of contexts, as indicated by four (or more) of the following:

1. Suspects, without sufficient basis, that others are exploiting, harming, or deceiving him or her;

2. Is preoccupied with unjustified doubts about the loyalty or trustworthiness of friends or associates;

3. Is reluctant to confide in others because of unwarranted fear that the information will be used maliciously against him or her;

4. Reads hidden demeaning or threatening meanings into benign remarks or events;

5. Persistently bears grudges, i.e., is unforgiving of insults, injuries, or slights;

6. Perceives attacks on his or her character or reputation that are not apparent to others and is quick to react angrily or to counterattack ;

7. Has recurrent suspicions, without justification, regarding fidelity of spouse or sexual partner.

"It does not occur exclusively during the course of Schizophrenia, a mood disorder with psychotic features, or another psychotic disorder and is not due to the direct physiological effects of a general medical condition."[49]

Paranoid Personality Disorder starts with the criterion "distrust and suspiciousness of others." My question is, "Isn't this a perception?" Yes it is. Can we teach someone how to trust and not be suspicious? It might be very hard if their past experiences and transference issues suggest that they should be distrustful and suspicious of others. Remember that a person cannot be diagnosed with a disorder if they are under the influence of drugs or alcohol. I had a client once who would hide inside a refrigerator box inside her house in case "they" could see inside her home. She slept in that box. However, despite her behavior, she was under the influence of drugs, so she could not be diagnosed with Paranoid Personality Disorder.

If a person grows up in a family involved in crime, they might learn not to trust anyone. Some people have difficulty trusting others because they cannot trust themselves. If that is the case, then that is exactly where you can start to help them.

A few paragraphs ago, I put the word, "they" in quotations when speaking of the woman who hid in the cardboard box. I did this because in my experience most people with paranoia cannot tell me who "they" are, but everyone seems to "know" who "they" are. One day I was riding on Utah's light-rail train system, called Trax. There was a man sitting in a seat looking at the young woman in front of him. On Trax, you sit so close your knees are almost touching the person in front of you. The problem was that the man was talking out loud to himself about this young woman. He would also look out the window every once in a while and tell himself a joke and laugh. This young woman was obviously disturbed and at the next stop got up and walked down to a seat on the far side of the train. I was intrigued with this man and could see that he had some suspiciousness. He began looking at all the people around him, slowly moving from one to the next, and as he did so, everyone turned their head and looked away from him. I wondered if I could make myself one of "them" to him. When he looked at me, I kept my eyes focused on his eyes and did not flinch. He quickly turned his head and stared out the window until the next stop where he got off without ever looking back at me or anyone else.

With a personality disorder, a person's distrust and suspiciousness is not focused on one individual or a defined group. It encompasses anyone and everyone that can be labeled as "them." It is a scary world to live in, not trusting people and wondering if everyone is out to get you. These people suspect, without sufficient basis, that others are exploiting, harming, or deceiving them. They are preoccupied with unjustified doubts about the loyalty or trustworthiness of friends or associates. They are reluctant to confide in others because of unwarranted fear that the information will be used maliciously against them. They read hidden demeaning or threatening meanings into benign remarks or events. They persistently hold grudges. They are unforgiving of insults, injuries, or slights. They perceive attacks on their character or reputation that are not apparent to others and are quick to react angrily or to counterattack. They have recurrent suspicions, without justification, regarding the fidelity of their spouse or sexual partner.

This life is a very lonely one if you have Paranoid Personality Disorder. I want to share some thoughts from a class I took on Schizophrenia. Even though this is not the subject at hand, the lesson is applicable to paranoid personality disorder as well as all the other personality disorders.

Schizophrenia Class

I worked in the Utah State Prison from April 2000 to April 2002. I attended a class on Schizophrenia that was sponsored by the prison. It was the best class I have ever been through, but I never want to do it again. As I walked into the classroom, I was handed a headset with a tape deck and told to put on the headphones and turn on the tape (for the young readers, it was like turning on a MP3 player but a much older version). When I did, I heard three noises: one was nonstop cussing, the second was an unintelligible whisper in the background, and the third was an ambience like sound or white noise.

Throughout the class, we were to be participating in several work stations, and we would receive instructions at each one. I was also told to keep the tape playing the entire time. At one work station, I was asked to name the last five presidents of the United States. I said, "President Bush, President Clinton," and my mind went completely blank! I felt so dumb. That was an easy question but I could not think with all those sounds going through my head. At one station I was asked to read a paper and then answer the questions that followed. I read the little story but when I came to the questions, I could not remember a single thing I had read. Once again, that was very frustrating. I went to another station where the person told me five numbers and wanted me to repeat them back. Guess what? I could not do it. At the last station, I sat at a table with some other participants. We each had a little book in front of us. Each page in the book gave us a shape to create with six toothpicks. After creating the first shape, we were to turn the page and start on the second shape and so on.

The first page told me to make two squares out of the six toothpicks. I sat there knowing that if I was to create two squares, sharing one side, then I would need at least seven toothpicks. The "teacher" started walking around the table yelling at us to hurry up. My brain kept telling me it was impossible; I only had six toothpicks of equal size. As the "teacher" was yelling at us, I saw some of the other participants turn the page in their book as if they achieved the two squares, and I thought, "You cheaters! There is no way to do this. You are just turning the page so the teacher won't yell at you." I was going crazy because I could not figure it out, and I could not even think straight. So I started to take my headset off. It had been 45 minutes with all those noises going through my head. I figured I was willing to be yelled at for a moment of silence. Just then the instructor said, "Okay you can take off your headsets now." I could not believe my luck. I would have peace and quiet, and I was not even going to get yelled at. Apparently I was not the only frustrated one. The "teacher" told us that one participant once got so mad at her for yelling at him during this exercise that he actually stood up and grabbed his chair and threw it at her across the room. These are professionals taking this class and someone "lost it" that bad? We then processed the experience together.

We discussed how hard it was to remember anything. The instructor taught us that when interacting with people with Schizophrenia, we need to remember they do not think, process, or remember things like we do or as easily as we do. Sometimes we yell at them for forgetting an assignment or forgetting to take out the trash. We need to have more empathy for them and be more patient. The difference between what I experienced and their lives is that I could take the headset off, and they unfortunately cannot.

After that class, as I was driving home on I-15 southbound, I was alone in my car and found myself saying out loud, "You're okay. You don't have any voices in your head. Just calm down. You're alright." I was truly grateful for the experience once my head calmed down a bit, but I never want to do that again.

By the way, here's how you make the two squares out of six toothpicks: use four toothpicks to make a square. Then take two toothpicks and make an upside down "L" in the bottom right corner of the square with the ends going outside the square and leaving a small square.

Start Where They Are

We need to treat others with patience and understanding. As stated in Stephen Covey's <u>Seven Habits of Highly Effective People</u>,[50] we should "Seek first to understand then to be understood." Too often we forget that people do not always see things the way we see them. Your perception is unique and belongs only to you. We strive in life to share parts of our perception, but there is no one that sees everything exactly the way you do.

Going back to a person with Paranoid Personality Disorder, their perception might not make any sense to you or me, but I assure you, it is very real to them. We should never make fun of them. Instead, we should try to see things from their point of view and then proceed to work with them from where they are at.

A scene from a movie comes to mind. Have you ever seen the movie "Patch Adams[51]" with Robin Williams? In the beginning of the movie, Patch checks himself into a psychiatric ward of a hospital for suicide. His roommate is a man named

Rudy. Rudy is afraid of squirrels that do not really exist - but they do to him. He had not left his bed in weeks - not even to go to the bathroom - until Patch got there. At first Patch was even a little scared and surprised at Rudy's reaction to something that was not even there. But then Patch does an incredible thing. He goes along with Rudy's belief and pretends that he has a gun and starts to kill the squirrels. He goes from a hand gun to a machine gun and cleans up with a bazooka. He covers for Rudy so that he can run into the bathroom to relieve himself for the first time in weeks. Patch Adams did this by understanding Rudy's belief and helped Rudy starting from where Rudy was at. Helping Rudy was actually Patch's start in the "people" business, and he has never stopped helping them.

Too often we tell people they must think or be a certain way without helping them to get there or recognizing the process and time it takes to get there. In treatment we expect people to open up quickly and do everything we say right off the bat. Sometimes we forget to first go to where they are at and start the process from there. Maybe for a Paranoid Personality Disorder person, we might first understand their paranoia and agree with them that it is scary. We then would have a better chance of helping them change their perception. If we start out by telling them there is no one there and that it is all in their head, they might put up walls of defense and stop listening to us. They most likely will also stop sharing with us. I like the quote that says, "People don't care how much you know until they know how much you care."

Daily Inventory

If people have Paranoid Personality Disorder criteria, then I suggest they document their behaviors or traits by using this daily inventory chart every night (see below). The traits or behaviors on the left side are compared to the traits or behaviors on the right side at the end of each day. As they compare the two sides to each other, if they believe they have portrayed the left side trait completely, then they would put a "10" in the box under that particular day's date. If they feel they have portrayed the right side completely, then they would put a "0" in the box under that particular day's date. If they feel they have portrayed both sides then they have the flexibility to rate themselves between 10 and 0. After a few days, they can easily visualize where they need to put more of their focus by seeing which line has the least numbers day after day. They would focus their energy the next day on that particular item. Below is a blank daily inventory for Paranoid Personality Disorder that can be copied. Below the blank inventory chart is an example of a semi-completed chart.

Daily Inventory

Month _____ Year _____

BENEFITS
Strive for these

If this side--X

DRAWBACKS
Avoid these

If this side--O

EVALUATE YOUR DAY

Benefits (Strive for these)	1	2	3	4	5	6	7	8	9	10	11	12	13	14	15	16	17	18	19	20	21	22	23	24	25	26	27	28	29	30	31	Drawbacks (Avoid these)
you do not suspect that others are exploiting you																																suspects that others are exploiting, harming you
not preoccupied that friends are disloyal, untrustworthy																																preoccupied that others are disloyal, untrustworthy
share opening with others																																won't confide in others; fear of being exploitative
you do not read hidden messages in benign remarks																																reads hidden demeaning or threats into benign remark
forgives; lets go of resentments																																bears grudges; unforgiving of insults, injuries or slights
do not perceive attacks when others don't either																																perceives attacks against him when no one else does
you trust sexual partner to be faithful																																suspicions regarding fidelity of sexual partner

Every night compare the two sides

183

Daily Inventory

Month _____   Year _____

BENEFITS
Strive for these

If this side--10

DRAWBACKS
Avoid these

If this side--1

EVALUATE YOUR DAY

BENEFITS	1	2	3	4	5	6	7	8	9	10	11	12	13	14	15	16	17	18	19	20	21	22	23	24	25	26	27	28	29	30	31	DRAWBACKS
you do not suspect that others are exploiting you	9	8	8	9	8	1	8	9	2																							suspects that others are exploiting, harming you
not preoccupied that friends are disloyal, untrustworthy	1	2	8	2	3	2	7	2	2																							preoccupied that others are disloyal, untrustworthy
share opening with others	7	8	8	9	8	2	9	8	9																							won't confide in others: fear of being exploitative
you do not read hidden messages in benign remarks	2	1	3	2	2	3	8	2	1																							reads hidden demeaning or threats into benign remark
forgives; lets go of resentments	8	8	8	2	1	9	8	8	1																							bears grudges; unforgiving of insults, injuries or slights
do not perceive attacks when others don't either	2	1	8	3	2	9	9	8	9																							perceives attacks against him when no one else does
you trust sexual partner to be faithful	9	9	9	9	9	9	9	9	9																							suspicions regarding fidelity of sexual partner

Every night compare the two sides

Notice on this inventory that the person has struggled lately with being preoccupied that others are disloyal and untrustworthy as well as reading hidden demeaning or threats into benign remarks. So I would advise this person that tomorrow (being the 10th of the month) to focus on these two aspects only. Then I would discuss with him what he did to not get a lower number in one of those boxes. This will help him be empowered and help himself.

Schizoid Personality Disorder

Schizoid Personality Disorder is a, "Pervasive pattern of detachment from social relationships and a restricted range of expression of emotions in interpersonal settings, beginning by early adulthood and present in a variety of contexts, as indicated by four (or more) of the following:

1. Neither desires nor enjoys close relationships, including being part of a family;

2. Almost always chooses solitary activities;

3. Has little, if any, interest in having sexual experiences with another person;

4. Takes pleasure in few, if any, activities;

5. Lacks close friends or confidants other than first-degree relatives;

6. Appears indifferent to the praise or criticism of others;

7. Shows emotional coldness, detachment, or flattened affectivity.

"It also does not occur exclusively during the course of Schizophrenia, a mood disorder with psychotic features, another psychotic disorder, or a pervasive developmental disorder and is not due to the direct physiological effects of a general medical condition."[52]

Why would someone not enjoy or want a social relationship and therefore lack close friends? Why would they not enjoy or desire a close relationship, including being part of a family? Why would they almost always want to be alone? Why would they not want an intimate relationship with another person? Why would they take pleasure in few, if any, activities?

Is the answer not found in their perception? As a person distances themselves from others, they become even more of an odd-ball. After a while, even if they wanted to socialize, they may not be able to do so without help. They may have drifted too far away from the "norm" to get back by themselves.

My Roommate

I am not diagnosing my college roommate with Schizoid Personality Disorder, but he did display many of the diagnostic criteria. The only part of the criteria he does not meet (or at least I do not know that he does) is whether he started this behavior beginning in early adulthood. I met him in his thirties, so I cannot answer that question. I was told that he had been married one time, but it apparently did not last long. After that he hardly ever socialized. He would come home and go straight into his room. He only came out of his room to use the restroom or to get some food which he then took back into his room to eat. That is it. I lived with him for about three years, and I only saw his bedroom once. To this day, I do not know why he asked me to come into his room that one time. On the other hand, I had another roommate who was a social butterfly. He was constantly going out on dates or to gatherings just to be with people. He would often knock on the first roommate's door and ask him if he wanted to get out of his room and go on a double date or go to a party. The first roommate would yell at him to leave him alone. The social butterfly roommate seemed to have made some kind of a goal to get the first roommate out of the house.

So I do not know if my roommate had these features in early adulthood. I do not know if he just chose to have a chip on his shoulder after his divorce. But I do know that his life was lonely without friends. This must be what it is like to have Schizoid Personality Disorder.

Perceptions can change. This asocial person can learn to socialize and even to enjoy it. The hardest problem, though, is getting them to the point where they want to change their perception. My roommate did not want to talk and was "satisfied" being alone. I think he convinced himself that he was satisfied being alone, but deep inside he was longing for something he did not have. He appeared, to me, to be miserable.

Fear of Being Hurt

I know people who have chosen to distance themselves and even isolate themselves because they are afraid of getting hurt. My roommate's philosophy in life was, "Screw them before they screw me." There is a principle that says, **"The extent to which you are willing to be hurt is the extent to which you can love."** The reverse is also true, **"The extent to which you love is the extent to which you may be hurt."** The more we are willing to open up and share ourselves with others the more we can love and be loved. Some people express that they fear vulnerability. But if we are not vulnerable, we can never truly love or be loved. My experiences lead me to believe that the more vulnerable I become, the more people like me because they understand me.

A useful tool in this situation would be to take a piece of paper and draw a line down the middle. Write "Pros" on the right side of the page and "Cons" on the left side. Then write down the pros and cons of going out with a certain person or having a close relationship. What about always being alone? List the pros and cons of being alone. Write down an activity you are contemplating participating in and list the pros and cons of doing it. You get the idea. The paper clearly lists each pro and con and allows for you to weigh the two sides against each other and determine a course of action.

Criterion 6 reads, "Appears indifferent to the praise or criticism of others." Notice the word "appears." It does not say that it does not affect them. It says that it *appears* to not affect them. Lots of people like praise and lots of people do not. Some believe they are only worthy of criticism. I believe these people appear indifferent to either praise or criticism because to accept the praise would mean they are taking a risk on establishing a relationship, and they cannot do that. They do accept the criticism but because it hurts so much they do not show it for fear of establishing a relationship with another person who wants to show sympathy. They cannot let people know who they are, or they might be rejected. It is easier to be rejected for what you do rather than for who you are. At least this is what their perception says will happen.

Daily Inventory

If someone has Schizoid Personality Disorder criteria, then I suggest they keep track of their behaviors or traits by using this daily inventory (see below) every night before going to bed. The left-side traits or behaviors are compared to the right-side traits or behaviors at the end of each day. As they compare the two sides to each other, if they believe they have portrayed the left side trait completely, then they would put a "10" in the box under that particular day's date. If they feel they have portrayed the right side completely, then they would put a "0" in the box under that particular day's date. If they feel they have portrayed both sides then they have the flexibility to rate themselves between 10 and 0. After a few days, they can easily visualize where they need to put more of their focus by seeing which line has the least numbers day after day. They would focus their energy the next day on that particular item. Below is a blank daily inventory for Schizoid personality disorder that can be copied. Below the blank inventory is an example of a completed chart.

Daily Inventory

Month _____ Year _____

BENEFITS	DRAWBACKS
Strive for these	Avoid these
If this side--X	If this side--O

EVALUATE YOUR DAY

BENEFITS	1	2	3	4	5	6	7	8	9	10	11	12	13	14	15	16	17	18	19	20	21	22	23	24	25	26	27	28	29	30	31	DRAWBACKS
enjoy close relationships																																do not enjoy close relationships including family
hangs out with people																																almost always chooses solitary activities
interest in sexual experiences with another																																little interest in sexual experiences with another
takes pleasure in many activities																																takes pleasure in few, if any, activities
have close friends and confidants																																lacks close friends or confidants other than family
criticism hurts: enjoys praise																																indifferent to praise or criticism of others
empathetic with others; range of expressions of emotions																																emotional coldness, detached, or flattened affect

Every night compare the two sides

Daily Inventory

Month _____ Year _____

BENEFITS	DRAWBACKS
Strive for these	Avoid these
If this side--10	*If this side--1*

EVALUATE YOUR DAY

Benefit	1	2	3	4	5	6	7	8	9	10	11	12	13	14	15	16	17	18	19	20	21	22	23	24	25	26	27	28	29	30	31	Drawback
enjoy close relationships	1	2	3	9	8	8	9	1																								do not enjoy close relationships including family
hangs out with people	1	1	1	1	1	1	1	1																								almost always chooses solitary activities
interest in sexual experiences with another	1	8	7	2	3	3	8	1																								little interest in sexual experiences with another
takes pleasure in many activities	1	1	1	1	1	1	1	7																								takes pleasure in few, if any, activities
have close friends and confidants	9	3	2	3	3	8	3	2																								lacks close friends or confidants other than family
criticism hurts; enjoys praise	1	1	1	1	6	8	2	2																								indifferent to praise or criticism of others
empathetic with others; range of expressions of emotions	3	2	3	9	8	8	2	2																								emotional coldness, detached, or flattened affect

Every night compare the two sides

On this particular inventory, I would ask them to focus on hanging out with other people the following day. Since that criterion has not been met over the last eight days, I might even suggest that they not worry about anything else and just concentrate on that one thing. My next concern would be for them to take pleasure in any activity. I would have them make a list of things they like to do and then suggest that they do them. I would then focus their attention on making friends. You can see what I am doing. I simply take the information they have given about themselves and discuss with them how they can change their perception. Since they are the one filling out the inventory, they have a criterion themselves to meet before they can achieve a higher number in the box. Find out what it is, and pursue that with them.

Schizotypal Personality Disorder

Schizotypal Personality Disorder is, "A pervasive pattern of social and interpersonal deficits marked by acute discomfort with, and reduced capacity for, close relationships as well as by cognitive or perceptual distortions and eccentricities of behavior, beginning by early adulthood and present in a variety of contexts, as indicated by five (or more) of the following:

1. Ideas of reference (excluding delusions of reference);

2. Odd beliefs or magical thinking that influences behavior and is inconsistent with subcultural norms (e.g., superstitiousness, belief in clairvoyance, telepathy, or 'sixth sense'; in children and adolescents, bizarre fantasies or preoccupations);

3. Unusual perceptual experiences, including bodily illusions;

4. Odd thinking and speech (e.g., vague, circumstantial, metaphorical, overelaborate, or stereotyped);

5. Suspiciousness or paranoid ideation;

6. Inappropriate or constricted affect;

7. Behavior or appearance that is odd, eccentric, or peculiar;

8. Lack of close friends or confidants other than first-degree relatives;

9. Excessive social anxiety that does not diminish with familiarity and tends to be associated with paranoid fear rather than negative judgments about self.

"It does not occur exclusively during the course of Schizophrenia, a mood disorder with psychotic features, another psychotic disorder, or a pervasive developmental disorder"[53].

From the list described above, could this person's "acute discomfort with, and reduced capacity for, close relationships" be caused by perception? Discomfort is an uneasiness caused by one's thoughts. If I am not comfortable with you, it is because of my thoughts about you. It might be that I feel bad vibes coming from you, but even then I have thoughts that interpret those feelings. If I entertained my paranoid thoughts or if I was mind reading, then I would probably have a reduced capacity for a close relationship. That is why it says, "as well as by cognitive or perceptual distortions and eccentricities of behavior."

If you want a relationship to end, all you have to do is not forgive the other person for any of their faults. In other words, do not show any mercy for your spouse or anyone else. If my perception is that my wife is supposed to be perfect and I find out that she has a fault, she then does not meet my expectation. If I decide not to forgive her but instead to store up resentments, then those resentments will naturally pull us apart.

To be diagnosed with a Schizotypal Personality Disorder, five cognitive distortions or perceptual distortions must be met. The first is ideas of reference (excluding delusions of reference), meaning the person incorrectly interprets events in their lives as having a particular and unusual meaning just for them. They may be superstitious or believe that they have special powers or are able to read people's minds. They might believe they can see the future. They may have unusual perceptual experiences, including bodily illusions. So once again, we throw perception into the equation by saying, "unusual perceptual experiences." They have odd thinking and speech which might mean that they are

194

vague, circumstantial, metaphorical, overelaborate, or stereotyped.

I know people like this, but we do not diagnose them as Schizotypal. Similarly to Schizoid Personality Disorder, they too have a lot of suspiciousness or paranoid ideation. These people also tend to have inappropriate or constricted affect. Their faces do not usually have the appropriate expression for the topic at hand. Their behavior or appearance is odd, eccentric, or peculiar. They lack close friends or confidants other than first-degree relatives (previously discussed with the last personality disorder). They have excessive social anxiety that does not diminish with familiarity and tends to be associated with paranoid fear rather than negative judgments about self.

Creativity

It is becoming more obvious what is meant by personality being defined or caused by perception. So, can those with personality disorders learn to view life differently? I believe so. But on the other hand, why do they have to conform to society's view of things? If their way works for them, is that okay? I submit that we restrain creativity in our society and that we should be more open to it.

Here is an activity I do with my clients to stimulate creativity. I first put a shoe in the middle of the floor and then ask, "What can you use that shoe for?" When I have done this in group, I have heard more than 40 answers before I stopped it. The purpose is to generate creativity. Children are very creative, but society does not tend to promote creativity. Rather we promote seeing and doing things the way everyone else does them. At first, thinking of ideas of what we can do with a shoe is difficult for people until they open their minds to new and different possibilities. Even so, some still struggle with this assignment. A few examples of uses for the shoe are: a glass, a vase, a football, a Christmas tree ornament, a jewelry box, a frame, a hat, an ear muff, a pretend phone, and a weapon. After we have exhausted our minds with the endless possibilities, I then ask the question, "How many of you have ever bought a shoe to use it as anything other than a shoe?" No one ever raises their hand. Why? Why do we have to do the same thing everyone else does? Can we be creative?

Because society tends to value science and not the arts, the artistic people struggle to make ends meet and often times turn to crimes and end up in prison. I jokingly tell people the requirements to go to prison are: (1) you must know how to draw (prisoners are the best artists I have ever seen), (2) you must like to lift weights, (3) you must play the guitar, and (4) you must have tattoos. If society placed greater value on the arts than science, then we would likely see those current inmates making millions and the scientists and lawyers locked up in prison (that brought a smile to some of you and others it did not because of your perception).

Working With People Who Have Schizotypal Personality Disorder

Once I have stimulated creativity in the mind of people with Schizotypal Personality Disorder, then I set up a couple of scenarios with them and discuss the different interpretations there might be. All I am trying to do at this stage in treatment is to show that there are a variety of perceptions out there. Can I get this person to accept the fact that people see this life differently? Can I help him understand what we discussed in the first part of the book - that our perceptions might be wrong? As I lead him down this road, I turn to his own thinking and ask if it is possible for his own thinking to be wrong. That leads into questions about how to change his perception of the activities going on around him. I ask the questions and he gives the answers.

Here is an example of some questions I might ask someone who thinks he has super powers: Might your perception be wrong (after explaining about perception)?

Might my perception be wrong (this helps them to relax)? What would it mean to you if your perception was wrong? What if you really do not have super powers; could you still do super things? What if your mind-reading abilities did not always work correctly and you received the wrong message? What if you and I are the only normal ones in the world and everyone else is abnormal (this is my favorite and I have used it before and they seem to like it too)?

One day I said to a client, "If you and I are going to get along, you must understand something - I'm weird." My client then said, "I'm weird too." So I said, "Maybe you and I are the only normal ones in the world, and everyone else is abnormal. I'll make you a deal. If you accept me for my weirdness, then I'll accept you for yours." He agreed to that. I was able to make "weird" requests of him while reminding him that I am weird; therefore, he accepted my requests.

Some of my colleagues think they always have to be "professional," but I believe they are missing out on a lot of great opportunities to connect with people. Dr. Scott Miller[54] spends his life analyzing studies to see what really works. He once told me that studies have shown that the theory a therapist uses does not matter nearly as much in treatment as the relationship between the therapist and the client does. In fact Scott Miller made the most profound comment when indicating he had compared all types of treatment and found that, "Some of the treatment works some of the time with some of the people." You cannot get more real than that.

The point is that we need to relate to our clients even if their thoughts are off a little or a lot. Strides can only be made with people who have Schizotypal Personality Disorder if they feel they can relate to you or that you can understand them. We need to put ourselves in their shoes for a minute and see the world through their eyes. I had a client one day say to the medical director and myself, "I have a hard time trusting people and I have chosen to only trust one person and that's him (pointing to me)." Why? She trusted me because I was willing to relate to her. It is not important that they see our world right now. And who knows, maybe our perception is wrong.

Daily Inventory

If someone has Schizotypal Personality Disorder criteria, then I suggest they keep track of their behaviors or traits by using this daily inventory (see below) every night before going to bed. The left-side traits or behaviors are compared to the right-side traits or behaviors at the end of each day. As they compare the two sides to each other, if they believe they have portrayed the left side trait completely, then they would put a "10" in the box under that particular day's date. If they feel they have portrayed the right side completely, then they would put a "0" in the box under that particular day's date. If they feel they have portrayed both sides then they have the flexibility to rate themselves between 10 and 0. After a few days, they can easily visualize where they need to put more of their focus by seeing which line has the least numbers day after day. They would focus their energy the next day on that particular item. Below is a blank daily inventory for Schizotypal Personality Disorder that can be copied. Below the blank inventory is an example of a completed chart.

Daily Inventory

Month _____ Year _____

BENEFITS
Strive for these

DRAWBACKS
Avoid these

If this side--10

If this side--1

	1	2	3	4	5	6	7	8	9	10	11	12	13	14	15	16	17	18	19	20	21	22	23	24	25	26	27	28	29	30	31	
																				EVALUATE YOUR DAY												
incidents & events do not have special meaning for you																																ideas of reference (excluding delusions)
does not have odd beliefs or magical thinking																																odd beliefs or magical thinking; superstitiousness
does not have special power to see future or read minds																																unusual perceptual expereineces
thoughts and speech are logical																																odd thinking & speech
not suspicious or paranoid of others																																suspiciousness or paranoid ideation
wide range of expressions of emotions																																inappropriate or constricted affect
behavior conforms with society's expectations																																behavior or appearance is odd, eccentric or peculiar
has close friends																																lack of close friends other than family
no anxiety around socializing with others																																excessive social anxiety with paranoid fears

Every night compare the two sides

Daily Inventory

Month _____ Year _____

BENEFITS
Strive for these

If this side--10

DRAWBACKS
Avoid these

If this side--1

EVALUATE YOUR DAY

BENEFITS	1	2	3	4	5	6	7	8	9	10	11	12	13	14	15	16	17	18	19	20	21	22	23	24	25	26	27	28	29	30	31	DRAWBACKS
incidents & events do not have special meaning for you	7	9	8	8	9	2	8	8	3																							ideas of reference (excluding delusions)
does not have odd beliefs or magical thinking	2	2	2	3	1	8	3	2	2																							odd beliefs or magical thinking, superstitiousness
does not have special power to see future or read minds	8	9	1	2	8	3	4	7	8																							unusual perceptual experieneces
thoughts and speech are logical	8	8	1	7	1	2	2	8	9																							odd thinking & speech
not suspicious or paranoid of others	1	1	1	1	1	1	1	1	1																							suspiciousness or paranoid ideation
wide range of expressions of emotions	1	2	2	8	7	7	2	2	7																							inappropriate or constricted affect
behavior conforms with society's expectations	8	7	8	2	3	8	8	8	8																							behavior or appearance is odd, eccentric or peculiar
has close friends	8	2	2	3	1	8	8	2	2																							lack of close friends other than family
no anxiety around socializing with others	8	8	9	2	8	8	8	2	8																							excessive social anxiety with paranoid fears

Every night compare the two sides

This person needs to focus on his suspiciousness or paranoid ideations. He would also benefit from working on his odd beliefs or magical thinking. By no means are these daily inventories meant to be easy. They should stretch us and help us work on ourselves. It gives us a chance to track our progress every day.

Cluster B

Individuals who appear dramatic, emotional, or erratic.

Antisocial Personality Disorder Derived From Perception

In my line of work, I deal much more with Cluster B Personalities than Cluster A or C. These people keep my job exciting. I told my wife when I first began looking for a career, "I want a job that isn't boring." I found it with Cluster B Personalities.

The first Cluster B personality is the Antisocial Personality Disorder. In the Antisocial Personality Disorder, "There is a pervasive pattern of disregard for and violation of the rights of others occurring since age 15 years, as indicated by three (or more) of the following:

1. Failure to conform to social norms with respect to lawful behaviors as indicated by repeatedly performing acts that are grounds for arrest;

2. Deceitfulness, as indicated by repeated lying, use of aliases, or conning others for personal profit or pleasure;

3. Impulsivity or failure to plan ahead;

4. Irritability and aggressiveness, as indicated by repeated physical fights or assaults;

5. Reckless disregard for safety of self or others;

6. Consistent irresponsibility, as indicated by repeated failure to sustain consistent work behavior or honor financial obligations;

7. Lack of remorse, as indicated by being indifferent to or rationalizing having hurt, mistreated, or stolen from another.

"Also, the individual is at least 18 years old, there is evidence of conduct disorder with onset before age 15 years, and the occurrence of antisocial behavior is not exclusively during the course of Schizophrenia or a manic episode."[55]

Since you probably do not have the DSM-IV book in front of you, Conduct Disorder is "A repetitive and persistent pattern of behavior in which the basic rights of others or major age-appropriate societal norms or rules are violated, as manifested by the presence of three (or more) of the following criteria in the past 12 months, with at least one criterion present in the past 6 months:

Aggression to people and animals:

1. Often bullies, threatens, or intimidates others,

2. Often initiates physical fights,

3. Has used a weapon that can cause serious physical harm to others (e.g., a bat, brick, broken bottle, knife, gun),

4. Has been physically cruel to people,

5. Has been physically cruel to animals,

6. Has stolen while confronting a victim (e.g., mugging, purse snatching, extortion, armed robbery),

7. Has forced someone into sexual activity.

Destruction of property:

1. Has deliberately engaged in fire setting with the intention of causing serious damage,

2. Has deliberately destroyed others' property (other than by fire setting).

Deceitfulness or theft:

1. Has broken into someone else' house, building, or car,

2. Often lies to obtain goods or favors or to avoid obligations (i.e., "cons" others),

3. Has stolen items of nontrivial value without confronting a victim (e.g., shoplifting, but without breaking and entering; forgery).

Serious violation of rules:

1. Often stays out at night despite parental prohibitions, beginning before age 13 years,

2. Has run away from home overnight at least twice while living in parental or parental surrogate home (or once without returning for a lengthy period),

3. Is often truant from school, beginning before age 13 years.

"Also noted is that the disturbance in behavior causes clinically significant impairment in social, academic, or occupational functioning. If the individual is age 18 years or older, criteria are not met for Antisocial Personality Disorder."[56]

Antisocial Personality Disorder is unique to all other disorders in one regard in that it is the only disorder that cannot be used as a "good" defense in court. If you were to say to a judge that you have Antisocial Personality Disorder and that is why you committed a crime, then he would tell you that he knows a place where they treat people who have Antisocial Personality Disorder; it is called prison. Most people in prison have Antisocial Personality Disorder in that they disregard the law. When they get out of prison, guess what? They break the law again. This is known as the "revolving door syndrome." We used to say that the slogan at the prison was, "We'll leave the lights on."

In the Antisocial Personality Disorder, "There is a pervasive pattern of disregard for and violation of the rights of others." These clients might steal or fight another person. I had a client, who was upset when I told her she had Antisocial Personality Disorder and she said, "That makes me so mad when you say that; I just want to get violent." I said, "That's exactly what I'm talking about." She then understood what she just said and laughed.

These people have what Daniel J. Bayse, in his book "As Free as an Eagle[57]" calls "Looking out for Number One." It says, "I'm NUMBER ONE! I can do anything I want! Say anything I want! Anytime I want! Anywhere I want! To anyone I want! And there is nothing that you or anyone else can do about it, PERIOD!" We often describe them as egocentric and apathetic. They do not seem to think the world exists without them. It is all about them. They have the answers to everything. Yet by definition, the answers are insane. In the drug world, insanity is defined as doing the same things over and over again and expecting different results. If these people have all the answers, then why on earth do they keep doing the same things that are clearly not working for them?

When I worked in the prison system (2000-2002), the recidivism rate for inmates was about 85%. One inmate told me after coming back to prison that he gets a high from paroling. So after he got out and got his high from paroling, he needed to get back to prison so that one day he could experience that high again. Now that is definitely insane. Why do these people not learn? Might it be their perception?

Story

Let me share a story from an inmate. His dad would often come home drunk and get violent with him. As he got bigger, he decided he was not going to put up with it anymore. His dad came home one day and he hit his dad over the head with a bat and knocked him out. When his dad came to, he told his dad that he would not put up with his violence any longer. A day or two later, his dad came home and knocked him to the ground and stood on his neck and stuck a gun to his face and said, "Beg me for your life!"

Let us take this scenario and ask ourselves, "Can we understand why he was the way he was with regards to the following criterion?" First he failed "to conform to social norms with respect to lawful behaviors as indicated by repeatedly performing acts that are grounds for arrest." Can we understand why he was involved with the law? Sure there are children out there who have ruthless parents and they still turn out alright, but they might be the exception and not the rule. It is my firm belief that children tend to follow the example of their parents more often than deciding to do the exact opposite of their parents. Hopefully as the child grows older, he begins to think for himself and decides if the path he is on is the path he wants to follow.

I explained to the inmates once that there are two worlds out there. One is a world of crime and drugs, and the other is a world free of illegal substances and unlawful behavior. I explained that both worlds try to ignore the other world. Drug addicts and criminals try to stay away from people of the other world either out of embarrassment or fear of getting caught. People who stay clean and obey the law ignore the other world because they do not want to admit that it might be happening within their own family or to ease their mind with regards to their own safety. The reality is that both worlds live together and among each other. I told the inmates at the prison that they have the power to choose which world they live in. If they wanted to go out and get a job and work 40 hours a week and provide for their family, they have the power to do so. One inmate raised his hand and said, "Webb, that's not the world I live in." I told him he was right, but nonetheless that world is still there and he can choose to live in it if he wanted to.

His perception is that he had no choice; he had to steal and rob to live. I was just trying to help him change his perception. I tried to engrave into the inmates' minds, "**There are always choices.**"

The second criterion is "deceitfulness, as indicated by repeated lying, use of aliases, or conning others for personal profit or pleasure." Everyone I know who intentionally breaks the law also lies about it. They justify or rationalize their behavior. I know a person who pawned his own mother's wedding ring for drugs. You see, he needed it. These people are impulsive, irritable, irresponsible, and reckless in regard to the safety of themselves or others.

We have already discussed impulsivity and irritability in an earlier chapter. Irresponsibility is a learned behavior. Behaviors are created by our thoughts and feelings. As discussed earlier, feelings are created by our thoughts. Our thoughts are generated by our perception. Thus, ultimately our behaviors are created by our perceptions. If I believe that I do not need to go to work if I do not want to, then I will not and I will get fired. If I believe I need to answer the phone when it rings and my child is in the bathtub, guess what I will do when the phone rings? I will leave the child unattended and answer it even while putting my child's life at risk. Some of these perceptions are not conscious, but they still control what we do. We call this impulsivity.

A thief might say, "I did not think about it. I just stole it because I needed it." What might we guess about his underlying perception? It might be, "It is okay to steal if I really need it." They might even say, "I'm not stealing from a person, I'm stealing from a company. They can afford to replace this. It's not coming out of their pocket; they have insurance and the insurance company will replace it." So again, "I'm NUMBER ONE! I can do anything I want! Say anything I want! Anytime I want! Anywhere I want! To anyone I want! And there is nothing that you or anyone else can do about it, PERIOD!"

No Rules

In one of the first counseling sessions with a client who has Antisocial Personality Disorder, I take them down to the basketball court at our facility. I tell them we are going to play a game of basketball with one rule: There are no rules. We then start to play. I might shoot the ball and make a basket and grab it again and shoot again. I might lower the hoop to 8 ½ feet so I can jump and put my hand up through the hoop and knock out any ball that they shoot. I sometimes run to another hoop and start shooting. After a couple of minutes, I ask them, "Are you having fun?" At first they usually are having fun, but after a while, they do not like it at all. I then ask, "What's the score?" They will tell me the score based upon typical basketball rules. I then ask them, "How do you know?" As they start to explain, they quickly realize that there are not any rules and therefore, there is not a score. I ask them, "Why aren't you having fun?" They tell me, "Because there aren't any rules." I then ask, "Are you telling me that in order to have fun, you must have rules?" They generally wait a minute, try to argue it then they say something like, "Yeah, I guess so." Then I tell them of a scene in a video that depicts this idea very well.

In the video, Spiritual Crocodiles,[58] a teenage boy is having a conversation with his conscience represented by another person who looks just like him. The boy had just become mad after talking to his mom about one of the house rules. His conscience says, "Rules are dumb right?" He agrees. Then his conscience snaps his little finger, and they are sitting in a convertible Ferrari on what appears to be an Arizona desert straight-away. The teenager cannot believe it. He is sitting in his dream car on the open road. He looks up and sees a police officer with his motorcycle standing in front of a speed limit sign that reads, "Speed Limit 55 mph." The boy looks at his conscience and says, "I'm in my favorite car and I have to drive 55 miles per hour?!!" His conscience questions, "Rules are dumb right?" "Right!" is his reply. His conscience then grabs his chin with his hand and turns his face toward the police officer and the speed limit sign. The letters and the numbers on the speed limit sign fall to the ground and "No Limit" appears on the sign. The police officer looks at the sign and then disappears. The boy looks at his conscience in awe and wonder, and his conscience hands him a pair of sunglasses. He puts them on with a big smile and takes off. To give the audience an idea as to how fast he is driving, he speeds by a hitchhiker, and the hitchhiker falls to the ground and rolls several times. The teenager keeps driving very fast. The camera then shows a diesel coming from the other direction. The camera focuses on the driver of the diesel with slow music playing in the background suggesting he is a slow driver. Just before the diesel gets to where the Ferrari is, he crosses over into the oncoming lane where the Ferrari is driving. And just before the two vehicles collide, the boy screams and suddenly is back in his bedroom.

The boy angrily asks, "Did you see that? That guy could have killed us!" His conscience said, "He didn't do anything wrong." He then said, "Didn't do anything wrong? He was in my lane!" His conscience then reminded him there were not any laws - just like he wanted. The conscience then asked "Which law did the truck driver break?" The teenager answered, "None." The conscience then asks, "So what did he do wrong?" "Nothing, except he was in my lane" was the boy's reply. The conscience then asked, "Were you in the correct lane?" The boy answered, "Yes" and his conscience asked him how he knew that. The boy answered, "Because the law says," and then he pauses and he realizes what he is saying. The conscience explains that rules are not there to make us mad but to help us find joy and safety.

My client and I further discuss that rules are there to help us not to hurt us. Rules are to help us be happy and safe. Maybe there is a senator out there who had their own agenda when they got a law passed and it seems pointless, but for the most part, the rules and laws are to help us be happy and safe. The reason we drive on the right side of the road is so we can get from one point to another safely and happily. The reason there is a law that prohibits us from drinking and driving is so people do not die and so that people do not have to go to prison for killing someone while driving drunk. Ultimately, they are there so we can be safe and happy.

The reason people who have Antisocial Personality Disorder have a difficult time playing the game of basketball with no rules is that these people choose their actions based upon rules. They do not like to hear that, because they believe the rules do not apply to them and they can do whatever they want. But my experience says that they choose behaviors that are the exact opposite of what the rules say. In other words, if the speed limit says 55 mph, they say, "Oh yeah, watch me drive faster." They take a look at the rule and then break it. Without rules, they do not know how to act because their actions are based upon the rules.

Through my little game of basketball without rules and without them knowing what lesson they are learning, they begin to change their perception. I ask them to name a rule that we have in our facility that they do not like. After doing so, I ask them what the purpose of the rule is. Is it just to make the residents mad? They begin to understand the purpose of rules. My dad taught me, "There is a reason behind every rule. If you can understand the reason, then it is easier to obey the rule." If we can just understand the reason, it is easier to follow the rule even if we do not necessarily agree with it. Some people who have Antisocial Personality Disorder tell me they get a high by getting away with something. Unfortunately, this is true and this is where we must help them see the consequences.

There was one factor that helped people to get out of prison after coming back time and time again. That factor was age. How many old men do you see in gangs? How many old people do you see rob banks? How many old men are out tagging or vandalizing? Very few elderly people get caught up in criminal behavior. They simply outgrow it. Their perception changes as to what is enjoyable. Maybe their perception changes when they have their own children. Maybe their perception changes the closer they get to death.

Many people who have Antisocial Personality Disorder say that they want to be free to do whatever they want. However, society is set up so that if you want your freedom, then you must use your agency to choose to follow the rules of the land. If you use your agency to choose to break the rules, then your freedom gets restricted or taken away from you. I ask people what they value most in life and they often respond by saying the power to choose what they believe to be right for them. When I ask inmates what they value most, they almost always say freedom. If they truly valued freedom over everything else in life, why would they not follow this simple principle to maintain their freedom? Why do they break the rules that result in their freedom being taken from them? Do they understand? Or are they lying to themselves and they do not really value freedom at all but rather just wish they could do anything they wanted to and have no consequences? Their perceptions are clearly skewed in this regard.

What they really want is agency to do whatever they want and they want everyone else's agency to be taken away. They want everyone else to be forced to do what they want. Now, to a certain degree is not that what we all want? When we get mad at people for not doing what we want or thinking the way we want them to, are we not really wanting their agency to be taken away and forcing them to do what we want. How many of you hate stupid people? Why? Because they do not do what you would have them do or say what you would have them say. You want their agency taken away and lined up with your choices. Can you see that?

I believe there are two types of people - those who can learn from others and those who must learn for themselves. Whether those who learn the hard way can cross over and become someone who learns from other's mistakes is all based upon their perception. What I like to do is ask the people with an Antisocial Personality Disorder if they think they can cross over and what they need to do to make the change. They know themselves better than I do, so only they know what they need to do.

There is a program out there to help people who have Antisocial Personality Disorder. In my experience, it works like a charm. The program is called "Why Try."[59] If I struggle with someone in my counseling session, I can always rely on the principles taught in this program to help them and also help me in my role as a therapist. I give a lot of thanks to both Christian Moore and Hans Magleby for their work with the Why Try program. Basically Why Try leads the client through simple steps to understand different principles. Each principle has a picture with it that helps in understanding it better. Each principle also has a song that helps implant the principle into our minds. It is a fantastic program, and I highly recommend it.

Apathy, Empathy, Sympathy

Apathy is a common trait in people with Antisocial Personality Disorders. Apathy means "Without feeling." Empathy means "Understanding how one feels." Sympathy is "Feeling how one feels."

All crimes are committed with apathy towards the victim. I made that same statement once in prison, and an inmate said to me that he believed he really felt for his victim and that is why he did not shoot him. I told him if he had empathy or sympathy towards the victim, he would never have put a gun in his face. I simply cannot believe anything else is true in those situations.

My goal with my clients is to teach them to be empathetic. I do not want them to be sympathetic. It is okay to be sympathetic with people who are really close to you, but if your emotions are controlled by others' emotions, then you may cross over into codependency. We need to be in control of our own feelings.

To help my clients learn to be empathetic, I place two clients out in the middle of the group with all the other clients surrounding them. I tell the ones watching that their role in this role play is to be the judges. I give the two clients in the middle a role to play, and I have the ones on the outside judging their roles as to whether they were apathetic, empathetic, or sympathetic. Then I ask the clients in the middle to tell me a crime they committed, whether or not they were caught. Both clients then share their crimes, and I pick one for the role play.

One day I had a client tell me that he had stolen money from a company. I told that client that he was now going to have the opportunity to make amends with the owner of the company. The other client would represent the owner. I told the first client that his job was to put himself in the owner's shoes and imagine what it must have been like to have all that money stolen from his company. I am trying to change his perception by getting him to look at the situation from another perspective. I have heard clients say, "Well, it's not like I'm stealing from a person." Or, "Company X has insurance so the company won't lose." Or, "He can afford it; he's rich." All these thoughts are apathetic, and now I want a change of perception, and I want my clients to feel empathetic.

I said, "Imagine being the owner and having all that money lost. What if he was counting on that money to buy his children Christmas gifts? He went home feeling so down and had to face his wife and tell her they would not be having Christmas like they had planned. The children would be sad.

213

Even if the insurance company ends up paying the owner, the owner's family is affected by it." We just do not know the extent to which we have an impact on other people. What we do know is that all of our actions, for good or for bad, have a ripple effect and many people are impacted by them.

The clients then begin to role play. After a while, I stop the role play and ask the judges about what they saw. More often than not they say that the client was apathetic in their apology. Sometimes they say she was empathetic. Rarely do they say that the client was sympathetic. If the client was not empathetic, than I give them another chance after they have received feedback from their peers.

Another scenario I have given is as follows: "Imagine finding out that the drug you sold to someone actually killed that person. Now you get a chance to meet her daughter. How would you make amends?" I remind him that we are working on being empathetic and ask him, "Can you relate at all?" Maybe my client has never had a mother die from drugs. So what I try to do is to get him to make a connection with a similar event. Has he ever had a family member die? If not, has he ever had a pet die? All I want is for him to make a connection to the best of his ability so that he can start to understand what it must be like to be that daughter grieving for her mother.

My client might say in this situation, "I just found out that I'm the one who sold your mother the drugs that ended up killing her. I want to apologize with all my heart. I've been getting treatment so that I'll never contribute to someone's death again. I can't imagine how you must feel to have lost your mother. My mother is still alive, but I remember when I lost my grandma and how much that hurt me at that time. Losing your mother must be so much more painful."

Again, empathy is only trying to understand how one feels. We will never be able to completely understand how another person feels, but we can come close with our own personal experiences if we will but try. If my clients can

214

imagine what it must be like to be the other person, then they would never commit a crime against that individual because they understand how the person feels.

Often when we apologize we say, "Will you forgive me?" This question is very inappropriate. When a perpetrator asks a victim if she will forgive him, he is setting up the victim to be victimized again. What I mean by that is, maybe the victim is not yet ready to forgive the perpetrator. So when the question is asked and the victim says, "No" or, "Not yet," then the perpetrator says, "See, I apologized and you will not forgive me. Who's the bad guy here?" Isn't the question, "Will you forgive me?" a given when you apologize to another human being? We do not need to ask that question. What is the real purpose of our apologizing? Is it to get forgiveness from the other person or are we apologizing because it is the right thing to do according to our value system?

Daily Inventory

If someone has Antisocial Personality Disorder criteria, then I suggest they keep track of their behaviors or traits by using this daily inventory (see below) every night before going to bed. The left-side traits or behaviors are compared to the right-side traits or behaviors at the end of each day. As they compare the two sides to each other, if they believe they have portrayed the left side trait completely, then they would put a "10" in the box under that particular day's date. If they feel they have portrayed the right side completely, then they would put a "0" in the box under that particular day's date. If they feel they have portrayed both sides then they have the flexibility to rate themselves between 10 and 0. After a few days, they can easily visualize where they need to put more of their focus by seeing which line has the least numbers day after day. They would focus their energy the next day on that particular item. Below is a blank daily inventory for Antisocial Personality Disorder that can be copied. Below the blank inventory is an example of a completed chart.

Daily Inventory

Month _____ Year _____

BENEFITS
Strive for these

DRAWBACKS
Avoid these

If this side--10

If this side--1

	1	2	3	4	5	6	7	8	9	10	11	12	13	14	15	16	17	18	19	20	21	22	23	24	25	26	27	28	29	30	31	
																	EVALUATE YOUR DAY															
conformed to social norms; obeyed the law																																failure to conform to social norms; broke the law
honest in all dealings																																deceitfulness; lying, use of aliases, conning others
actions were thought out																																impulsivity or failure to plan ahead
calm and collected																																irritability and aggressiveness; physical fights or assaults
regarded the safety of self and others																																reckless disregard for safety of self or others
responsible; met work and financial obligations																																irresponsible; failure with work or financial obligations
empathetic toward others																																lack of remorse; justifies having hurt, mistreated or

Every night compare the two sides

216

Daily Inventory

BENEFITS
Strive for these

If this side--10

Month _____ Year _____

DRAWBACKS
Avoid these

If this side--1

EVALUATE YOUR DAY

	1	2	3	4	5	6	7	8	9	10	11	12	13	14	15	16	17	18	19	20	21	22	23	24	25	26	27	28	29	30	31	
conformed to social norms; obeyed the law	7	7	8	2	3	2	8	7	2																							failure to conform to social norms; broke the law
honest in all dealings	2	2	2	2	7	2	1	3	2																							deceitfulness; lying, use of aliases, conning others
actions were thought out	2	2	7	2	3	6	2	7	2																							impulsivity or failure to plan ahead
calm and collected	3	3	7	7	7	2	2	8	9																							irritability and aggressiveness; physical fights or assaults
regarded the safety of self and others	7	7	2	3	2	2	7	1	1																							reckless disregard for safety of self or others
responsible, met work and financial obligations	2	7	7	7	7	7	7	1	2																							irresponsible; failure with work or financial obligations
empathetic toward others	2	2	2	1	2	2	7	2	2																							lack of remorse; justifies having hurt, mistreated or

Every night compare the two sides

This person should focus on being honest. They should also focus on being empathetic toward others. If we break our personality down into the criteria, then we can have a clear understanding of what we need to do to change. It is very beneficial to do it this way with a person who has Antisocial Personality Disorder because they are evaluating themselves, and no one is telling them what to do. They get to measure their own life and decide for themselves what they need to work on.

Borderline Personality Disorder Derived From Perception

Let us look at the criterion of Borderline Personality Disorder. According to the DSM-IV it is "A pervasive pattern of instability of interpersonal relationships, self-image, and affects, and marked impulsivity beginning by early adulthood and present in a variety of contexts, as indicated by five (or more) of the following:

1. Frantic efforts to avoid real or imagined abandonment. (**Note:** Do not include suicidal or self-mutilating behavior covered in Criterion 5);

2. A pattern of unstable and intense interpersonal relationships characterized by alternating between extremes of idealization and devaluation;

3. Identity disturbance: markedly and persistently unstable self-image or sense of self;

4. Impulsivity in at least two areas that are potentially self-damaging (e.g., spending, sex, substance abuse, reckless driving, binge eating). (**Note:** Do not include suicidal or self-mutilating behavior covered in Criterion 5);

5. Recurrent suicidal behavior, gestures, or threats, or self-mutilating behavior;

6. Affective instability due to a marked reactivity of mood (e.g., intense episodic Dysphoria, irritability, or anxiety usually lasting a few hours and only rarely more than a few days);

7. Chronic feelings of emptiness;

8. Inappropriate, intense anger or difficulty controlling anger (e.g., frequent displays of temper, constant anger, recurrent physical fights);

9. Transient, stress-related paranoid ideation or severe dissociative symptoms"[60]

People with Borderline Personality Disorder like crisis in their lives. If they do not naturally have one, they will create a crisis just to have one. Most of the time, their crisis involves other people, not just themselves. That is why one of the criteria says, "pattern of instability of interpersonal relationships." A common thing they do is they tell Person A something about Person B then they tell Person B something about Person A. They get these two people pitted against each other and then sit back and play the innocent role and watch. If you have a child who is has Borderline Personality Disorder, then you might find yourself in a lot of arguments with your spouse because of this child. It is not your spouse's fault, but rather it is being set up by your child.

Their perception says that people abandon them. Therefore they will do anything and everything to "avoid real or imagined abandonment." Notice the word, "imagined." If they believe they might be abandoned, they will do whatever it takes to feel secure in that relationship. They might say to their spouse, "If you leave, then I'm going to tell everyone that you are having an affair." They often question their partner if they are just a few minutes late coming home. They might ask if they are seeing someone else, or they might just come straight out and accuse them of cheating on them. They are so afraid of abandonment that if they fear they might lose their partner, they might actually get another boyfriend on the side before the break-up occurs so that they are not left alone.

Another aspect that might be seen in people with Borderline Personality Disorder is the fear of abandonment to the point that they might go to the extreme in showing love.

They might cling onto their partner so much it actually pushes their partner away. John Grey in his book, "<u>Men Are from Mars, Women Are from Venus</u>"[61] talks about the need for a man to go into his cave (a place of escape). When the woman comes pounding on the door of the cave demanding that he comes out, it actually pushes the man farther away from her. She misinterprets it as him not loving her, and so feels she must push harder or pound louder on the cave door. This vicious cycle continues. If the woman would just back off and give the man his space for a little while, then he will naturally emerge from the cave and show his affection. The woman in this scenario is a perfect example of what a person with Borderline Personality Disorder might do or perceive.

People with Borderline Personality Disorder have, "A pattern of unstable and intense interpersonal relationships characterized by alternating between extremes of idealization and devaluation." The best example I can give of this is from a male client of mine who walked into my office one day and said, "Jason, just because I hate you doesn't mean that I don't love you." All I could say was, "I understand." People with Borderline Personality Disorder love someone one day and hate them the next day. It might not even take a day (or an hour) for them to switch between the two. If you have to ask yourself about a family member or friend, "I wonder if she's going to hate or love me tonight," they might have Borderline Personality Disorder.

You can understand why people with Borderline Personality Disorder act the way they do. It is because they have an "identity disturbance." They have a "Markedly and persistently unstable self-image or sense of self." They have feelings of worthlessness, and they try and hide it behind their actions or by getting everyone else to act out in their crisis to take away the attention from themselves. This unstable self-image is based upon their own thoughts or perceptions rather than anything tangible. He finds himself in a vicious cycle where he feels bad and acts out or gets into a crisis and then the crisis lowers his self-image because he "did it again" and the pattern repeats.

Since the person's (with Borderline Personality Disorder) image of themselves fluctuates and they are afraid of being abandoned, they will often act impulsively in at least two areas that are potentially self-damaging (e.g., spending, sex, substance abuse, reckless driving, binge eating). These behaviors are intended to help their image, but they actually do the opposite. Remember it is not about what is real but is rather about their perception of what they need to do to improve their image or their chances of staying in a relationship.

They are known for their "Recurrent suicidal behavior[s], gestures, or threats, or self-mutilating behavior[s]." Do you know someone who cuts themselves? That is a good indication they might have Borderline Personality Disorder, and it at least warrants a look into the possibility. I had a client one time who burned herself. She took a lighter and burned her forearm then scratched off her burnt skin and burned herself again. I saw another self-mutilating behavior one time that really surprised me; a woman self-mutilated by sewing letters or pictures into her arm. Multiple piercing and tattoos can also fall into this category of self-mutilating behavior (despite the current popularity of it). There are several reasons why a person might self-mutilate, but in my experience, it is generally used as an escape. They want to get rid of their emotional feelings so they turn to physical pain because it is easier to endure. There are also endorphins in the brain that are jump started when one is in pain. I have heard several clients describe this as a "high."

Some people with Borderline Personality Disorder use their self-mutilating behaviors or suicidal threats as a means of manipulating others. I know a man who dated a girl and she threatened to kill herself every time he talked about leaving her. Despite the threats, and they might follow through on their threats, we must not allow that possibility to stop us from doing what we want or getting out of a dysfunctional relationship. We need to understand that they are responsible for their actions and we are not. The more we give in to such behavior, the more we reinforce it and will have to deal with it again and again as it becomes stronger and stronger. He finally left and she didn't kill herself.

Their moods are unstable. They might be pleasant one moment and irritable the next. They might experience a lot of anxiety or even a panic attack and then be perfectly fine. They often experience "Inappropriate, intense anger or difficulty controlling [his] anger (e.g., frequent displays of temper, constant anger, recurrent physical fights)." They have learned that their moods or temper can be used effectively to get what they want. They also use them because of their chronic feeling of emptiness. When one feels empty inside, they often turn to maladaptive behaviors in a desperate attempt to fill the void. I refer you to earlier chapters where we already discussed how our moods, feelings, and anger are caused by our perceptions.

The last criterion is, "Transient, stress-related paranoid ideation or severe dissociative symptoms." We discussed these symptoms and how they are related to perception when we discussed Cluster A Personalities.

One counselor said, "I know if I'm dealing with a person who has Borderline Personality Disorder because I want to hit him/her during treatment." Another person said, "If you want to know if someone has Borderline Personality Disorder, then ask the people that live or work with them." One other Therapist said, "Why do we get mad at these people. They are doing their job. Yet when they do their job of acting out we act surprised." Expect them to do their "job." Help them see what they really want in life and how to best achieve their goals.

Daily Inventory

If someone has Borderline Personality Disorder criteria, then I suggest they keep track of their behaviors or traits by using this daily inventory (see below) every night before going to bed. The left-side traits or behaviors are compared to the right-side traits or behaviors at the end of each day. As they compare the two sides to each other, if they believe they have portrayed the left side trait completely, then they would put a "10" in the box under that particular day's date. If they feel they have portrayed the right side completely, then they would put a "0" in the box under that particular day's date. If they feel they have portrayed both sides then they have the flexibility to rate themselves between 10 and 0. After a few days, they can easily visualize where they need to put more of their focus by seeing which line has the least numbers day after day. They would focus their energy the next day on that particular item. Below is a blank daily inventory for Borderline Personality Disorder that can be copied. Below the blank inventory is an example of a completed chart.

Daily Inventory

Month _____ Year _____

BENEFITS
Strive for these
If this side--10

DRAWBACKS
Avoid these
If this side--1

EVALUATE YOUR DAY

BENEFITS	1	2	3	4	5	6	7	8	9	10	11	12	13	14	15	16	17	18	19	20	21	22	23	24	25	26	27	28	29	30	31	DRAWBACKS
dealt with feelings of abandonment																																frantic efforts to avoid real or imagined abandonment
a pattern of stable and healthy relationships																																a pattern of unstable and intense relationships
clear understanding of identity and sense of self																																identity disturbance; unstable self-image or sense of self
actions were thought out																																impulsive
no thoughts of self-harm																																suicidal gestures or threats, or self-mutilating behaviors
mood seemed to be stable throughout the day																																affective instability; quick mood changes
feeling worthwhile																																chronic feelings of emptiness
anger managed and controlled																																inappropriate, intense anger or difficulty controlling anger
no paranoia or dissociative symptoms																																stress-related paranoid ideation or dissociative

Every night compare the two sides

Daily Inventory

Month _____ Year _____

BENEFITS
Strive for these

If this side--10

DRAWBACKS
Avoid these

If this side--1

EVALUATE YOUR DAY

BENEFITS	1	2	3	4	5	6	7	8	9	10	11	12	13	14	15	16	17	18	19	20	21	22	23	24	25	26	27	28	29	30	31	DRAWBACKS
dealt with feelings of abandonment	3	3	3	3	2	7	3	2	7																							frantic efforts to avoid real or imagined abandonment
a pattern of stable and healthy relationships	7	1	1	2	3	1	8	2	2																							a pattern of unstable and intense relationships
clear understanding of identity and sense of self	7	1	1	2	3	1	8	2	2																							identity disturbance; unstable self-image or sense of self
actions were thought out	1	1	1	1	1	1	1	1	1																							impulsive
no thoughts of self-harm	9	9	9	9	4	9	9	9	8																							suicidal gestures or threats, or self-mutilating behaviors
mood seemed to be stable throughout the day	8	7	6	2	7	6	9	7	8																							affective instability; quick mood changes
feeling worthwhile	0	0	0	0	5	0	0	0	0																							chronic feelings of emptiness
anger managed and controlled	8	8	8	4	4	8	7	9	8																							inappropriate, intense anger or difficulty controlling anger
no paranoia or dissociative symptoms	7	6	9	8	7	7	7	2	7																							stress-related paranoid ideation or dissociative

Every night compare the two sides

This person has a profound identity disturbance. Even though there are other categories that also need to be improved, it might be a good idea to work on this one first. Sometimes it is helpful to work on the "worst" one first. Then after feeling confident with that, move on to the next "worst" one. If we try and bite off too many at the same time, we sometimes get overwhelmed. Anyone can work on one issue at a time. Anyone can work on one issue for one day. I have a second definition of insanity which varies from the one mentioned earlier. It is, "Doing different things and expecting the same results." How absurd to think that if I change the direction I'm driving that I will end up at the same place I was going before. We set ourselves up for failure by thinking this way with regards to treatment.

Histrionic Personality Disorder Derived From Perception

Histrionic personality disorder is a "Pervasive pattern of excessive emotions and attention seeking, beginning by early adulthood and present in a variety of contexts, as indicated by five (or more) of the following:

1. Is uncomfortable in situations in which he or she is not the center of attention;

2. Interaction with others is often characterized by inappropriate sexually seductive or provocative behavior;

3. Displays rapidly shifting and shallow expression of emotions;

4. Consistently uses physical appearance to draw attention to self;

5. Has a style of speech that is excessively impressionistic and lacking in detail;

6. Shows self-dramatization, theatricality, and exaggerated expression of emotion;

7. Is suggestible, i.e., easily influenced by others or circumstances;

8. Considers relationships to be more intimate than they actually are"[62]

People with Histrionic Personality Disorder have the perception that if they are not the center of everything, then they have no value or are inferior to those who are at the center. They are excessively emotional because of this perception. They also tend to use their emotions as a form of manipulation to get what they want. These emotions are not always negative emotions and in fact they are flattering emotions at times.

They often times dramatize or exaggerate their expression of emotions as if they were on stage. They might extend the sound of certain letters in words. For example, she might say, "But daaaaaadddyyyyyyy." They often times act like little children even when they are adults (physically and chronologically at least). They might whine or even throw a fit just like a little child.

They must be the center of attention. If they go to a party or if they have a friend over, they must dominate the conversation. If you ask a crowd of people to be quiet for a minute or two, these people are uncomfortable and fidgety and make little comments under their breath to be funny and break up the silence. They struggle with boredom rather than learning to embrace it.

This idea of being the center of attention crosses over into another aspect or criterion of the diagnosis and that is that their "Interaction with others is often characterized by inappropriate sexually seductive or provocative behavior." Their boundaries are often thin and vague. They do not understand where to stop, so they find themselves going against their own value system at times to get the approval of others. Their speech might be of a nature that invites or turns another person on. They might come across as wanting a sexual relationship with that person and that may just be the case.

They consistently use physical appearance to draw attention to self. A woman might wear a low-cut blouse to show her cleavage which is just another attempt to get people to focus on her. It does not matter whether the attention is purely physical or sexual or if it is out of a genuine concern for the person; it is all the same to them. This provocative style of appearance is not limited to when they are around people of the opposite sex. They will dress like that around those of the same sex or just walking down the street alone. Remember they always want others to notice them, always.

These women who have Histrionic Personality Disorder (and it is not just limited to women) will often get their breasts augmented. They might also get their tummies tucked as well as "fixing" other parts of their body. They will go to extremes to get noticed. One client told me that she got her breasts augmented after she broke up with her boyfriend to "show him what he was missing." When confronted on such behavior, she did not see anything wrong with it and even justified it.

Even though she flaunts herself and gets the worst of the worst to notice her, she considers that relationship to be more intimate than it is. The man might just be using her, yet she believes he is her knight in shining armor. Her relationships are therefore short-lived, and she is soon on the hunt again. She acts like the predator until she finds her prey. Then she acts like the helpless prey until she is caught.

She might fool one into believing she really cares for him, but in reality he is merely filling a void and being used. She will believe she has found her one and only after one date and even tell him that he is all she needs. Yet, she will go to another party with him and almost ignore him in order to be the life of the party. She needs the attention of everyone at the party and is not satisfied with the attention of her new "one and only."

The people with Histrionic Personality Disorder might display rapid shifting and shallow expression of emotions. The reason for this is because their emotions are actually shallow. They are not usually genuine but rather a mask (even to themselves) to fulfill their need. If they feel discounted, they can leave the relationship and get someone else because at the parties everyone loves them.

They are also the one at the party who will eat a live worm or cricket. They will do the crazy stunts no one else is willing to do because they want approval and attention. There is no holding them back. The only limit is their imagination and what others tell them.

They might have a style of speech that is excessively impressionistic and lacking in detail. They might try to impress everyone with their knowledge of language even when the conversation is just chit-chat. They might try to talk about something they have little knowledge about. In other words, they are a dilettante. Did you catch my attempt to be histrionic in my last sentence? A dilettante is someone who talks about something he knows little or nothing about. A person with Histrionic Personality Disorder might have the perception, "If I appear to be smart, others will pay attention to me." However, the reality is that if you want others to understand you and you want to understand everyone else, then know the big words but use the little words.

The last criterion to be mentioned is that people with Histrionic Personality Disorder are easily influenced. You can probably guess why. If someone is so concerned about being the center of attention, they are easily persuaded to do something if they believe it will make others like them better. They follow the trends of society. They believe they need to follow what the models or movie stars are doing. They pay attention to the tabloids. They care about being in the in-crowd. In a sense, they give up their own agency to the whims of the day.

Daily Inventory

If someone has Histrionic Personality Disorder criteria, then I suggest they keep track of their behaviors or traits by using this daily inventory (see below) every night before going to bed. The left-side traits or behaviors are compared to the right-side traits or behaviors at the end of each day. As they compare the two sides to each other, if they believe they have portrayed the left side trait completely, then they would put a "10" in the box under that particular day's date. If they feel they have portrayed the right side completely, then they would put a "0" in the box under that particular day's date. If they feel they have portrayed both sides then they have the flexibility to rate themselves between 10 and 0. After a few days, they can easily visualize where they need to put more of their focus by seeing which line has the least numbers day after day. They would focus their energy the next day on that particular item. Below is a blank daily inventory for Histrionic Personality Disorder that can be copied. Below the blank inventory is an example of a completed chart.

Daily Inventory

Month _____ Year _____

BENEFITS
Strive for these
If this side--10

DRAWBACKS
Avoid these
If this side--1

EVALUATE YOUR DAY

Benefits	1	2	3	4	5	6	7	8	9	10	11	12	13	14	15	16	17	18	19	20	21	22	23	24	25	26	27	28	29	30	31	Drawbacks
does not need to be center of attention to feel O.K.																																uncomfortable when not the center of attention
not sexually seductive or provocative																																inappropriate sexually seductive or provocative
emotions maintained and shared deeply																																rapid shift and shallow expression of emotions
does not seek attention by looks																																use physical appearance to draw attention to self
speaks so others can understand																																use of excessively impressionistic speech
emotions managed within normal range																																dramatic, theatrical, & exaggerated emotions
not easily influenced by others or circumstances																																suggestible: easily influenced by others
sees relationships for what they are																																thinks relationships more intimate than they are

Every night compare the two sides

Daily Inventory

BENEFITS — Strive for these

DRAWBACKS — Avoid these

Month _____ Year _____

If this side--10 · *If this side--1*

EVALUATE YOUR DAY

BENEFITS (Strive for these)	1	2	3	4	5	6	7	8	9	10	11	12	13	14	15	16	17	18	19	20	21	22	23	24	25	26	27	28	29	30	31	DRAWBACKS (Avoid these)
does not need to be center of attention to feel O.K.	1	2	2	2	2	2	3	6	2																							uncomfortable when not the center of attention
not sexually seductive or provocative	7	4	4	9	8	8	9	9	9																							inappropriate sexually seductive or provocative
emotions maintained and shared deeply	6	4	6	4	6	4	6	4	6																							rapid shift and shallow expression of emotions
does not seek attention by looks	0	0	0	0	0	0	0	0	0																							use physical appearance to draw attention to self
speaks so others can understand	8	8	8	4	4	3	7	3	3																							use of excessively impressionistic speech
emotions managed within normal range	6	2	2	3	6	2	2	2																								dramatic, theatrical, & exaggerated emotions
not easily influenced by others or circumstances	2	2	3	6	3	2	2	1	2																							suggestible; easily influenced by others
sees relationships for what they are	3	4	6	3	4	3	3	6	2																							thinks relationships more intimate than they are

Every night compare the two sides

This person needs to focus on not seeking attention through her physical appearance. There is nothing wrong with looking nice, but the meaning behind it is what counts. It is important to focus on being okay with ourselves even when we are not the center of attention. We should try to listen twice as much as we speak. Another good assignment for this person is to write down what her goals are. Then as she starts to act in certain ways, she can ask herself if her actions are taking her towards her goals or away from them. She can also see whether or not her goals are shallow.

Narcissistic Personality Disorder Derived From Perception

Narcissistic personality disorder is "A pervasive pattern of grandiosity (in fantasy or behavior), need for admiration, and lack of empathy, beginning by early adulthood and present in a variety of contexts, as indicated by five (or more) of the following:

1. Has a grandiose sense of self-importance (e.g., exaggerates achievements and talents, expects to be recognized as superior without commensurate achievements);

2. Is preoccupied with fantasies of unlimited success, power, brilliance, beauty, or ideal love;

3. Believes that he or she is 'special' and unique and can only be understood by, or should associate with, other special or high-status people (or institutions);

4. Requires excessive admiration;

5. Has a sense of entitlement, i.e., unreasonable expectations of especially favorable treatment or automatic compliance with his or her expectations;

6. Is interpersonally exploitative, i.e., takes advantage of others to achieve his or her own ends;

7. Lacks empathy: is unwilling to recognize or identify with the feelings and needs of others;

8. Is often envious of others or believes that others are envious of him or her;

9. Shows arrogant, haughty behaviors or attitudes"[63]

I have worked with several people with Narcissistic Personality Disorder in my career. In the beginning of my career, I wanted to know how to treat Narcissistic Personality Disorder; I wanted to know what worked. I looked up narcissism on the internet and learned that I should confront them on their behavior. I should also expect that when I do this they will get defensive and angry. Then as they begin to accept the confrontation, they will get depressed and then suicidal. If I can get them past the suicide state, then they have a good chance. As you can imagine, this formula did not excite me much.

People with Narcissistic Personality Disorder like themselves too much. However, if you get down deep inside of them, which is extremely difficult for reasons I will talk about later, you would find a person with a very low self-esteem, and their narcissistic behaviors are only a mask. Notice in the diagnosis "A pattern of grandiosity," and here is the key, "in fantasy or behavior" and not in their belief system. They have a need for admiration. They believe that this admiration will increase their self-esteem but it actually will not. In fact their extreme need to be admired is manifested in such a way that turns people off, and they do not give them the admiration they are looking for. They are actually setting themselves up for less admiration.

They have a grandiose sense of self-importance. They exaggerate achievements and talents and expect to be recognized as superior without commensurate achievements. They may not have achieved anything special in life yet they want the whole world to recognize the happy face sticker they got on their kindergarten paper. I know one in particular who has money and a career because of his father yet he expects everyone to admire him.

People with Narcissistic Personality Disorder are so involved in themselves that if someone tells them something they do not want to hear, they simply ignore the person as if they are not worthy enough to even look their way. They believe they are "special" and unique and can only be understood by, or should associate with, other special or high-status people (or institutions). Therefore, if you do not fall into their special or high-status category, then they simply disqualify everything you say.

Because they believe that they are special, then it is a privilege for you and me just to talk to them. I have heard two clients in my career say that the only reason they were in treatment was because they wanted me to feel good and think that I was helping someone. In other words, they were in treatment simply because it was an honor for me to be their therapist, and they did not want to take that away from me.

These people are preoccupied with fantasies of unlimited success, power, brilliance, beauty, or ideal love. It is all part of their perception. They do not have any tangible proof of this. One client grew up believing he was the most beautiful man in the world because his mother told him so. As he got older, he reported using his good looks to get whatever he wanted. He stated that he could have any woman he wanted because he was so good looking. Another client was asked if he had ever paid someone for sex and his response was, "With this face do you think I need to pay someone for sex?" And yet another client just before making Dream Catchers during a recreation group was asked if he knew what a Dream Catcher was. He said, "Yes. It's a girl who catches me."

Back to the good looking client mentioned above, after entering our treatment program he said, "I even used my looks to get through my last rehabilitation program, but then I came here and you wouldn't let me use my looks. In fact, you teach that looks are nothing and that it's all about who I am on the inside, and I don't like myself." It was a moment where he had a change of perception. He did not like the new perception because he couldn't get anything he wanted but he believed the new perception to be true.

People with Narcissistic Personality Disorder have a sense of entitlement (i.e., unreasonable expectations of especially favorable treatment or automatic compliance with their expectations). This is because they believe they are to be admired because they are so much better than the rest of us. One client came into treatment and sat in the groups but would not participate or open up. After a while, she said it was because she believed she was better than everyone in the room, and since she was not as bad off as they were, she did not need to be processed. She walked around expecting everyone to move for her or bow to her every need. Since she wanted favorable treatment, she lied about her life so that she would not have to admit to all her problems. Later in treatment, her lies were brought up by her father, but by that time she had burned all her bridges and no one could trust her.

People with Narcissistic Personality Disorder are interpersonally exploitative (i.e., takes advantage of others to achieve his or her own ends). They believe that others are on the earth for their use. This characteristic reminds me of the kings' attitudes from way back when. The king would do what he wanted and did not have a second thought about the impact his will had on the peasant people. If in the end the king got what he wanted, that was all that mattered to him. This is the kind of person who wants their mom and dad to give them more independence and then turns around and asks for money, the car, or whatever they want.

For a discussion on empathy, see the section under Antisocial Personality Disorder titled, "Apathy, Empathy, Sympathy." A big difference between people with Narcissistic Personality Disorder and people with Antisocial Personality Disorder is that the latter does not care about anyone but themselves, and the former believes that you exist for their benefit. The activity mentioned in the "Apathy, Empathy, Sympathy" section is a good activity for people with Narcissistic Personality Disorder as well.

They are often envious of others or believe that others are envious of them. Remember that deep down inside them is a low self-esteem. They might be envious of others, but they cannot come off that way and so must elevate themselves even more. They might push others down (figuratively speaking) so that the other person must look up to them. They do this by belittling them to their face or talking about them behind their backs. They try and get others to focus on their qualities and not others. They set themselves up to be envied by others. They show arrogant haughty behaviors or attitudes.

As an example, I was talking to a woman with Narcissistic Personality Disorder (NPD) on the phone one day, and the conversation went like this:

Me: "Hello."

NPD: "Hi, this is [so and so]. I left you a message. Did you get it?"

Me: "No."

NPD: "Well I left it with [a coworker of yours]."

Me: "I haven't seen him today, so I haven't received it."

NPD: "Well, it was really important!"

Me: "I didn't receive it."

NPD: "I need to come in tomorrow and talk to you about all the bad behaviors of my husband so you can fix him."

Me: "That's not going to happen because I don't work on Saturdays" (this conversation occurred on a Friday).

NPD: "Is there anybody else I can meet with?"

Me: "No. I'm your husband's therapist and if you come up here, you need to meet with me. How about meeting next week?"

NPD: "No. I can't. I need to meet with you tomorrow."

Me: "That's not happening."

NPD: "Did you know that he is on my insurance and I'll just take him off of my policy, and then you won't get paid to treat him!" (At this point she had begun to yell at me, so I hung up the phone. The phone rang again shortly thereafter and I answered it.)

Me: "Hello."

NPD: "I think we were disconnected."

Me: "No we weren't. I hung up on you."

NPD: (In the most arrogant voice possible) "You hung up on me?"

Me: "Yes."

NPD: "That's not very professional."

Me: "I guess I'm a sick twisted freak."

NPD: "What?"

Me: "I guess I'm a sick twisted freak."

NPD: 'What?"

Me: "I guess I'm a sick twisted freak."

NPD: "Well what are you going to do about hanging up on me?"

Me: "Nothing."

NPD: "Well let's get this straight. Because you hung up on me, you can't meet with me."

Me: "Okay." She hung up the phone.

Her husband was sitting next to me at the time and said, "I never even thought about hanging up on her." He got a new perception right then. I told him that we do not need to take abuse in any form. He was planning on getting a divorce and said that she would never take a look at her side of an issue but rather she always blamed him for everything. Did you notice in the conversation that it was apparently an honor for me to talk to her? I should have rearranged my schedule to talk to her because it was a privilege for me to even have a minute of her time.

It is a difficult thing to work with people with Narcissistic Personality Disorder. First of all, we must approach them from a friendly point of view (in their eyes or from their perception), so that they will put us on the same playing level as themselves. Otherwise, they will discount everything we say because we are not worthy of them. However, if we can get them to see us as a person of intelligence, who wants to help, then they are more likely to open up and hopefully share with us their inadequacies and low self-esteem. At that point, there is hope.

We then need to teach them that no one is better than anyone else, and no one person is worse than another. To teach them how important they really are, I mention to them what I have already stated under the Personalization section in the Depression chapter, and that is if you think you are that important, just put your fist into a bucket of water and pull it out and see what kind of hole you left. To the world we mean nothing. If we died today, our family and close friends would take time out of their busy schedules to mourn, but the world as a whole would most certainly go on without us. Now if you want to know how important you are to God, the answer is infinitely important, beyond our comprehension. And so is everyone's worth to God.

Service is a great tool to use with people with Narcissistic Personality Disorder. I like to take them to a facility where people are disabled or elderly. As they get out of themselves to help others, they find a love through being selfless. It is a new concept and a whole new perception for them. I had one client that I got mad at because when I took him to a state-run facility where people were in wheelchairs and most of them could not even talk, he asked me for some gloves before he pushed the wheelchairs. I could not believe my ears, but he had been diagnosed with Narcissistic Personality Disorder and had a "holier than thou" attitude.

Daily Inventory

If someone has Narcissistic Personality Disorder criteria, then I suggest they keep track of their behaviors or traits by using this daily inventory (see below) every night before going to bed. The left-side traits or behaviors are compared to the right-side traits or behaviors at the end of each day. As they compare the two sides to each other, if they believe they have portrayed the left side trait completely, then they would put a "10" in the box under that particular day's date. If they feel they have portrayed the right side completely, then they would put a "0" in the box under that particular day's date. If they feel they have portrayed both sides then they have the flexibility to rate themselves between 10 and 0. After a few days, they can easily visualize where they need to put more of their focus by seeing which line has the least numbers day after day. They would focus their energy the next day on that particular item. Below is a blank daily inventory for Narcissistic Personality Disorder that can be copied. Below the blank inventory is an example of a completed chart.

Daily Inventory

Month _____   Year _____

BENEFITS
Strive for these

If this side--10

DRAWBACKS
Avoid these

If this side--1

EVALUATE YOUR DAY

Benefits (Strive for these)	1	2	3	4	5	6	7	8	9	10	11	12	13	14	15	16	17	18	19	20	21	22	23	24	25	26	27	28	29	30	31	Drawbacks (Avoid these)
not more important than anyone else																																grandiose sense of self-importance
no fantasies of unlimited success, power, love																																fantasies of unlimited success, power, love
sees himself/herself as equal to others																																belief that he/she is special
does not need the praise of others																																requires excessive admiration
no sense of entitlement																																sense of entitlement
respects others																																takes advantage of others to achieve his/her own end
empathetic towards others																																lacks empathy; won't identify with others
not envious of others nor believes others of him/her																																envious of others; belief that others envy him/her
humble																																arrogant, haughty behaviors or attitudes

Every night compare the two sides

244

Daily Inventory

Month _____ Year _____

BENEFITS
Strive for these

If this side--10

DRAWBACKS
Avoid these

If this side--1

EVALUATE YOUR DAY

BENEFITS	1	2	3	4	5	6	7	8	9	10	11	12	13	14	15	16	17	18	19	20	21	22	23	24	25	26	27	28	29	30	31	DRAWBACKS
not more important than anyone else	4	5	4	4	4	6	6	6	6																							grandiose send of self-importance
no fantasies of unlimited success, power, love	7	8	7	4	4	7	8	8	7																							fantasies of unlimited success, power, love
sees himself/herself as equal to others	0	1	0	1	1	1	0	0	0																							belief that he/she is special
does not need the praise of others	8	8	5	5	4	7	7	8	8																							requires excessive admiration
no sense of entitlement	4	5	4	4	8	8	9	8	8																							sense of entitlement
respects others	9	9	9	8	8	9	9	8	8																							takes advantage of others to achieve his/her own end
empathetic towards others	4	3	8	3	8	4	7	7	8																							lacks empathy; won't identify with others
not envious of others nor believes ohters of him/her	1	1	1	2	1	0	1	1	2																							envious of others; belief that others envy him/her
humble	5	7	4	3	6	6	2	3	3																							arrogant, haughty behaviors or attitudes

Every night compare the two sides

This person should focus on his belief that he is better than everyone else. He believes that others are envious of him. He also has a strong belief that he is of great importance. Serving others would be a great task for him to do. Helping him see himself for who he is and not what he has would be helpful. If he could see himself as a child of God and then see others as children of God then that would put everyone on the same level.

Cluster C

People who appear anxious or fearful.

Avoidant Personality Disorder

Avoidant personality disorder is, "A pervasive pattern of social inhibition, feelings of inadequacy, and hypersensitivity to negative evaluation, beginning by early adulthood and present in a variety of contexts, as indicated by four (or more) of the following:

1. Avoids occupational activities that involve significant interpersonal contact, because of fears of criticism, disapproval, or rejection;

2. Is unwilling to get involved with people unless certain of being liked;

3. Shows restraint within intimate relationships because of the fear of being shamed or ridiculed;

4. Is preoccupied with being criticized or rejected in social situations;

5. Is inhibited in new interpersonal situations because of feelings of inadequacy;

6. Views self as socially inept, personally unappealing, or inferior to others;

7. Is unusually reluctant to take personal risks or to engage in any new activities because they may prove embarrassing."[64]

First we begin with Avoidant Personality Disorder. These people have a pattern of social inhibition, feelings of inadequacy, and hypersensitivity to negative evaluation. You can see how these three criteria all deal with perception. Their perception affects their personality.

They sometimes avoid occupational activities that involve significant interpersonal contact because of fears of criticism, disapproval, or rejection. Their fears are derived from their perceptions. These types of fears would be included under the subsection 'Erroneously Predicting the Future' as discussed in the section on Depression. Their fears are made up from their thoughts. These thoughts are illogical, irrational, and absolutely false. However, I do not invalidate their feelings because all feelings are valid. If I can get my client to tell me why they are afraid, then I can help them change their perception by changing their thoughts.

The other thing I would do here is ask why they care so much about what others think or say about them. Why is their self-worth based upon what others say or think and not on what God thinks of them? With regards to this fear, I would also have them take a piece of paper and draw a line down the middle. Then I would have them write above the left-side column, "Pros" and write "Cons" above the opposite side. I would have them list on the left side all the benefits of being fearful of criticism, disapproval, or rejection. On the right side, I would have them list all negative aspects that come from being fearful of criticism, disapproval, or rejection. Then I would have them compare the two sides with the pros and cons staring them in the face.

They may be unwilling to get involved with people unless they are certain of being liked. With their unwillingness, I would have them list why people might dislike them. I would explain that some people will like them and some people will not, but that is just part of life, and we cannot please everybody. I would try and get them to identify their values and get in touch with God. Then I would teach them that happiness is based upon living in accordance with their values and is not based upon what others think of them.

They might show restraint within intimate relationships because of the fear of being shamed or ridiculed. You can understand how hard it is to treat someone with such an ingrained perception of fear. These fears may have begun when they were little and were made fun of by family members or children in school. Schools are the ideal setting for children to be shamed or ridiculed by other students. For example, starting in junior high and then in high school, the boys are required to take showers after their P.E. class. I do not know about your school, but in my school we all had to stand around a pole with showerheads all around the pole. More developed boys mercilessly made fun of less developed boys. This could easily initiate fears in the underdeveloped student with regards to future intimate relationships. The opposite of fear is faith. So how do we get rid of fear? We replace it with faith.

They might be preoccupied with being criticized or rejected in social situations. Once again, I go back to school as an ideal place for these fears of criticism and rejection to be planted. Junior high students are the most ruthless kids in the world. I guess this is where children begin to find their places in society as they begin to approach the adult world. Some would say that this is where the survival of the fittest begins. Sadly though, the weakest fall to the wayside even though they may be very strong in some other areas. It only seems to matter that they are weak in the areas that their peers tell them.

They may be inhibited in new interpersonal situations because of feelings of inadequacy. Many of the criteria listed above for this disorder may appear to be the same or similar, but the point is that these people are avoidant in all aspects of life and not just one. In other words, they are avoidant at work, at home, in relationships, in society, with making new friends, etc. These feelings of inadequacy are all encompassing. They cannot escape these feelings when they measure their life by other people's yardsticks, so that is what I teach my clients not to do.

A story was told to me of a handicap child who was running in the Special Olympics. If you do not know much about the Special Olympics, their message is that everyone is a winner. After a particular race, all the children were standing on the platform receiving their gold medals. As the presenter put a medal on one little girl, she raised her hands high in the air and yelled, "I did it." Her parents were in the audience and started to cry, obviously moved by the occasion. An insensitive man said to them, "Why are you crying? Everyone gets a medal." The mother turned to this man and said, "That was the first time she's ever said a word in her entire life." You see, this little girl did not care what the world thought. She did not care that everyone got a medal. She measured her life by her own yardstick, and that yardstick said she was a winner.

One yardstick that I am completely opposed to is a scale. Scales do not tell us how much our bones weigh, or how much the liquid in our bodies weighs, or how many fat cells we have. All it says is that, according to the professionals (and I would like to know who made them the professionals), if you are a female between the ages of 20 and 22 and you are 5'8" tall, then you should weigh a certain amount on the scale. The scales do not take into account genetics or race. What I tell my clients is that if they want to get in shape, then they should exercise until they feel good and not until the scale tells them they feel good. In some tribes in Africa, the heaviest women are chosen first for marriage because it is a sign of wealth. So in that country, the yardstick is different than it is here. Here some women kill themselves either through suicide or a slow death through starvation because of our society's yardstick. So you can see how detrimental it is to measure our lives by other people's yardsticks.

The avoidant person may view himself as socially inept, personally unappealing, or inferior to others. Their perception leads them into a vicious cycle where they stop trying and watch the world move on in technology and other aspects and they feel more and more inept. They might take a chance and try to socialize but find themselves out of tune with what is going on and become convinced that they are socially inept and inferior to others. They feel unappealing and rejected, and their fears are reinforced by their perceptions.

They are unusually reluctant to take personal risks or to engage in any new activities, as they may prove embarrassing. They forfeit a lot of things they would love to do because of what others may think or say. They do not take risks and do not understand that part of learning and growing is making mistakes and learning from them. Their perception says that they must be perfect or they are a total loser. This is dichotomous thinking. In order to not appear to be a loser, they give up the opportunity to be a winner because they are unwilling to take any risk that may prove embarrassing.

Daily Inventory

If someone has Avoidant Personality Disorder criteria, then I suggest they keep track of their behaviors or traits by using this daily inventory (see below) every night before going to bed. The left-side traits or behaviors are compared to the right-side traits or behaviors at the end of each day. As they compare the two sides to each other, if they believe they have portrayed the left side trait completely, then they would put a "10" in the box under that particular day's date. If they feel they have portrayed the right side completely, then they would put a "0" in the box under that particular day's date. If they feel they have portrayed both sides then they have the flexibility to rate themselves between 10 and 0. After a few days, they can easily visualize where they need to put more of their focus by seeing which line has the least numbers day after day. They would focus their energy the next day on that particular item. Below is a blank daily inventory for Avoidant Personality Disorder that can be copied. Below the blank inventory is an example of a completed chart.

Daily Inventory

Month _____ Year _____

BENEFITS
Strive for these

DRAWBACKS
Avoid these

If this side--10

If this side--1

EVALUATE YOUR DAY

BENEFITS	1	2	3	4	5	6	7	8	9	10	11	12	13	14	15	16	17	18	19	20	21	22	23	24	25	26	27	28	29	30	31	DRAWBACKS
goes to events without fear of criticism, disap-proval.																																avoids events; fears criticism & disapproval & rejection
involved despite being liked or not																																not involved unless certain of being liked
intimate without fear of being shamed & ridiculed																																restraint in intimacy; fear of being shamed & ridiculed
not worried or concerned about being criticized																																preoccupied with being criticized or rejected
free in new relationships; not inadequate																																inhibited in new relationship; fear of inadequacy
views self as social and equal to others																																views self as socially inept, unappealing or inferior
takes some risks even if it may be embarrassing																																won't take risks or try new things; may be embarrassing

Every night compare the two sides

Daily Inventory

Month _____ Year _____

BENEFITS	DRAWBACKS
Strive for these	Avoid these
If this side--10	If this side--1

EVALUATE YOUR DAY

BENEFITS	1	2	3	4	5	6	7	8	9	10	11	12	13	14	15	16	17	18	19	20	21	22	23	24	25	26	27	28	29	30	31	DRAWBACKS
goes to events without fear of criticism, disap-proval.	1	1	0	5	0	1	1	0	0																							avoids events; fears criticism & disapproval & rejection
involved despite being liked or not	6	6	4	4	5	5	6	7	6																							not involved unless certain of being liked
intimate without fear of being shamed & ridiculed	7	8	9	7	8	5	5	8	8																							restraint in intimacy; fear of being shamed & ridiculed
not worried or concerned about being criticized	1	1	1	1	1	1	1	1	1																							preoccupied with being criticized or rejected
free in new relationships; not inadequate	6	7	6	4	3	4	4	6	6																							inhibited in new relationship; fear of inadequacy
views self as social and equal to others	3	3	3	2	3	6	7	5	5																							views self as socially inept, unappealing or inferior
takes some risks even if it may be embarrassing	6	6	7	6	4	3	4	6	4																							won't take risks or try new things; may be embarrassing

Every night compare the two sides

This person should focus on not worrying about being criticized. He also needs to work on his relationship with God. With God's approval, he would not care so much about what others think. He needs to worry more about lining up his actions with God's values and realizing that some will like him and some will not. If someone tells him they do not like him, then he can simply put their name down on the list of people who do not like him and then hang out with the people who do.

Dependent Personality Disorder

Dependent Personality Disorder is, "A pervasive and excessive need to be taken care of that leads to submissive and clinging behavior and fears of separation, beginning by early adulthood and present in a variety of contexts, as indicated by five (or more) of the following:

1. Has difficulty making everyday decisions without an excessive amount of advice and reassurance from others;

2. Needs others to assume responsibility for most major areas of his or her life;

3. Has difficulty expressing disagreement with others because of fear of loss of support or approval. **Note:** Do not include realistic fears of retribution;

4. Has difficulty initiating projects or doing things on his or her own (because of a lack of self-confidence in judgment or abilities rather than a lack of motivation or energy);

5. Goes to excessive lengths to obtain nurturance and support from others, to the point of volunteering to do things that are unpleasant;

6. Feels uncomfortable or helpless when alone because of exaggerated fears of being unable to care for himself or herself;

7. Urgently seeks another relationship as a source of care and support when a close relationship ends;

8. Is unrealistically preoccupied with fears of being left to take care of himself or herself."[65]

A person with Dependent Personality Disorder needs to be taken care of to such a point that it leads to submissive clinging behavior and fear of separation. They can become so dependent that if you tell them they need to separate from the other person; they might actually experience physical withdrawal symptoms similar to a drug addict coming off of drugs. It is amazing to watch the similarities.

They have difficulty making everyday decisions without an excessive amount of advice and reassurance from others. If left to themselves, they doubt their abilities and freeze up. They do not have the self-esteem and confidence they need to make their own choices. By not making their own choices, they never get the chance to see the results of their own decisions. It is easier to do what others tell you to do because that way, if something goes wrong, you are not to blame. The downside is when things go well you do not get the credit or feel the sense of satisfaction either. Your self-esteem and confidence cannot increase. In fact, your self-esteem does not even stay stagnant but actually begins to decline, as you face the reality that you cannot make your own decisions due to your fear of making a mistake. This helps satisfy the need for others who assume responsibility for most major areas of your life. This sounds a lot like a person in a co-dependent relationship.

Can you see how a change of perception would benefit this person? If their perception would allow them to take a little risk and make their own decision, then they stand to benefit from it whether it turns out good or bad. If it turns out good, then their self-esteem and confidence increases. If it turned out bad, they have the opportunity to learn that success often comes from failure. I like the quote, "It matters not if you try and fail and try and fail again; it matters a whole lot if you try and fail and fail to try again."

People who have Dependent Personality Disorder have difficulty expressing disagreement with others because of fear of loss of support or approval. This was discussed in the previous chapter; but let me just say that if their perception centered more around what God thinks than what man thinks, they would be better off. If they can change their perception to allow them to disagree without worrying about losing support or approval from others, then they would be able to do so. It is the idea of, "Let's agree to disagree." Their perceptions are stopping them from expressing their true feelings.

They have difficulty initiating projects or doing things on their own (because of a lack of self-confidence in judgment or abilities rather than a lack of motivation or energy). Notice in the criteria that they do not avoid completing projects because of a lack of motivation but rather because of their perception of their judgment or abilities is minimal. There is a lot of wasted potential in this individual. Dr. Frankl said that everyone is unique in the sense that what one person has to offer society cannot be duplicated by anyone else (or everyone else) no matter how hard we try. When the person who has Dependent Personality Disorder does not give to society what he has to offer, society loses.

They go to excessive lengths to obtain nurturing and support from others, to the point of volunteering to do things that are unpleasant. The only way I know how to get people to stop caring about what others think is to get them in touch with God and get His "thumbs up" in their life. Once they know that God loves them, they do not have to rely on what others think. People with Dependent Personality Disorder want the nurturance and support from others because that tells them they are okay. But can you see how others might take advantage of their vulnerability? And often times they do, but the people who have Dependent Personality Disorder do not see it because all they want is the other person's support.

People who have Dependent Personality Disorder feel uncomfortable or helpless when alone because of exaggerated fears of being unable to care for themselves. Their perception exaggerates their fear and stops them from being independent. Often times their thoughts say, "What if I succeed? Then I'll have to keep succeeding and I don't know if I can." Or another one I've heard is, "If I succeed then others will expect more from me; it's easier to be helpless." These thoughts or perceptions help to paralyze them.

When a close relationship ends, they urgently seek another relationship as a source of care and support. This person is similar to a person who has Borderline Personality Disorder in the sense that they fear abandonment and must quickly find a new relationship. People who have Dependent Personality Disorder, however, are lost without a host. I use the analogy that people who have Dependent Personality Disorder are parasites who feed off of a host, and when the host goes away, the parasite must find another host to survive.

They are unrealistically preoccupied with fears of being left to take care of themselves. Once again we see the perception or fear of not being able to care for themselves thus creating fear and anxiety. This fear is what keeps people home rather than going out into society on their own. I know people who are 30 to 40 years old who are still at home with mom and dad because of their fear of caring for themselves. Their perception or fear controls their life.

One thing they do over and over to see how their relationship is going is they take the other person's emotional temperature. In other words, they ask questions like, "Are you mad at me?" Or they state it as a fact, "You are mad at me," even when you are not mad. If you don't answer a phone call or text within a certain time frame they might text you, "I don't blame you for being mad at me." It is a form of manipulation that should not be given any attention. Tell them, "I will not respond to such questions or statements. If I'm mad at you then I will tell you." Then, hold your boundaries. Tell them you will only talk to them on Fridays or whatever schedule you set up. Remember, setting boundaries is the easy part. Holding boundaries is the hard part, and I promise you they will test them to see how flexible your boundaries are. Be strong. Your boundaries are there to protect you not hurt them.

Daily Inventory

     If someone has Dependent Personality Disorder criteria, then I suggest they keep track of their behaviors or traits by using this daily inventory (see below) every night before going to bed. The left-side traits or behaviors are compared to the right-side traits or behaviors at the end of each day. As they compare the two sides to each other, if they believe they have portrayed the left side trait completely, then they would put a "10" in the box under that particular day's date. If they feel they have portrayed the right side completely, then they would put a "0" in the box under that particular day's date. If they feel they have portrayed both sides then they have the flexibility to rate themselves between 10 and 0. After a few days, they can easily visualize where they need to put more of their focus by seeing which line has the least numbers day after day. They would focus their energy the next day on that particular item. Below is a blank daily inventory for the Dependent Personality Disorder that can be copied. Below the blank inventory is an example of a completed chart.

Daily Inventory

Month _____ Year _____

BENEFITS
Strive for these

If this side--10

DRAWBACKS
Avoid these

If this side--1

EVALUATE YOUR DAY

BENEFITS	1	2	3	4	5	6	7	8	9	10	11	12	13	14	15	16	17	18	19	20	21	22	23	24	25	26	27	28	29	30	31	DRAWBACKS
makes decisions by oneself																																difficulty making decisions without excessive advice
assumes responsibility for one's own life																																needs others to assume responsibility for your life
able to disagree without fear of losing approval																																difficulty expressing disagreement for fear of loss of approval
initiates projects because of a belief that it can be done																																difficulty initiating doing things because of lack of self-confidence
finds nurturance from within																																goes to excessive lengths to obtain nurturance and support
comfortable with self and able to care for self																																feels uncomfortable when alone for fear of unable to care for self
can be alone without needing a relationship																																seeks another relationship soon after a close one just ended
confidant to take care of self																																unrealistically preoc-cupied with fears of being left to care for self

Every night compare the two sides

Daily Inventory

BENEFITS
Strive for these

If this side--10

DRAWBACKS
Avoid these

If this side--1

EVALUATE YOUR DAY

Benefit	1	2	3	4	5	6	7	8	9	10	11	12	13	14	15	16	17	18	19	20	21	22	23	24	25	26	27	28	29	30	31	Drawback
makes decisions by oneself	2	3	2	2	2	6	2	2	3																							difficulty making decisions without excessive advice
assumes responsibility for one's own life	5	6	2	2	2	2	3	2	3																							needs others to assume responsibility for your life
able to disagree without fear of losing approval	3	2	3	4	5	6	6	4	3																							difficulty expressing disagreement for fear of loss of approval
initiates projects because of a belief that it can be done	2	2	4	3	6	2	1	1	1																							difficulty initiating doing things because of lack of self-confidence
finds nurturance from within	3	6	6	6	6	6	4	4	4																							goes to excessive lengths to obtain nurturance and support
comfortable with self and able to care for self	4	3	3	4	6	7	6	4	4																							feels uncomfortable when alone for fear of unable to care for self
can be alone without needing a relationship	9	9	9	9	9	9	9	9	9																							seeks another relationship soon after a close one just ended
confidant to take care of self	6	4	4	4	7	8	7	8	9																							unrealistically preoc-cupied with fears of being left to care for self

Every night compare the two sides

This person's greatest need is to learn to make decisions himself. He must also assume responsibility for his own life. He needs to take the risk of deciding himself what he will and will not do. He must not care so much about what others think about him but instead he needs to do things for himself. If he is still living at home, it would be fantastic for him to move not only out of the house, but all the way out of town away from his parents so that he is forced to make life decisions on his own. He will learn that he can do it which will reinforce a new perception of "I can" verses his current perception which is, "I can't".

Obsessive-Compulsive Personality Disorder

Obsessive-compulsive personality disorder (OCPD) is different from obsessive-compulsive disorder (OCD) as described earlier. OCPD is, "A pervasive pattern of preoccupation with orderliness, perfectionism, and mental and interpersonal control, at the expense of flexibility, openness, and efficiency, beginning by early adulthood and present in a variety of contexts, as indicated by four (or more) of the following:

1. Is preoccupied with details, rules, lists, order, organization, or schedules to the extent that the major point of the activity is lost;

2. Shows perfectionism that interferes with task completion (e.g., is unable to complete a project because his or her own overly strict standards are not met);

3. Is excessively devoted to work and productivity to the exclusion of leisure; activities and friendships (not accounted for by obvious economic necessity)

4. Is overconscientious, scrupulous, and inflexible about matters of morality, ethics, or values (not accounted for by cultural or religious identification);

5. Is unable to discard worn-out or worthless objects even when they have no sentimental value;

6. Is reluctant to delegate tasks or to work with others unless they submit to exactly his or her way of doing things;

7. Adopts a miserly spending style toward both self and others; money is viewed as something to be hoarded for future catastrophes;

8. Shows rigidity and stubbornness."[66]

OCPD is a disorder of perfectionism and may include hoarding things. This person "is preoccupied with detail, rules, lists, order, organization, or schedules to the extent that the major point of the activity is lost." Have you ever known someone who tries so hard to make the activity fun by scheduling every single minute that no one has fun? When I was in school, I had a professor once tell us as a class, "I want you to have fun with this project." People who have OCPD struggle with such assignments because their focus is too much on getting it right and following the rules. They lose the "fun" in it. When I do experiential activities with my clients, the main goal is for my clients to learn about themselves. People who have OCPD get so caught up in whether the group is doing things right that they miss the point of the activity - to learn about themselves.

They "show perfectionism that interferes with task completion." When I get a new client in treatment, I have them write their autobiography so that I can learn about them more quickly. One of the rules I give them is that they cannot start over, throw away, scratch out, or delete anything. They can, however, add to it. The reason I say this is because I have so many clients who believe their papers have to be perfect. When they see a mistake (in their perception), they throw the paper away and never finish the assignment because it is not perfect. I explain the only way to have a perfect paper is that the autobiography is completely honest.

The next criterion states that people who have OCPD are workaholics. Not because they need the money, but because they have to be perfect. They literally spend hours and hours wasting their employer's money just to produce a perfect project. They miss out on activities with family and friends because of their "need" to work.

They are "overconscientious, scrupulous, and inflexible about matters of morality, ethics, or values (not accounted for by cultural or religious identification)." This overconscientiousness is due to their perception. Their perception tells them they must be 100% perfect with no exceptions. If they make a mistake in ethics, values, or morality, they believe they are broken, damaged, and worthless. There is nothing wrong with wanting to do the best we can, but we have to accept the fact that we are humans and we do make mistakes. That does not make us broken, damaged or worthless.

People who have OCPD are unable to discard worn-out or worthless objects even when they have no sentimental value. This might seem contradictory to perfection, but the thought process seems to be that "discarding something would be wasting it." There may be the thought that "I may need it later, and if I throw it away, I won't have it." This criterion does not fit everyone with OCPD, but it certainly describes many.

They are reluctant to delegate tasks or to work with others unless the others will submit to exactly their way of doing things. The project has to be perfect and if someone else will not do it perfectly (according to the perception of the person who has OCPD), then the person who has OCPD will just do it himself to ensure perfection. These people get frustrated with others and often times say, "I'll just do it myself." The other person might not understand the frustration being displayed at them, but in reality it is not even about them. People who have OCPD have an internal need for perfection caused by their own perception of perfection. One perception that would help them change would be, "So what?" If they could ask themselves this question whenever something is not perfect and then follow through and answer it logically, it would help them see the irrational thoughts they are having.

People who have OCPD adopt a miserly spending style toward both self and others. Money is viewed as something to be hoarded for future catastrophes. Remember, they have a need to be perfect not only now but also in the future. They want to prepare for any future catastrophes so much that they do not enjoy any of their hard-earned money in the present. This does not include people who are saving up for a particular item or event but is rather a person who views money as something to be hoarded. I have had clients who felt $1000 in the bank account was great. I have dealt with a woman who had $100,000 in her bank account and panicked because it was not enough.

They show rigidity and stubbornness. Things, events, projects, and details must be perfect. When others do not comply with their perception of perfection, they get upset and stubborn. As mentioned above, it is not because of anything the other person has done but it is to satisfy an internal requisite brought on by their own perception.

A big difference between people who have OCD and people who have OCPD is the people with OCD know it is all in their heads; people with OCPD do not. People with OCPD think the whole world should be more like them. They have no need for treatment because they are close to perfection and the counselor needs to focus on their spouse who is not perfect. They are very difficult to treat for this very reason. People with OCD want to get rid of their obsessions or compulsions while people with OCPD are convinced they are living the right way while those around them are not.

Daily Inventory

If someone has Obsessive-Compulsive Personality Disorder criteria, then I suggest they keep track of their behaviors or traits by using this daily inventory (see below) every night before going to bed. The left-side traits or behaviors are compared to the right-side traits or behaviors at the end of each day. As they compare the two sides to each other, if they believe they have portrayed the left side trait completely, then they would put a "10" in the box under that particular day's date. If they feel they have portrayed the right side completely, then they would put a "0" in the box under that particular day's date. If they feel they have portrayed both sides then they have the flexibility to rate themselves between 10 and 0. After a few days, they can easily visualize where they need to put more of their focus by seeing which line has the least numbers day after day. They would focus their energy the next day on that particular item. Below is a blank daily inventory for the Obsessive-Compulsive Personality Disorder that can be copied. Below the blank inventory is an example of a completed chart.

Daily Inventory

Month _____ Year _____

BENEFITS Strive for these **If this side--10**	EVALUATE YOUR DAY (1-31)	DRAWBACKS Avoid these **If this side--1**
enjoys activities without losing focus on details		preoccupied with details so that point of activity is lost
completes tasks regularly whether perfect or not		perfectionism interferes with task completion
enjoys leisure time and friends		devoted to work to the exclusion of leisure activities and friends
flexible with matters of morality and values		overconscientious, inflexible with matters of morality, or values
can discard objects		unable to discard worn-outworthless objects even with no value
delegates tasks and allow others to do it their way		won't delegate tasks unless they submit to his way of doing it
money is spent without feeling it's taboo		money is hoarded not spent, adopts a misery spending style
flexible and open with others		shows rigidity and stubbornness

Days: 1 2 3 4 5 6 7 8 9 10 11 12 13 14 15 16 17 18 19 20 21 22 23 24 25 26 27 28 29 30 31

Every night compare the two sides

Daily Inventory

Month _____ Year _____

BENEFITS Strive for these *If this side--10*		DRAWBACKS Avoid these *If this side--1*

EVALUATE YOUR DAY

Benefit	1	2	3	4	5	6	7	8	9	10	11	12	13	14	15	16	17	18	19	20	21	22	23	24	25	26	27	28	29	30	31	Drawback
enjoys activities without losing focus on details	3	2	2	3	4	5	2	3	2																							preoccupied with details so that point of activity is lost
completes tasks regularly whether perfect or not	1	1	1	1	1	1	1	1	1																							perfectionism interferes with task completion
enjoys leisure time and friends	4	5	6	6	3	3	4	4	6																							devoted to work to the exclusion of leisure activities and friends
flexible with matters of morality and values	1	1	1	1	1	1	1	1	1																							overconscientious, inflexible with matters of morality, or values
can discard objects	9	9	9	9	9	9	9	9	9																							unable to discard worn-out/worthless objects even with no value
delegates tasks and allow others to do it their way	7	4	4	3	4	4	6	6	6																							won't delegate tasks unless they submit to his way of doing it
money is spent without feeling it's taboo	8	7	8	9	8	5	9	9	9																							money is hoarded not spent; adopts a misery spending style
flexible and open with others	3	3	2	3	6	5	3	2	6																							shows rigidity and stubbornness

Every night compare the two sides

269

This person should focus on completing tasks without insisting on perfection. According to the chart, they do not have a single day where this was not a problem for them. I would suggest that they forget about all the other criteria and focus on this one only for now. After working on this for a few days, I would give them the same advice but in regards to their "over conscientiousness and inflexibility with regards to morals, ethics, and values." They should then focus on enjoying the activity without getting lost in the details. Their perception is so engrained in their head that taking on one issue at a time would be plenty and very beneficial.

Section V: Summary

Final Chapter or Is It?

In the first chapter of this book, I was sitting on the deck of a cruise line enjoying peace and relaxation. I discussed that I was going to be in court testifying that a woman should lose her child to the state. Here is the rest of the story.

While I was standing outside the courtroom, I began to get nervous and felt butterflies in my stomach. I stood on the second floor of the courthouse looking over the rail at people walking into the building. I imagined that I was on the deck of the cruise line again looking overboard at the white waves and the sun reflecting off the water. I imagined that beautiful sun setting in the horizon with nothing between me and the sun except the breathtakingly beautiful ocean. My favorite day on the cruise was the day we had at sea with nothing to do. I found it so relaxing to just look overboard and watch the waves lap against the ship. I was able to recapture that relaxing feeling in the courthouse that day through those powerful memories.

I was invited into the courtroom and asked to take the witness stand. After being sworn in, I took my seat. I was again very nervous, so I put myself back on the cruise ship in my memory again and I found peace. I did this little exercise in between every question. I must have been the calmest person to ever sit on that witness stand. I would carefully answer the question asked of me and then go back to the deck of the ship and watch the sunrise and listen to the waves. That scene has become my "happy place," and I go there when I need to relax.

So how was it that I could be so relaxed when everything around me said that I should be very nervous? It was my perception of what was going on. I actually convinced my mind (which is the part of my body that causes stress, anxiety, and nervousness) that I was on a cruise ship enjoying the beautiful surroundings with nothing to do but rest and enjoy the scenery. How did I do it? I simply changed my perception. I imagined it in my mind's eye.

(Before I move on, you probably want to know what happened in court. The state did take this woman's baby away and gave her to a friend of the family in another state to raise her child. What about the mother? She continues to struggle with her alcoholism and has a very unstable life.)

Perception Affects the World

In 1992, I traveled to Jerusalem for my first semester of college. As part of the curriculum, I studied the Jewish and Muslim cultures. I remember sitting in a classroom listening to a Jewish leader talk about the history of the Jews and why Jerusalem, especially the Temple Mount, belonged to the Jews. I walked out of that class thinking, "The Jews are right." I then walked into a class where a Muslim leader spoke to us about their history and why Jerusalem, especially the Temple Mount, belonged to the Muslims. I walked out of that class thinking, "The Muslims are right." To this day, I am convinced there is no answer to their dilemma because the beliefs of each side are too deeply rooted and not likely to change.

Because both cultures have different perceptions, they live their lives in ever-increasing opposition to each other, and they have for thousands of years. The government even supports this conflict to the point that if you are a Jew, your car has a yellow license plate, but if you are Arab, your car has a blue license plate. Now if a car with a yellow license plate drives through an Arab part of town, the chances are good that the Arabs will flip the car over and light it on fire. The opposite is true as well.

A co-student of mine thought it would be funny to wear a Jewish Kippah (Yarmulke) and walk through an Arab part of town. As he walked back to the college from the city, a few

Arab men stormed up to him and ripped the Kippah off his head and thrust it into his chest and said, "You're lucky we know you're an American. If you ever do that again, we will piss all over you." In the student's naïve perception, he thought it was a joke. To someone who lives in Jerusalem and understands the conflict, there is nothing funny about it, as so many lives have been lost over this intense issue.

While I was a missionary in Chile, I lived in a small town called Requinoa. I was told that missionaries had not been in that town for quite some time because there was an ongoing community war between one subdivision and another. I was told that my companion and I would be the first missionaries called back into this community.

I was fed by a lady I called, "Mamita." My Mamita strongly urged us to be in before dark. She said our lives would be at risk if we did not follow her advice. So here I had a perception (should I choose to adopt it) that could paralyze me and prevent me from doing the work I was sent there to do.

I received a new companion who was Chilean, but he had grown up in a different part of the country from where we lived. His family was well-off, so he was dealing with some fears of his own. He had played an electric guitar in a Chilean rock band before his mission. He played the guitar by ear which we decided to use for our benefit. There were groups of men sitting in the streets, playing guitars, smoking, drinking, and essentially loitering. I walked up to these men and asked to borrow their guitar. One of them handed me their guitar, and I then handed it to my companion and said to the men, "Name a song, any song." They would then name a song, and my companion would play it perfectly. They loved us. Pretty soon, we were playing soccer with them in the streets, and we felt safe around them.

We started coming home at 10:00 p.m. My Mamita was so upset and worried by this. She told us to come home sooner because of the great danger we were in. I tried to convince her that we had made friends with the "good" people and the "bad" people; therefore we were not an enemy to any of them. We felt safe. I lived there for a short two months and never had a problem. I again suggest that the main difference between the different groups and us was our perception. I felt welcomed by the "good" and the "bad" in Chile, and I felt welcomed by both the Jews and the Arabs.

If I can just understand my perception and realize that my perception may be wrong, then I become more open to others' perceptions. Whether or not I agree with them does not seem to be the deciding factor as to whether or not we are friends. What seems to matter is my ability to let them have their own perception - period. We can share our perceptions with each other and even disagree, but in the end, we are still friends.

It Divides Us

I have a good friend who is a Methodist. He grew up in the southern United States and tells me about how the Baptists and the Methodists hate each other down there. He said they just cannot accept each other for their differences. Now I know that is not universally true. I know of a Methodist who loves a Baptist very much. But my friend's perception comes from living on a street in a neighborhood where religion dominated the conversations and everything else.

I lived in Brandon, Florida, for the summer of 1992 before I went to Jerusalem. In church one day, a man stood up and said, "It's great to see a bunch of Yankees and Confederates sitting in church today and getting along without fighting." I did not have a clue what he was talking about! I thought the civil war ended more than a century ago. But then my Methodist friend moved in by me, and he explained to me that the conflict and feelings between the North and the South are still alive and well in the South, even today. As he was trying to sell his house in the South, a neighbor threatened him that if he sold his house to a Black family, he (the neighbor) would burn his house down. I am completely dumbfounded by

274

this. My perception was that this was something I read about in history books in school. In other words, it was an event that happened in the past, not the present. It is quite obvious to me that some of these "past" perceptions are holding strong in the present.

At the end of the 1990's, I was involved in opening a residential substance abuse program. It took a long time to do so because of the attitude of "not in my backyard" caused by the neighbors of our treatment center. The facility was located in the midst of a wealthy neighborhood full of very nice expensive homes. The fight got so bad that some of the neighbors cut our telephone lines, stopped our sewage system, broke our water lines, shot out the light above our trout pond, took the largest trout out and filleted it and left it on the deck for us to see, shot a hole in one of the counselor's car windshield, blocked our driveway, reported drug use on the facility, reported that we had underground tunnels where we hid people, and used political power illegally.

It was a tough time for us because our intentions were pure and wholesome. We only wanted to help addicts recover. Some of the neighbors were in recovery themselves, but they did not want anyone to know, so they would approach us privately and tell us they wished us the best. On the other hand, some of the neighbors wanted to tar and feather us. Perceptions were across the board.

We were told, upon opening our treatment facility; that we needed to hold an open house for everyone living within 100 yards of the facility. I made invitations for all the homes within 100 yards, and for some reason I made the invitations on off-white paper. The night of the open house, lots of people showed up. Some even showed up with an invitation on pure white paper, suggesting that copies of my original invitation had been distributed to homes farther than the 100-yard requirement. One lady approached me that night and screamed in my face, "Get out of my backyard!" I said, "We would like to explain to you what we do." She screamed again, "I don't care what you do. Get out of my backyard!" We had moved into an old polygamist compound and the neighbors told us they wanted the polygamists back.

That night as I drove home on a road filled with luxury homes, much like the ones our "neighbors" at the treatment center owned, I said to myself, "I would rather live with a bunch of addicts than a bunch of rich people any day." I then thought, "Am I doing the same thing these rich people are doing?" They are judging us and now I am judging them. I thought about the rich people that I knew personally who were very nice. I reminded myself that I shouldn't overgeneralize and say, "All rich people" or "all drug addicts" or "all the neighbors" were a certain way. That simply was not true. That night I really had to fight my perception and be open to another perception.

Objectify

I recently learned that the way we segregate ourselves is by objectifying other people. This is also how we can torture or beat up another human being. This is also how we can belittle or emotionally abuse another human being. Simply put, we do not view them as a human being with feelings and emotions and a story to tell. Instead we objectify them and see them as an object to be used for our gain or simply an obstacle standing in the way of getting what we want.

I was taught by the Anasazi Group, a wilderness rehabilitation center in Arizona, that when we view others as human beings we also honor ourselves. We honor ourselves because we too are human beings. As we value others as humans and because we are humans too, then we must also have value. However, when we objectify others, we betray ourselves. We betray ourselves because if they are nothing more than an object and they are humans, then we too must be worth nothing more than an object because we are humans too. So, by the way I treat other human beings, I either honor myself or betray myself. This became an "Ah, ha!" moment in my life. It changed my perception.

Soon after learning this, I was standing in a bank waiting to deposit a check. There were three people in front of me in line, and two people were already working with the tellers. It seemed that minutes had passed and nothing was happening. I began to get restless. I thought, "Maybe I should turn around and ask out loud to the other bank workers sitting at their desks, 'Could we get some help up here?'" I then stopped and realized that I had objectified the people in front of me. I was not thinking of them as human beings with a story to tell. I was seeing them as an obstacle to getting what I wanted (i.e., deposit my check and go home).

As I changed my perception, I calmed down. I looked at the man in the front of the line and I pictured him going home to a family. I pictured his little boy running up to him and jumping on his lap and being excited that daddy was home. I imagined these people having lives with good and bad in it. I started to feel for them. I got outside myself and by doing so I paradoxically honored myself. I left the bank peaceful and happy about my new insights or perceptions.

Later I was driving home and was behind a few cars driving 5 mph slower than the speed limit on a one-lane highway. I started to go nuts and anxiously looked for a chance to pass. Then the thought crossed my mind, "You are seeing these human beings as obstacles to getting what you want." Once again, I had to stop myself and see their humanness. Once again, the process brought me tranquility. Because I too am human, I fall short of remembering this all the time, and I still find myself objectifying people. But this just shows me how much I need to work on changing my perception. But to change my perception, I must be willing to accept the fact that my perception might be wrong.

Shocking For Worms

I used to fish a lot when I was a child, but I never actually caught a fish. Then one day when I was 16 years old, I went fishing with my friend, Mark. I caught a fish and Mark told me I had to kill it. I asked him to do it, but he declined. I asked him how to kill it, and he told me to slap it against a rock. I did not like the idea, but I figured if I was going to do it I would need to hit it pretty hard so it would not live through it. I slammed the fish so hard, the chain in the fish's mouth ripped through his mouth and gills. I was so disgusted that I gave up fishing. I gave all my gear to my brother, and told him I never wanted to fish again.

When I got married, I quickly discovered that my in-laws liked to fish. I reconsidered and picked up fishing again for one purpose - to learn how to take the fish from the lake to the plate. I wanted to learn how to fish as a survival skill in case I ever needed it. My boss at work (not my boss at home) offered to teach me how to fish without killing the fish. I was intrigued and went ice fishing with him to learn. He had a fishing hut that we fished in. When he caught a fish, he took it off the line, opened the hut door, and threw the fish out onto the ice. He closed the door and said, "When we leave, it will be dead, but we don't actually have to kill it." I am not necessarily trying to encourage this type of killing, but it was a different perception. (By the way, it was the same boss who told me I could make jerky out of any kind of meat. I tried it with ground beef. It was difficult but I made it.)

Next, I did not want to spend so much money for worms to take fishing. My boss told me how to shock worms out of the ground, so I did not have to buy them. He told me to take a small extension cord, strip the ends, and attach the ends to two different screwdrivers. He then told me to water the grass. I was to plug the extension cord in and stand on a piece of wood (wood is not a conductor of electricity). Once I was on a piece of wood I was to take both screwdrivers and plunge them both into the grass saturated with water.

Before you read on, you should know that I am not the brightest light in the harbor, and I do not recommend you do what I did. I stuck the screwdrivers into the ground. Nothing happened. I wondered what was wrong. I took the screwdrivers over to the metal shed in my backyard and touched the screwdrivers to the shed. Nothing happened. I wondered what was wrong. I grabbed both screwdrivers in my hands. Nothing happened. I thought that maybe the outlet wasn't working. I took my setup and went into the bathroom where I had shaved earlier so I knew that outlet was working. I plugged the extension cord into the bathroom outlet, and I touched the screwdriver to the screw that was holding the light plate onto the wall. An explosion occurred. The wall was black and my wife yelled from the other side of the house, "What was that?!" I was frantically wiping down the wall, spraying an air freshener, and yelling to my wife, "It was nothing."

My perception was innocent. I was not raised with much electrical or construction knowledge. If there was a problem in my house, my dad would call someone to come over and fix the problem. I never learned how to fix things. My grandpa was an auto mechanic, and he hated the lifestyle so much that he refused to teach his children about cars in an effort to prevent them from being mechanics like he was. So I did not know much about electricity, and I learned a lot that day. My kids taught me even more when they stuck two keys into an electrical outlet in my house and saw "fire" come out of the wall. My electrician told me that if both the boys were touching each other when they had done that, they would have been fried because there would have been a closed circuit, but fortunately they were not touching each other.

Back to my point, if my perception was different, as it is today, then I would never have touched the screwdrivers to the metal shed. If my perception was different, as it is today, then I would never have grabbed the screwdrivers with both my hands. If my perception was different then, as it is today, I would never have taken the screwdriver into the bathroom and touched it to the screw in the wall.

Children's Perception

Children see the world much differently than we do. I walked by my boy the other day and told him, "It's time to take a shower." About 15 minutes later, my wife walked by him and said, "Didn't your father tell you to take a shower?" My boy responded, "No, he just said it was shower time." Now whether or not this was truly his perception or he was just trying to manipulate I am not exactly sure. I have my opinion of course, but that is my perception.

One night another of my boys (I have five of them) came walking in my bedroom, and I believe he was actually walking in his sleep, and actually I hope that he was. He walked into my bedroom closet and dropped his pants and was about to use our laundry chute as a urinal. My wife and I quickly stopped him and helped him into the bathroom. The next day, my boy did not remember a thing. That night, however, his perception was reality to him, though he was way off the mark.

When I was a child, my sister used to walk in her sleep. On one occasion, she sleep-walked right out of the house and continued on down the street where a cop found her and brought her home. On another occasion, she walked around the block and ended up at a friend's house where she knocked on the door. When they answered in the middle of the night, she told them that I was beating her up, and she needed to spend the night at their house. That was not true, but that night her perception was reality to her.

April Fool's Day was approaching a while back, and my wife and I were explaining to our son what a prank was. It later became obvious that his perception was different than ours. On the evening of April Fool's Day, my wife went to hop in bed, and she pulled the covers on the bed down and found ketchup all over the sheets. My boy thought that would be a funny prank. Our perception that night was "That's funny that he thinks that way, but it definitely is not funny." He did not get in trouble, but we did sit him down and taught him what a prank is and what it is not.

As parents, we sometimes get after our children when we have not done enough to teach them. One mother got after her toddler for walking into the street. The mother said to her, "Didn't I tell you not to get off the sidewalk?" The little girl responded, "Mommy, what's a sidewalk?" Do we teach our children sufficiently before we get after them? If we have taught them verbally, what have we taught them nonverbally? Have you ever spanked your child because they hit their brother or sister? Did you happen to say, "We don't hit in this family?" Are we hypocritical? Remember, nonverbal communication is far louder than verbal communication. Children's perceptions are founded in the lifestyle the parents give them.

Cocaine Poem

Children see the world differently than we do. We often get upset with them because we expect them to see the world the way we do. We expect them to be as intelligent as we are. We expect them to be 100% obedient. Yet we do dumb things and expect others, including our children, to accept us for our weaknesses. We aren't 100% obedient to the law. We mess up at times. For example, we might go 5 mph over the speed limit. What I am trying to say is that we are all hypocrites at times. What we want to be are hypocrites in progress.

Here is a poem which shows the perception of a daughter whose father was using cocaine:

COCAINE

Cocaine means

Heartache

Swollen Cheeks

And puffy eyes

Crying Alone

Confused

It means waiting...

Waiting for my dad

Listening for a car

Speeding up the driveway

To rescue me

I never heard one

He never came

Waiting...

I've waited and waited...

14 years I've waited

Hoped

Trusted

Wished

Dreamed

For him to come

He never came

Cocaine means

Lies

And

Lies

Cocaine stole my dad

By

Andrea Miller[67]

Maybe it is time we see the world through other people's eyes, especially the eyes of our children. How great it would be for all of us to be more like a child whose perception of life has not yet been distorted by the evils of the world. We could walk around loving everyone, accepting everyone, and playing all day long. My dad used to tell me, "If we want the children to grow up being innocent and childlike forever, then we need to kill all the adults in the world." Adults have a way of pushing their perceptions onto vulnerable children and we end up messing them up.

You probably know of children who had to grow up too fast because, for whatever reason, their mom or dad or both were not around. These children are hurt by having to gain an adult perception of the world with all its responsibilities and accountabilities. How sad! How tragic! Perception affects everything. Perception becomes everything.

Summary

Here is a story I picked up many years ago. The source is unknown.

Two battleships assigned to the training squadron had been at sea on maneuvers in heavy weather for several days. A man was serving on the lead battleship and was on watch on the bridge as night fell. The visibility was poor with patchy fog, so the captain remained on the bridge keeping an eye on all activities.

Shortly after dark, the lookout on the wing of the bridge reported, "Light, bearing on the starboard bow."

"Is it steady or moving astern?" the captain called out.

Lookout replied, "Steady, captain," which meant we were on a dangerous collision course with that ship.

The captain then called to the signalman, "Signal that ship. We are on a collision course. Advise: You change course 20 degrees."

Back came a signal, "Advisable for you to change course 20 degrees."

The captain said, "Send: I'm a captain, change course 20 degrees."

"I'm a seaman second class," was the reply. "You had better change course 20 degrees."

By that time, the captain was furious. He spat out, "Send: I'm a battleship. Change course 20 degrees."

Back came the flashing light, "I'm a lighthouse."

We changed our course.

The ship's course was quickly altered. Can you see how every aspect of our lives is affected by our perception? Can you see how our attitude is affected by our perception? Now the question is - Do you believe you can change your perception and change your life? We have a banner at work which reads, "Choices." We display it between two trees right in front of the facility so everyone coming in can read it. It reminds us that we all have choices. We no longer need to be victims of our circumstances - we can choose to be survivors. We no longer need to be acted upon - we can choose to act for ourselves.

The choices we have include our thoughts and thus our perceptions. It is hard to do. I will be the first to tell you that it is hard to be in control of our perception, which is fine because that means we are on the right track.

One Last Story

I would like to share one last story to illustrate that sometimes we just do not have a clue as to what is going on. When I was a teenager I was playing Nintendo over at my friend Chris' house. His parents were working and we were there with his younger brother Nick. Nick was bugging us and kept walking up to us and then walking away. The last time he walked up to us I reached out and pushed him away. My foot (unaware to me) was on his foot and he fell straight back and hit his head on the ground.

He began to cry. He kept crying. About ten minutes later Chris called his mom at work and she tried to talk to Nick but he was crying too much to talk so she decided to come home. Chris and my perception was, "He's being a baby. He's such a wimp." Chris even said what many people have said, "If you don't stop crying I'll give you something to cry about!" Nick's mom finally got home and Nick was still crying. She decided to take him to the doctor's office. It had been about 30 minutes since I pushed him. After they left it was back to peace and quiet for us. We were once again caught up in ourselves with no thought of Nick.

We then got a phone call from Chris' mom. She told us that when I pushed Nick down and he hit his head, he began to bleed in his head. He was drowning in his own blood and we didn't know it. Nick was taken by Life-Flight to the hospital where they were preparing for an emergency brain operation. With the blessings of heaven, Nick's bleeding stopped while on the helicopter. The hospital kept Nick for a few days watching him to make sure the bleeding didn't start up again. I bought Nick that year's baseball set to make amends and apologize. I would like to take this opportunity to tell Nick, "I'm still sorry."

How were we supposed to know that he was dying? How were we supposed to know that he wasn't just being a baby? I think this is a great story to illustrate that sometimes we just don't know the whole story. Sometimes we cannot see the whole picture and we insist that our perception is right.

Imagine that I am standing on the Rocky Mountains and the only thing I can see is a big rock in front of my face. I adamantly declare that I know exactly what is in front of me. What I do not know-because I cannot see it all-is that I am standing on a beautiful mountain range that expands for miles and miles and miles. There are people skiing on it, driving on it, living on it, fishing on it, etc.

Might my perception be wrong? It sure was the day I pushed Nick. If Chris had not called his mom to complain about Nick's crying, only God Himself could tell us what would have happened to Nick. My life could have been so different today. I could have been charged with killing him had he died. I could have spent many years in detention. Therefore, we must be willing to look at situations from different perceptions rather than always demanding that our perceptions are right.

Conclusion

The first step in the process of changing our perceptions is to recognize our perceptions as just that - OUR perceptions. The second step is to understand and believe that our perceptions might be wrong. Since there is a possibility that OUR perceptions might be wrong, the third step is being willing to entertain other perceptions. The more we work on looking at situations from other people's perceptions, the easier seeing other's perceptions becomes. The more we see them, the more we are able to imagine different perceptions in our mind. The fourth step would be choosing a perception that we like and that does not make us depressed, anxious, or upset.

In the beginning, I explained that we all live in a bit of a fairy tale. I choose to live in a happy fairy tale. My fairy tale is one where everyone is trying their best. One that says good things do come my way. One that says we all have good qualities in us, but sometimes we do dumb things. I like the world I live in. It feels good. I feel happy.

I hope this book has been helpful. I hope it has given you new thoughts and beliefs. I hope it helps you become your ideal self. I hope you can find your new world that is full of joy and happiness.

Section VI: Two Bonus Papers

The Part Pride Plays In the 12-Steps

As I read the 12-Steps, I could not help but see how pride affects almost every step. A person must truly swallow their pride if they want to make it through the 12-Steps and remain clean and sober throughout their life. A prideful person simply cannot successfully work through all 12-Steps and live a clean and sober life because their pride would not allow it. Throughout this paper, I will point out exactly how pride affects each step and how it affects all of us. I will also show what we can do to swallow the pride to allow us to embrace the steps and overcome our addictions and live a happier life.

The word "pride" is not too well understood. In this paper, we will refer to pride as a fault and will only refer to pride in the negative sense. For our purposes, self-esteem and pride are two different characteristics. Most of us are prideful without even knowing it. We are simply ignorant to the fact.

So, what is pride? What comes to your mind when you think of pride? The Webster dictionary lists the following definition: an unduly high opinion of one's self, haughtiness, and arrogance.[68] I would also like to add conceit and being self-centered. Surely, as an addict, you were only thinking of yourself when you just had to have that high. You may have even stolen money from your loved ones just to get one more buzz. The only relationship that mattered was the one you had with your chemicals.

You thought highly of yourself and your needs and gave no thought to others. Daniel J. Bayse, the author of the book, "Free as an Eagle,"[69] calls this the "Looking out for number one" attitude. It says, "I'm NUMBER ONE! I can do anything I want! Say anything I want! Anytime I want! Anywhere I want! To anyone I want! And there is nothing that you or anyone else can do about it, PERIOD!" Do these definitions and this attitude of pride ring a bell? Do any of them fit your life?

Selfishness is a key characteristic of a proud person. He wonders how everything is going to affect him, and he does not consider how it will affect anyone else. Self-conceit, self-pity, self-fulfillment, self-seeking, and self-gratification are all that matters. Looking out for number one - period!

We are all quite familiar with these definitions, and although they are elements of pride, we are still missing the main element of pride. The main element of pride is enmity. It could be enmity towards God (as you understand Him), or it could be enmity towards others. Enmity is defined as "hatred toward, hostility to, or a state of opposition." It is the power by which the evils of today wish to reign over the good.

This could simply be by hating the policeman who arrested you. Did you deserve to be arrested? Think of the number of times you should have been arrested and you were not caught. Again I ask, "Did you deserve to be arrested?" Do you hold a grudge against the people who try to keep society clean? Are you upset with the judge or your parole/probation officer? Are you hostile with those you work with? Do you think the world is out to get you so you live your life in a state of opposition to everyone around you?

Ezra Taft Benson said, "Pride is essentially competitive in nature. We pit our will against God. When we direct our pride towards God, it is the spirit of "my will and not thine be done."[70] The proud person is always seeking after his own interests and addictions, not the things which are just and right. You may have chosen alcohol or drugs over your family, health, jobs, friends, schooling and even self-care. Did you give a thought to what was right?

Did you care about anything besides your next high? And when you got that high, did you feel like you had conquered whatever it was that was challenging you? Maybe it was the law, your family, friends, or even your conscience. This is the enmity of pride.

If we seek after our own will and do not care about others, we allow our desires, appetites, and passions to go unbridled. A horse is controlled by putting a bridle over him and allows him to be controlled or restrained. We too must control or restrain our desires, appetites, and passions. Think of all the incest, rapes, robberies, murders, and for that matter all crimes, that occur because someone is not controlling or restraining their desires, appetites, and passions? What would this world be like if everyone practiced self-control? Children would not be afraid to play outdoors at night. Women would feel secure walking through a parking lot alone at night. Violent gangs would not even exist. Our streets would be free of illegal drugs. This would be ideal for all of us, but it must start on an individual basis.

One thing the proud person cannot accept is the authority of others. This includes parents, police, judges, and even counselors. He does not want others giving him directions for his life. He thinks he is smarter than the rest of the world. He might think or even say, "You don't know what it's like to be me." He thinks he is stronger than others and that he can handle himself just fine. The proud person thinks it somehow lowers his position if he accepts the authority of others in his life. Disobedience is essentially pride.

Too often I hear residents complaining about "this" or "that" in their recovery program, and they think they have a better plan. Usually after listening to their plan, it sounds more like chaos than a better plan. Sometimes we just have to accept directions from others. We need to trust that a drug and alcohol rehabilitation counselor knows more about what works in recovery than an addict does.

There is a story of a father who was working down in a deep hole in his backyard. His son came out to bring him lunch, and as he carefully peered over the edge of the hole, he could not see anything but blackness. His father yelled up to him to go ahead and drop his lunch down to him. The boy could not see his father but dropped the lunch anyway, and the father caught it. Then his father asked the boy if he wanted to eat lunch with him, and of course the boy did. The father told the boy to jump and promised to catch him. The boy was scared and said, "But I can't see you." The father responded, "It's okay. I can see you, and I will catch you." The boy jumped and trusted his father to catch him which he did.

Just like the little boy, we too must trust others who can see clearly. Maybe it is your counselors in rehabilitation.

Maybe it is the other members of Alcoholics Anonymous or Narcotics Anonymous. Or maybe it is God (Step 2 and 11).[71] Sometimes, we have to jump even when we cannot see where we will land (Step 3).[72] We may have to move to a new city so we are not living in the midst of our relapse triggers. When we do not trust others and only trust our own ideas, this is pride.

The proud person has a hard time being corrected or confronted. He throws his defense mechanisms up to cover his frailties or failures and to protect his feelings from getting hurt. "Well, he had it coming to him," or "She deserved it; she was asking for it," are just a couple of his rationales. He points the finger at the other person and never at himself.

When we fight against our higher power we become rebellious, hard-hearted, stiffnecked, unrepentant, puffed up, and easily offended. Are you offended easily? Do you blow up at your spouse or children or parents when they ask where you have been or who you have been with? How dare they question you? Do you think it might be because they actually care about you? Or do you really believe they are out to get you?

Another problem with pride is the enmity it causes toward others. Every day we are tempted to make ourselves look better than others. We make fun of other people thinking if we push them down, they will have to look up to us. We want to be the one on top even at a great cost, and somehow we think this makes us look and feel better.

Ezra Taft Benson said, "The proud wish everyone would agree with them. They aren't interested in changing their opinions to agree with others."[73] I would add that the proud person thinks he knows it all and knows what is best despite his history.

The proud person fights against others by pitting himself against their intellects, opinions, works, wealth, talents, or any other measuring device. In the words of C.S. Lewis, "Pride gets no pleasure out of having something, only out of having more of it than the next man ... It is the comparison that makes you proud: the pleasure of being above the rest. Once the element of competition has gone, pride has gone."[74]

It is the idea of keeping up with or even having more than the Jones' next door. With pride, we are not satisfied with life unless we have more "things" than our neighbors. For example, if the neighbors buy a new car, we suddenly need a new truck. If they buy a new boat, we go out and buy a house boat. We feel like we must always be one step in front of them. All too often, we find ourselves in out-of-control debt because our pride allowed us to go that far.

History abounds with evidence of the severe consequences of pride in individuals, groups, cities, and nations. Pride always leads to destruction. Just look back to the Los Angeles Riots in 1992. Pride caused people to fight, loot businesses, start fires, and destroy their own neighborhood. Pride is a major factor in all wars, and it killed millions of Jews in World War II alone.

The proud person is more concerned about what others think of him rather than what his Higher Power thinks of him. He is more concerned about getting caught by another person and do not realize that God has already caught him. By thinking like this, we allow others to control us because we want to please them. We hand our independence over and become dependent on the thoughts and judgments of others. The world shouts louder than the whisperings of encouragement from within. The rationalizations and justifications of men override our own judgment.

Pride loves the praise and acceptance of men more than approval from their Higher Power. We would be much happier if we cared more about pleasing God than in impressing men. This is what Step 3 is all about.

Some people do not care if they make enough money to pay their bills, they only care that they are making more money than their co-worker or neighbor. They just want to be a cut above the rest. This is the enmity of pride.

Again quoting Ezra Taft Benson, "Pride is a fault that can readily be seen in others but is rarely admitted in ourselves. Most of us consider pride to be a fault of those on the top, such as the rich and the learned, looking down at the rest of us. There is, however, a far more common ailment among us—and that is pride from the bottom looking up. It is manifest in so many ways, such as fault-finding, gossiping, backbiting, murmuring, living beyond our means, envying, coveting, withholding gratitude and praise that might lift another, and being unforgiving and jealous."[75]

Pride results in gangs that are built up to get the power, gain, and glory of the world. Gangs have caused so much damage to our society, and as long as they are around, there will yet be more hearts broken, more unnecessary deaths, and so much wasted potential. They place so much value on territory and feel a need to control it. They do not consider the loss, they only think of their own pleasure and gain. Tagging, for example, is seen by gangs as an expression of themselves. They even call it "art" and take no thought to the damage that it does or the money it will cost another to cover it up or remove it.

Pride also manifests itself as contention. Arguments, fights, spouse abuse, unhealthy dominion, generation gaps, divorces, riots, child abuse, and other disturbances fall into this category of pride.

If there is excessive contention in our home, it will destroy our family. It may even cause us to lose loved ones, maybe forever. Children run away from such homes, and the parents have little hope of seeing them again. Contention spans the spectrum from a hostile spoken word in anger to wars that rage on for years.

The proud person is easily offended. He takes life too seriously and takes the words spoken to him too personally. He almost looks for opportunities to take offense.

The proud person is slow to forgive. He thinks if he takes his time to forgive someone then that leaves the other person in his debt for a longer period of time. He also does this to justify his injured feelings. One of our residents at the rehab went home for a weekend visit. When he returned, he told me the first thing his father said to him was, "Why are you even trying? You are no good, and you can never change!" I feel sad for this father who is so full of pride. The proud person holds grudges and withholds forgiveness to justify his injured feelings.

The proud person looks to the world for acceptance and value. He might feel inferior at home so he looks for friends who are living in the gutters in order to make him look better. He feels important and worthwhile if he sees a large number of people beneath him in achievement, beauty, or intelligence. "Pride is ugly. It says, if you succeed, I am a failure" (Ezra Taft Benson).[76]

It is so hard to teach a proud person. He will not change his mind or opinion because if he does, that would be admitting he was wrong. He definitely cannot handle being wrong and must always be right, no matter what the cost; even if that means losing his family over a small issue.

Pride adversely affects every relationship we have. It affects our relationships with our parents, siblings, and children. It hurts our relationships with our counselors, employers, and co-workers. It even affects our relationship with our Higher Power. Our pride determines how we treat others. It also affects how we take what is dished out to us.

Pride automatically puts up walls between us and others. It segregates us by race, riches, education, religion, or any other differences there may be. Proud people cannot be unified. Unless we come together and stick together, we will not survive. That is why we have groups like Alcoholics Anonymous or Narcotics Anonymous - to help us eliminate any divisions so that we might be unified in our struggle. With the help of our Higher Power and love and support from those around us, we are strengthened so that we might fight this illness.

Think of what your pride has cost you in the past. Think of what pride is costing you now. And if you do not change, think of what you can lose because of your pride. It might be your family or your job. It may be your friends or your Higher Power. It may even be your own life.

How much happier would our homes be if our pride did not stop us from admitting when we were wrong. Is that not what the steps teach us - to admit when we are wrong (Step 10)?[77]

We think keeping "it" a secret is much better. But one secret leads to another until it snowballs into such a tremendous problem that is causes an avalanche. By that time, it is too late to stop the damage, and if we are to survive, we must start a slow clean-up process. Unlike real snow, this snow does not melt away by itself.

If these things are reminding you of your life, understand this: pride affects all of us. Some people have more pride than others. Some of us experience a greater amount of pride at certain times in our lives and less at other times. There is hope for all of us. We can change this vicious cycle of pride that feeds on itself. How?

The antidote for pride is humility. Going back to the dictionary, humility means showing a consciousness of one's shortcomings. It means being unpretentious or being modest or meek. It is having a broken heart.

It seems to me that we can learn from our past and from what is going on around us and we can choose to humble ourselves. We can allow the difficulties and hardships of life to teach us and humble us.

We can choose to humble ourselves by conquering enmity towards others. This means we start to see others as equals and try to help them and lift them up.

We can choose to humble ourselves by living our program and graduating from rehab and working on ourselves first.

We can choose to humble ourselves by receiving counsel and correction from our counselors and those around us who are equipped to help us.

We can choose to humble ourselves by giving of our time, talents, and everything with which we are blessed.

We can choose to humble ourselves by admitting we are powerless over alcohol or drugs and that our life has have become unmanageable (Step 1).[78]

We can choose to humble ourselves by coming to believe that a power greater than ourselves can restore us to sanity (Step 2).[79]

We can choose to humble ourselves by submitting our will and our life over to the care of God as we understand Him (Step 3).[80]

We can choose to humble ourselves by making a searching and fearless moral inventory of ourselves (Step 4).[81]

We can choose to humble ourselves by admitting to God, to ourselves, and to another human being the exact nature of our wrongs (Step 5).[82]

We can choose to humble ourselves by being entirely ready to have God remove all our defects of character including pride (Step 6).[83]

We can choose to humble ourselves by asking God to remove our shortcomings, and that would include pride (Step 7).[84]

We can choose to humble ourselves by making a list of all persons we have harmed and become willing to make amends to them all (Step 8).[85]

We can choose to humble ourselves by making direct amends to such people wherever possible, except when to do so would injure them or others (Step 9).[86]

We can choose to humble ourselves by continually taking a personal inventory and when we are wrong, admitting it (Step 10).[87]

We can choose to humble ourselves by seeking, through prayer and meditation, to improve our conscious contact with God as we understand Him, praying only for knowledge of His will for us and the power to carry that out (Step 11).[88]

We can choose to humble ourselves by attending our Alcoholics Anonymous or Narcotics Anonymous meetings and sharing our message with other addicts (Step 12).[89]

As we can see, we cannot even make it through the 12-Steps unless we first humble ourselves. Pride is intertwined in all that we do. When we find a mistake in a sweater we are crocheting, we need to undo the sweater back to the mistake to take it out. We must clean out our insides first by overcoming our pride.

Pride is a stumbling block. We will never be happy with ourselves or have a close family or a united community as long as we allow pride to run our lives. Let us choose to humble ourselves. We can all be at the top of our game if we just "Dig down deep to get to the bottom to stay on top." Let's get rid of the pride that is weighing us down. We can do it. I know we can.

-Jason Webb 2/18/99

De-Degrading Women

I was sitting in a meeting once and a client asked how his attending strip joints and watching women strip is degrading to women. I believed he was serious and that he could not see the big picture, so I wrote the following paper on the subject:

According to the Webster's New World Dictionary[90], degrade means: 1) to demote, 2) to lower in quality, moral character, dignity, etc., debase, dishonor, etc. According to the Merriam-Webster Dictionary[91] degrade means: 1) to reduce from a higher to a lower rank or degree, 2) debase, corrupt, and 3) decompose. With regards to how society treats women, any of these definitions can be used and do accurately portray the objectifying of women.

To begin we must understand that every girl, young lady, and woman is a daughter of God. Their value is infinite in His eyes. He has blessed them with tenderness and compassion. He blesses them to bring forth His precious children and bonds them together in a way that man cannot comprehend. I heard someone say one time that when God created man, He thought He better try again and created woman. After creating woman, He was satisfied. Women have tender feelings, which is pleasing unto God. He created women to be women and not to be men.

To degrade a woman is to take her from this high status of princess to the Most High King and lower her status by making an object out of her. In today's world, women have become sex objects. In the definitions listed above, notice that it does not matter whether or not the woman agrees to it. It is the same - degradation.

When men go to strip joints and pay a woman to take her clothes off for them, they are degrading her by making her an object of their lust. They objectify her. She means nothing more to him than a means by which to become sexually stimulated. In the song "Scarlet Fever"[92] by Kenny Rogers, he sings about going to a strip joint and watching young Scarlet. The lyrics read "Watch young Scarlet's body come alive." Notice, we do not watch Scarlet come alive, but rather just her body. We demote her, lower her in moral character, and reduce her to a lower status - that of being a body and not a human being or a daughter of God. He later sings, "She's a night club teaser, Not paid to notice me" so she is taught to objectify the viewers as well, but "She had a way of making a man believe She danced for only him."

Some men say, "If I'm paying her and she's willing to strip for money, than we both win." That is true from a capitalist point of view only. It is not true if we take into account anything other than money. Even from a capitalist point of view, the stripper is still being degraded because now she is given a monetary value. No longer is her worth infinite, but the audience sets a price on her worth.

When a stripper is dancing, there is no thought about her feelings. The crowd does not care if she is struggling in life and feels trapped. They do not care if she is lonely, depressed, or even suicidal. They only care about themselves. Some men tell themselves they are in love with her, but they are just sexually attracted to her body and have no real knowledge of or feelings for the actual person. Once again, she is viewed as a mere object.

I have worked with several women who had worked as strippers, and they all reported a low self-esteem. When a woman's value is tied to her body, which is only "good" for a few years, how can anyone expect them to feel self-worth?

An article was written this past year comparing self-esteem to self-worth. The author said that self-esteem came from man or society and that it is based upon what others thought about us. If we are good at sports and others cheer for us, then our self-esteem is high. If we wear the right pants (according to the popular trends), then we have high self-esteem. The flip side is also true. If we wore glasses as a child and were made fun of, we would have low self-esteem because our peers did not approve of us. Or if as an adult, we have fun running around and playing with the children and someone comments to us that we should not be acting that way, our self-esteem drops as we give heed to their words.

Self-worth on the other hand is God given. It is given at birth and everyone is given the exact same amount - infinite worth. As I think of my own children, I loved them right when they were born. What did they do for me? They did nothing for me. How did they earn my love? They did not. I love them because they exist and because they are a part of me. As fallible humans, we have a hard time understanding that an infallible God loves us as we love our own children simply because we exist and are a part of Him. Sure we make mistakes, but so do our children and we keep on loving them. We feel bad that they have to hurt or suffer, but we still love them, and God too follows this pattern.

The author summarizes by saying that we should not care or worry about self-esteem but rather should be focused on self-worth. If we truly saw each other's infinite worth, would we objectify them in any way? I do not believe so.

Let us turn to a related topic - pornography. Surely we can use the same arguments against pornography as we can against stripping. The model or actress is someone's daughter, and she is also a daughter of God. But the viewer does not care. The viewer does not care that her self-esteem is so low that in order to compete in this field, she makes herself throw up to be thin. When she gains three pounds, she believes she is fat, and photographers may even tell her she is fat. The viewer does not follow her home and see her use methamphetamines to quickly lose the weight. They do not see her crying in the corner of her bedroom because she believes she has no value without her body. She is not valued as an individual or someone with a brain or feelings. She is only valued according to her size and how it compares to others. And then to add salt to the wound, how must she feel after all the starving, throwing up, and dieting to be thin enough for her photo shoot only to have her picture taken and then put into a computer and edited and air-brushed because she still does not look good enough.

If you have ever looked into the eyes of one of these models, you would have noticed that her beautiful smile was a fake smile. You can see it in the pictures. Her so-called smile is a fake smile, and if you look even harder, you can see the pain in her eyes. Maybe that is why the eyes are known as the window to the soul.

One of the problems with viewing pornographic material is that our unbridled sexual appetites are never satisfied. Again, "You can never get enough of what you don't need, because what you don't need won't satisfy you." There is no satiable level within us for pornographic material. So we need more and more and turn to something stronger. We start watching adult movies, but they too cannot quench our thirst and eventually we start acting on our impulses. We cheat on our spouses, or we turn to criminal activities such as molestation and rape. I have never met a sex offender who did not start out with "just" pornography. With pornography, the viewer objectifies women more and more as the severity of his addiction worsens.

To be a sex offender, one cannot have empathy or sympathy for the victim at the time of the crime. The offender only has apathy, and when one is apathetic, there are no limits to what he will do. That is how someone can rape or kill another person - they do not feel anything for the victim. They are only concerned about themselves and fulfilling their needs.

During World War II, the newspapers and magazines published pictures portraying the enemy as the devil or a rat or some other object that belittled them. Thus, we felt justified in killing the Japanese because after all they were not people; they were devils or rats. Similarly, in our talk and actions, we belittle women which justify our seeing them and treating them as sex objects.

For example, if a blond joke is told, are we talking about men or women? We are talking about women, of course. Why do we do that? To state that these women do not have brains and thus cannot be good for anything, except for things of a sexual nature. We talk about women living their lives by emotions and it being "that time of month again." Since she is not seen as an intellectual person, she must not be "normal." Instead we make her less than "normal" and degrade her by doing so which allows us to view her as a sex object and not an equal to man.

Pictures of beautiful women with almost no clothing on are plastered onto billboards that read "Bud Light" at the bottom. What are these billboards about? Is it really promoting beer, or is it stating that beer helps strip women of their clothing so the man can have his sex object. There is even a country song out right now that says "Tequila makes her clothes fall off." What is society doing to women? And why are women being brained-washed into accepting this stereotype instead of fighting it?

Throughout history women have fought for their rights to work and vote and dress as they please, and essentially the right to be equal to men. But they never fought as a whole to not be seen or treated as a sex object. Individually sexual harassment cases have skyrocketed in recent years as women began fighting for their rights to be free of inappropriate behavior in the work place. Why has anyone not sued Hollywood for sexual harassment? Instead we pay them money to see it and laugh at it.

Why has anyone not sued the beer companies for their billboards? Why has anyone not sued the networks whose television shows promote degradation to women like nothing else? Society in general has succumbed to the vain imaginations of those preying on us for money. So we have become blind and have hardened our hearts. We have become desensitized to things of a sexual nature thus allowing more and more to be shown to us. We simply do not realize the impact this material has on us and everyone around us.

Swearing is another example of degrading women by degrading our bodies. Every cuss word has to do with a body, its function, or its progress. When we use such terms we are belittling our bodies and making it easier to degrade our bodies but more specifically women's bodies. Now, I do not want you to go through every one in your head to see if it applies. Just trust me.

Do you understand what I am trying to say?

So what can we do? My first suggestion is that we recognize our own behavior that contributes to the degradation of women. Speak of women with respect. In the Hispanic culture, it is a terrible insult to say anything derogatory about anybody's mother. Why can we not defend our mothers, and wives, and sisters with such love? And why can we not treat all women with love and respect? Whatever happened to standing up when a woman enters the room? I am not saying that we have to do this, but can you see that the respect once shown to women has gone right down the drain? Do we open doors for the women in our lives or any other woman for that matter? In part, I blame this lack of respect for women on the women's movement. The most vocal group of women said they did not want to be treated differently or inferior. I do not think they should be treated as inferiors, but I absolutely think they should be treated differently because they are not men – they are women. The behaviors showing respect to women could have and should have stayed.

Women can stop men from acting the way they do. They can make comments when men are being inappropriate around them rather than laughing or justifying it with, "He's just being a man." Being a man is no excuse to mistreat or disrespect a woman. There is no excuse for that. Why not change the old attitude of "boys will be boys" to "boys will be gentlemen." We excuse our behaviors so that others will accept it. The more we accept poor behavior, the more they will push the boundaries and excuse that behavior as well. How far will we allow them to go?

We must stop buying pornographic material in all its forms. We have to stop attending strip joints. Let us stop telling jokes that belittle women or laughing at such jokes. We need to turn the television off when the material is offensive. We have to get upset at the filth being broadcast; otherwise, we condone it by not fighting against it.

Another attempt at justification I have heard from married men is "Just because I'm on a diet doesn't mean I can't look at the menu." Once again, we have degraded women by making her a menu item, something to buy or something to look at. As that man objectifies other women, he begins to treat his wife differently as well. Gandhi[93] taught that we cannot live one part of our life one way and another part another way. He said that we are one soul, and that soul is affected by everything we do. So it is when we treat other women with disrespect, we begin to treat our own wives with disrespect.

The safest and best advice I give married men is "When you look at another woman and the thought goes through your mind that she is pretty, stop that conscious thought. Even as the sentence starts, distract yourself so as not to finish the sentence. If that were to happen with every conscious thought about another woman, you would never cheat on your spouse." Someone asked me if I thought it was actually possible to do that. From my own experience, the answer is yes. Also, we have the ability to stop conscious thoughts because they are conscious. In stopping these thoughts, we refuse to degrade women.

But is it a compliment to tell a woman she is sexy? No, unless it is one on a list of things you like about her and not just one thing you have labeled her as. Because if sexy is the only trait you like about her, you are viewing her as a sex object. If you are in love with this person and have already shared a list of traits you like about her, then sexy could be something that would actually compliment her.

Is it a compliment to tell a woman she is pretty? I guess that depends on what your definition of pretty is? Who are you comparing her to? And is she pretty because of what society tells you? I went to school with a famous television star and in high school she was not anyone big and popular. She moved to California and starred on a television show and she became this very popular and "gorgeous" woman because society said she was. Why was she not before she made it on television? Why do we think people on television are "hot"? Is it just because Hollywood says they are? Let us choose to think for ourselves.

Women, do not get your breasts augmented. Do not get your face lifted. Do not get Botox injections. Do not get your tummy tucked. Do not have liposuction to shrink your buttocks. So many women wear a fake mask on the outside and expect others to value what they have on the inside, when they do not value it themselves. Make a man earn you. Make sure he values you for who you are and what you look like; not what they want you to be or look like. Do not give in to their lustful desires by changing who you are. You are of infinite worth just the way you are.

It is my hope that both men and women can value women for who they are - daughters of God. Every one of them - the ones on television and the ones who are not - are of infinite worth. Let us treat them as if God, their father, was watching us; for He is. As we do so, we will gain more respect for ourselves and others and increased joy as we line up our actions with God's values.

-Jason Webb 2005

References

[1] Kiyosaki, R. T., & Lechter, S. L.   Rich Dad's Retire Young, Retire Rich: How to Get Rich Quickly and Stay Rich Forever!. New York: Hachette Book Group USA. (2007).

[2] Michael, George. (1984). Song: Wake Me Up Before You Go-Go. Single by Wham from the album *Make It Big*. Produced by George Michael. Label by Columbia Records (US/Canada) Epic Records.

[3] Merriam-Webster, Incorporated. (1997). The Merriam-Webster Dictionary; Tenth Edition. Springfield, Massachusetts, U.S.A.

[4] Collodi, Carlo. (1883). The Adventures of Pinocchio. Italy. Reprinted by Everyman's Library and published by Alfred A. Knopf (a division of Random House, Inc.) and separately, in paperback, by J. M. Dent (a division of Weidenfeld & Nicholson Ltd.) in the United Kingdom.

[5] Adams, Hunter C. "Patch", M.D. (born May 28, 1945 in Washington, D.C.) is an American physician, social activist, citizen diplomat, professional clown, performer, and author. He founded the Gesundheit! Institute in 1972. Each year he organizes a group of volunteers from around the world to travel to various countries where they dress as clowns, to bring hope and joy to orphans, patients, and other people.

[6] Burns, David D. (1999). Feeing Good: The New Mood Therapy Revised and Updated. New York: Harper.

[7] Ibid.

[8] The Andy Griffith Show is an American sitcom first televised

by CBS between October 3, 1960 and April 1, 1968.

[9] Cavuto, Neil Patrick. (Born September 22, 1958). is an American television anchor and commentator on the Fox Business Network and host of three television programs, *Your World with Neil Cavuto* and *Cavuto on Business*, both on the Fox News Channel and *Cavuto* on sister channel Fox Business Network. He is the senior vice president and managing editor of business news for the Fox Business Network.

[10] Nichols, Mike (Director). (1991). Movie: Regarding Henry. Starring Harrison Ford, R.M. Haley, Stanley H. Swerdlow, & Julie Follansbee.

[11] Brown, T. Graham, Burch, Bruce, & Hewitt, Ted. (1998). Song: Wine into Water. Single by T. Graham Brown from the album Wine into Water. Produced by Gary Nicholson & T. Graham Brown. Recorded by Sound Emporium, Omni Studio & Marshal Morgan Studio in Nashville, TN.

[12] Selye, Hans. (January 26, 1907 — October 16, 1982) was a Canadian endocrinologist of Austro-Hungarian origin and Hungarian ethnicity. Selye did much important factual work on the hypothetical non-specific response of the organism to stressors. While he did not recognize all of the many aspects of glucocorticoids, Selye was aware of this response on their role. Some commentators considered him the first to demonstrate the existence of biological stress.

[13] Carlson, Richard. (1996). Don't Sweat the Small Stuff-And It's All Small Stuff. New York: Hyperion.

[14] Merriam-Webster online dictionary. http://www.merriam-

webster.com/dictionary/anxiety

[15] Bourne, Edmund J. (2005). The Anxiety & Phobia Workbook, Fourth Edition. Oakland: Hew Harbinger Publications.

[16] Frankl, Viktor E. (1997). Man's Search for Meaning. New York: Pocket.

[17] Frankl, Viktor E. (1986). The Doctor and the Soul: From Psychotherapy to Logotherapy. London: Vintage.

[18] American Psychiatric Association: Diagnostic and Statistical Manual of Mental Disorders, Fourth Edition, Text Revision. Washington, DC, American Psychiatric Association, 2000.

[19] Lucas, George. (1977). Movie: Star Wars Episode V: The Empire Strikes Back. Screenplay by Leigh Brackett & Lawrence Kasdan. Starring: Harrison Ford, Mark Hamill, & Carrie Fisher.

[20] Broderick, Carlfred Bartholomew. (2008) The Uses of Adversity. Salt Lake City: Deseret Book.

[21] Jeffrey K. Zeig (born 6 November 1947), is the founder and director of the Milton H. Erickson Foundation. He has edited, co-edited, authored or coauthored more than 20 books on psychotherapy that appear in eleven foreign languages.

[22] Williams, Mary Beth, Poijula, Soili, & Nurmi, Lasse A. (2002). The PTSD Workbook. Oakland: New Harbinger Publications.

[23] Oz, Frank. (1991). Movie: What about Bob? Starring:

Murray, Bill, Dreyfuss, Richard & Hagerty, Julie.

[24] Mallinger, Allan E. & Dewyze, Jeannette. (1992). Too Perfect: When Being In Control Gets Out Of Control. New York: Ballantine Books (a division of Random House, Inc.).

[25] AA World Services Inc. (2009). Alcoholics Anonymous 4th Edition. New York: Alcoholics Anonymous World Services, Inc.

[26] George, Derek, Tirro, John & White, Bryan. (1998). Single: Imagine That. Sung by Diamond Rio. Produced by Michael D. Clute, Diamond Rio. Label by Arista Nashville.

[27] Dr. Brent A. Barlow was a BYU professor of marriage, family, and human development. He has written several books and lectures. He was awarded the Outstanding Teacher Award from Southern Illinois University in 1974. He received the Outstanding Teacher Award from the University of Wisconsin-Stout in 1977. He again received the Outstanding Teacher Award from Brigham Young University in 1998. In 2004 he got the Recognition, Chair, 1998-2004 Governor's Commission on Marriage in Utah.

[28] Holmes, Rupert. (1979). Song: Escape. Written and produced by Rupert Holmes. From the Album: Partners in Crime. Label by Infinity/Geffen.

[29] Stein, Joseph. (1971) Musical: Fiddler on the Roof. Music by Jerry Bock. Lyrics by Sheldon Harnick. Based off the book: Fiddler on the Roof which was originally titled Tevye (1894).

[30] Dr. John Lewis Lund is a native of Olympia, Washington. He holds degrees in sociology and education from Brigham

Young University. A second Master's degree was pursued in Educational Psychology at the University of Washington in Seattle. In 1972 Brigham Young University awarded him the degree of Doctor of Education. Because of his emphasis in research, he completed the equivalent of a Doctoral Minor in Statistics. He has several books and CDs including: Avoiding Emotional Divorce, How to Hug a Porcupine: Dealing with Toxic and Difficult to Love Personalities, and For All Eternity.

[31] Brigham Henry Roberts was born March 13, 1857 in Warrington, Lancashire, United Kingdom. He died September 27, 1933. He was a historian, and politician.

[32] Gray, John. (1992) <u>Men Are From Mars, Women Are From Venus.</u> New York: HarperCollins

[33] Beattie, Melody. (1992). <u>Codependent No More: How to Stop Controlling Others and Start Caring.</u> Center City: Hazelden.

[34] Beattie, Melody. (1989). <u>Beyond Codependency: And Getting Better All the Time.</u> Center City: Hazelden.

[35] The Holy Bible, King James Version. Matthew 18:21

[36] Joe McQuaney and Charlie Parmley have several recorded CDs about A.A. and the Big Book. These talks can be found on http://www.sobrietytalks.com/shop/?cat=15.

[37] <u>The Holy Bible</u>, King James Version. Matthew 5:44 & Luke 6:28.

[38] Brigham Henry Roberts was born March 13, 1857 in Warrington, Lancashire, United Kingdom. He died September 27, 1933. He was a historian, and politician. The quote comes from <u>Gospel and Man's Relationship to Deity</u>, pp. 289-90.

[39] Frankl, Viktor E. (1986). The Doctor and the Soul: From Psychotherapy to Logotherapy. London: Vintage.

[40] Frankl, Viktor E. (1997). Man's Search for Meaning. New York: Pocket.

[41] Brown, Hugh B. (1961). Continuing the Quest. p. 345-346. Salt Lake City: Deseret Book Company.

[42] Lewis, C.S. (2004). Collected Letters of C.S. Lewis. P. 262. New York: HarperCollins.

[43] Johnson, Jamey. (2005). The Dollar. Single written and sung by Jamey Johnson. Produced by Buddy Cannon. Label by BNA.

[44] Dr. Chuck Jackson is described as a "cross between John Dewey and Robin Williams", Chuck has presented hundreds of workshops, seminars and keynote addresses to audiences throughout the United States and Canada. The demand for his services grows out of his unusual style of presentation. He takes the stage clad in bib overalls, indicative of his native Oklahoma origins. He has the uncanny ability to move audiences from laughter to tears and back again through the effective use of humor, music and poetry. (see: http://www.speakersguild.com/education/jackson.html)

[45] Covey. Stephen R. (1990). The 7 Habits of Highly Effective People: Powerful Lessons in Personal Change. New York: Free Press.

[46] Kiyosaki, Robert T. (2000). Rich Dad, Poor Dad: What the Rich Teach Their Kids About Money—That the Poor and Middle Class Do Not! New York: Business Plus.

[47] Ramsey, Dave III (born September 3, 1960) is an American financial author, radio host, television personality, and motivational speaker. His show and writings strongly focus on encouraging people to get out of debt.
Ramsey's syndicated radio program The Dave Ramsey Show is heard on more than 500 radio stations throughout the United States and Canada.

[48] American Psychiatric Association: Diagnostic and Statistical Manual of Mental Disorders, Fourth Edition, Text Revision. Washington, DC, American Psychiatric Association, 2000.

[49] Ibid.

[50] Covey. Stephen R. (1990). The 7 Habits of Highly Effective People: Powerful Lessons in Personal Change. New York: Free Press.

[51] Shadyac, Tom (1998). Movie: Patch Adams. Screenplay by Steve Oedekerk. Starring: Robin Williams, Daniel London, and Monica Potter.

[52] American Psychiatric Association: Diagnostic and Statistical Manual of Mental Disorders, Fourth Edition, Text Revision. Washington, DC, American Psychiatric Association, 2000.

[53] Ibid.

[54] Scott Miller is one of the founders of The Institute for the Study of Therapeutic Change (ISTC) located in Chicago Illinois. Scott and his partners' common passions resulted in several books and dozens of articles, and culminated in the

APA best selling, *The Heart and Soul of Change*. Scott introduced Barry to the most revolutionary idea to hit psychotherapy in decades—namely, the use of client-based feedback to tailor services and improve effectiveness known as Outcome Rating Scale (ORS) and Session Rating Scale (SRS) *(See:* http://www.talkingcure.com/contactUs.asp*)*.

[55] American Psychiatric Association: Diagnostic and Statistical Manual of Mental Disorders, Fourth Edition, Text Revision. Washington, DC, American Psychiatric Association, 2000.

[56] Ibid.

[57] Bayse, Daniel J. (1991). As Free As an Eagle: The Inmate's Family Survival Guide. Laurel: American Correctional Association.

[58] Church Educational System (1993). Spiritual Crocodiles. Video created after Elder Boyd K. Packer's talk given in 1976. Salt Lake City: LDS Motion Picture Studio.

[59] The Why Try Organization was founded by Christian Moore, LCSW, who is now recognized internationally as a leading advocate for at-risk youth. The Why Try Program is a simple, hands-on curriculum which helps youth overcome their challenges and improve outcomes in the areas of truancy, behavior, and academics. See www.whytry.org.

[60] American Psychiatric Association: Diagnostic and Statistical Manual of Mental Disorders, Fourth Edition, Text Revision. Washington, DC, American Psychiatric Association, 2000.

[61] Gray, John. (1992) Men Are From Mars, Women Are From Venus. New York: HarperCollins

[62] American Psychiatric Association: Diagnostic and Statistical Manual of Mental Disorders, Fourth Edition, Text Revision. Washington, DC, American Psychiatric Association, 2000.

[63] Ibid.

[64] Ibid.

[65] Ibid.

[66] Ibid.

[67] Reprinted with the permission of Andrea Miller

[68] Neufeldt, Victoria (Editor in Chief). (1989). Webster's New World: Compact School & Office Edition. New York: Prentice Hall.

[69] Bayse, Daniel J. (1991). As Free As an Eagle: The Inmate's Family Survival Guide. Laurel: American Correctional Association.

[70] Benson, Ezra, Taft. (1989, May). Beware of Pride. Ensign. pp. 4-7.

[71] AA World Services Inc. (2009). Alcoholics Anonymous 4th Edition. New York: Alcoholics Anonymous World Services, Inc.

[72] Ibid.

[73] Benson, Ezra, Taft. (1989, May). Beware of Pride. Ensign. pp. 4-7.

[74] Lewis, C.S. (1952). Mere Christianity, New York:

Macmillan, pp. 109–10.

[75] Benson, Ezra, Taft. (1989, May). Beware of Pride. Ensign. pp. 4-7.

[76] Ibid.

[77] AA World Services Inc. (2009). Alcoholics Anonymous 4th Edition. New York: Alcoholics Anonymous World Services, Inc.

[78] Ibid.

[79] Ibid.

[80] Ibid.

[81] Ibid.

[82] Ibid.

[83] Ibid.

[84] Ibid.

[85] Ibid.

[86] Ibid.

[87] Ibid.

[88] Ibid.

[89] Ibid.

[90] Neufeldt, Victoria (Editor in Chief). (1989). Webster's New World: Compact School & Office Edition. New York: Prentice

Hall.

[91] Merriam-Webster, Incorporated. (1997). The Merriam-Webster Dictionary; Tenth Edition. Springfield, Massachusetts, U.S.A.

[92] Rogers, Kenny. (1983). Song: Scarlet Fever. Words by Mike Dekle. From the album: We've Got Tonight.

[93] Mohandas Karamchand Gandhi (pronounced: [ˈmoːɦəndaːs ˈkərəmtʃənd̪ ˈgaːnd̪ʱi]; 2 October 1869 – 30 January 1948), commonly known as Mahatma Gandhi, was the preeminent leader of Indian nationalism in British-ruled India. Employing non-violent civil disobedience, Gandhi led India to independence and inspired movements for non-violence, civil rights and freedom across the world.

19327333R00171

Made in the USA
Charleston, SC
18 May 2013